Welcome *to the*
Roller Coaster

Welcome *to the*
Roller Coaster

Real Life Stories of
the Ups and Downs
of Foster Care

Written by
A group of anonymous Foster Moms
using the pen name
D.D. Foster to protect their identities

This labor of love contains true stories that come from real foster parents. We would like to thank all of the women that shared these stories that are so close to their hearts. While names, ages, and locations may have been changed in order to protect privacy, these stories are a true reflection of what it is like to be a foster parent.

We are also grateful to those that took those stories amd immortalized them in this complete work. We could not have done this without the diligent work of Leah Wentzel, Tamara Studley, Bobbie Shell and David Metting. Thank you for your proofreading, editing, and help in story building.

Welcome to the Roller Coaster

First Printing: December 2014
Printed in the United States of America

First Edition: December 2014

Scripture verses are taken from the King James Version of the Bible.

*"To every foster mom who has fought, is fighting,
or will fight for their foster child."*

Contents

Introduction

*T*he decision has been made, and you know without a doubt that you are not turning back. The eager anticipation of what lies ahead has your heart racing and your knees weak as you prepare yourself for the ride of your life. As you settle in and begin the initial uphill climb, your excitement slowly turns to fear of the downward spiral that is sure to come. The ride takes you on the highest of highs and the lowest of lows. It twists and turns at dizzying speeds and leaves you questioning your decision to ever get on in the first place. Eventually the ride comes to a standstill, and you have a moment to catch your breath. That is when it hits you. You have just taken the most amazing, thrilling, terrifying, and rewarding ride of your life.

Making the decision to become a foster parent is much like deciding to ride on a roller coaster. We wait with baited breath for the call that will change our lives. We face our fears of loss and inadequacy head-on. We struggle to deal with a broken system, and sometimes wonder why we ever chose to foster at all. We rejoice as we watch our children achieve milestones that no one ever expected them to reach. Our hearts swell with love at the feel of our foster children's hands in our own or the first time they look up at us with eyes yearning to trust. We grieve with them and attempt to comfort them through their pain. Despite the ups and downs, we look at these children and know without a doubt that this particular roller coaster is most definitely worth the ride.

Within these pages you will find the stories that often times stay tucked away in the heart of a foster mother. They are stories about children we will always love – the ones who have stayed, and the ones who have gone. No two journeys on this foster care roller coaster are the same. Each has its own unique highs and lows. Each one is special, and every story is worth sharing. While pain is inevitable in foster care, joy is at every turn. We have learned that this calling is not about us at all. We do this for the children, because they are worth it.

1

Waiting for Our Starfish

The typical response I get when I tell someone that I am a foster parent is, "I could never do what you are doing. It would hurt too much to give them back." Without even stepping into the world of foster care, people already know that it is a broken mess. As a foster parent, I have experienced this first hand.

I grew up hearing stories of foster care from my maternal grandmother. She and my grandfather were foster parents in the late 1960s. They fostered specifically for the extra income. I am sure initially it sounded like a great idea. You take care of a child, and make some extra money. How hard could it be? Then they were placed with a beautiful baby girl and fell in love with her. They immediately broke the cardinal rule of foster care. They wanted to keep her. My mother still remembers the precious baby girl who lived with them for eighteen months.

Back in those days, it was not assumed that foster parents would adopt when the child in their care became available for adoption. They were not even given the first chance to adopt. One day, out of nowhere, my grandmother was told to bring the baby to the office for a medical checkup. They took the baby into a back room and told my grandmother, "Thank you for your services. The baby will be adopted by someone else." The thought of not being able to say goodbye and the feelings of loss she must have felt as she left that building are unimaginable to me. I saw the emotion in her eyes and heard the emptiness in her voice as she told me the stories years later. I think it was then I decided to be a foster parent.

I had always imagined myself with more children than the typical American family. The thought of a husband, 2.5 children, and a dog just never quite seemed to be enough for me. The scary stories of kids being sent back to abusive and neglectful homes took a backseat to my desire to make a difference. After many discussions with my husband about foster care and adoption, we began the 30-hour, 10-week course to become a licensed foster home. We completed stacks of paperwork, and we listed our closest friends and family as character references. We chose the age range of newborn to three years old, and decided we would be open to boys and girls. We spoke in depth to our four biological children and explained that there would be babies coming to live with us who had no other place to stay. Our job was to love them until their parents were ready to take care of them again.

Our first placement came to us in late December of 2005, only days after we were certified by our county. A four-month-old baby boy named Colby came to us from another foster home that was closing. Colby was placed in foster care at two months old because someone called 911 as they watched his father shaking him in public. His mom had stood by and done nothing. Colby seemed developmentally delayed, and it was obvious that it took a while for him to bond with us. As a new foster parent, my life seemed to be consumed by visits at the Department of Social Services building and appointments at the doctor's office. After a few months with us, Colby's Early Intervention Evaluation showed that he qualified for speech, physical, and occupational therapies. Our busy schedule was now even fuller with therapies three days a week. Colby slowly progressed. As the weeks passed his parents barely worked their case plan. One day Colby's caseworker called and asked if we were interested in adopting him. My husband and I discussed this monumental decision for weeks. Could we handle a special needs child? What if he never talked or took his first steps? Would we continue to foster if we adopted him? We had so many unanswerable questions. We prayed for direction and clarity, and finally the decision was made. After seventeen months of living with us, Colby left us to go to an adoptive family. I dropped him off with his new family in a McDonald's parking lot and cried the whole way home.

For weeks after Colby left us I second-guessed our decision. I questioned if I truly heard from God, or just did what I thought would be easier for our family. Waking up every morning wondering if I gave "my" son to another family to adopt was at times unbearable, but as time went on, it became clear that God had a different plan for us.

On December 27, 2007 the phone rang again. It was the on-call worker asking if we would take a baby boy born two days earlier right on Christmas Day. He had been born a month early and had drugs in his system. Felix was a five-pound, beautiful, biracial baby boy. As I held him later that day, I prayed that God would give us the peace to walk through our time with him. His mother was given a case plan, and even though she was offered visits twice weekly to bond with him she declined. Drugs were more important to her. Felix's father was incarcerated only days after his birth. As the county worker searched for a suitable relative placement, we fell in love. This tiny boy captured our hearts. We were smitten.

Week after week went by and no family came forward for him. The county workers put the adoption bug in our ear, and we had high hopes of adopting this sweet baby boy. Three months after he was placed with us the worker called to tell us that his maternal grandmother wanted a visit. As I drove to the county building for his visit with his grandma I prayed that God would sustain me and give me the peace I so desperately needed.

Grandma seemed nice and asked normal questions regarding his development. I wanted to ask her where she had been for the last three months as Felix screamed while his tiny body went through withdrawals. Where was she when he first smiled at me and stole my heart? I left the meeting with her begging God to let us keep our sweet boy. Ten days later, three months and twelve days after he was placed with us, the county worker called to tell me that the judge had given custody to Grandma in court earlier that day. I was supposed to meet Grandma at the social services building less than twenty-four hours later to give Felix and his belongings to her. I was losing my boy.

That was the moment I realized how strong my desire to adopt really was. The next day, I met Felix's grandmother in the Department of Social Services parking lot. I kissed his sweet little head and handed him to her. Leaving that parking lot was the hardest thing I had ever had to do. It made it so final. In the days and weeks after Felix left I sunk into a depression. I had my own children to take care of and a house that needed to be cleaned, but I could not function. All I could think about was my sweet boy sleeping in an unfamiliar house. Deep down I knew that he would be ok, but would I?

For some reason my heart held on to the thought of him coming back to us. I selfishly hoped his grandmother was overwhelmed and would change her mind about raising him. I vividly remember asking God if He truly thought that I could handle the loss that foster care brings. I prayed for God to use our loss for His glory, and to bring the children into our care that He knew needed us most.

Two months went by before our next phone call from DSS (Department of Social Services) came. In May of 2008, after a busy day out with my family, I got a phone call at 9pm. It was the DSS supervisor asking if we would be willing to take a seven-month-old baby girl. She explained that the birth parents had been on her radar for quite some time, and the night before they had gotten into a physical fight. After arriving at the scene, the police called CPS (Child Protective Services). They called because, supposedly, the baby had been injured by falling off the couch. Without hesitation I said yes. I met the CPS worker at the local Walmart. She quickly introduced me to Rose and drove off. I brought Rose home with me and gave her a bath. She was very dirty and smelled heavily of smoke. It was pretty late by the time we were ready to settle down for the night. I snuggled her close, and prayed that God would give us the wisdom and strength to be the "parents" she needed. I remember clearly the look in her eyes that night as I held her close and fed her a bottle. It was as if her eyes were saying, "I want to tell you about where I came from, and I do not want to go back."

As time went by it was clear that Rose's biological mother was cognitively delayed. She would question the clothes I put on Rose for visits and would tell me what I should be feeding her, and she was completely off the mark. Rose was with us for ten months before we got a call from her social worker asking if we were interested in adopting her. My husband and I prayed and prayed for clarity about this decision. She was a healthy little girl meeting and exceeding developmental milestones. Our biological children loved her, and the thought of her living somewhere else broke our hearts. As much as we loved this beautiful baby girl, we felt she was not to be our daughter. Rose left us to live with her adoptive family in May of 2009. We met them in the parking lot of a Red Lobster and handed them all of her belongings. As I reached in to get her from her car seat for one last kiss, she smiled and laughed. I kissed her and then handed her over to her new family. Our hearts were broken. My husband and I cried together as we tried to order our lunch at Red Lobster. The poor waitress could not even understand us through our tears. After Rose left, we prayed for her and for her new parents. We prayed that God would redeem our loss and heal our broken hearts. Many times we questioned our decision to let her go, but we knew that God had made it clear that she was never ours.

The feelings of loss and emptiness once again began to overtake me. I remember being angry with God in a way I cannot even explain. How could He let us go through this again? Why were we being placed with children that became available for adoption only to have no peace about adopting them? This was not fair to our biological children or to us. Our desire to adopt was so strong. I just could not understand why these kids had to keep leaving. As time went on the hurt was still there, but I made the decision to trust that God's plans were better than my plans. Ephesians 3:20 says that God is able to do exceedingly and abundantly more than you could ever ask, dream, or imagine. I held tightly to that verse. Every day I had to make the choice to trust God's plan for my life. It was not easy. So many times I felt like God wanted me to understand that, even though I was hurting, life was not about me. These babies experienced love while they were here, and that is what they needed.

I struggled most with other people's opinions about foster care. In sharing our experiences they were quick to ask, "If it hurts so much, why do you continue to do it?" If I have learned anything in our journey through foster care it is that God has never promised us that life would be easy. We all have different kinds of struggles. Our biggest struggle was that we had to say goodbye to children who we had grown to love, while others had to bury their loved ones, or had other struggles that we had not. Life is not always easy. When our lives are lived with purpose, the struggles do not seem quite as hard because we walk through the sacrifices with hope. I think this is true, because what we are living for and working toward goes way beyond anything our human minds can comprehend. Trusting God is not easy especially when your human desires seem to contradict what God is telling you to leave in His hands.

Surrendering my desire to adopt and choosing to embrace the fact that I may never add to our family through adoption was hard, but because I knew God was in control I learned to be at peace. From May of 2009 until November of 2010 we constantly had foster children in and out of our care. We were blessed to have some for a few weeks and others for months. Watching these babies thrive and grow was such a blessing. Many times I had to rely on God's promise to never leave or forsake us. I still had to trust that God would redeem the losses we had suffered and believe that His timing would be perfect.

On a cold November day in 2010, I found myself looking around my quiet house with nothing to do. My children were at school, all my laundry and dishes were caught up, and even the bathrooms were clean. On a whim I called the home finder at the agency we foster through. As I jokingly explained to her that the house was quiet and that I needed another baby, she told me that at the very minute her phone rang she was putting my address into her GPS (Global Positioning System) because she wanted to stop by and talk to me. A bit shocked, I told her to come right over. When she got to my house she told me about a baby boy that was due the next month. She told me that the agency was considering this baby to be a pre-adoptive placement because his biological mom had two other children who were already in foster care and reunification did not seem possible. The biological dad was not an option because he was incarcerated. She wanted to know if we would consider fostering and possibly adopting him.

Usually when DSS or CPS calls, you have five minutes to make a decision on whether or not you will accept a placement. I had over a month to get ready to bring this sweet baby boy home from the hospital. Did we want him? Yes, of course! I immediately started crocheting a blanket and setting up the crib. I got a new infant car seat and had all his clothes washed and in drawers. The second week of December I called the home finder again to find out the baby's exact due date. She told me she thought it was December 16th. I waited, but I was very impatient. Looking at everything ready to go and wanting desperately to hold him reminded me of the feelings I had when I was pregnant with my biological children. I was already in love with this baby I had not even met, and in foster care that is a scary place to be.

I called the home finder again on December 17th to see if he had been born yet. She told me that she was sorry, but the biological mom had moved to a different county and the baby would be placed with a family who fostered through the county where she now resided. My heart sank. As I hung up the phone, God whispered to my heart, "I am bigger than a county line." It was exactly what I needed to hear to give me the strength to keep going. I did not move the crib that was already set up. In fact, I prayed every time I saw it. I prayed that God's plan for this baby would be fulfilled, and I prayed that He would give us the grace to wait. Exactly one week later my cell phone rang. The home finder was calling to see if we could come in for a meeting about a baby. The same baby! He was due to be born over Christmas break. She wanted to make sure we understood what was expected of us and to fill us in with some details about the biological family. I reminded her of what she told me a week earlier and she said, "Well, I guess he is just meant to be with you guys."

When my husband and I went in for the meeting we found out he had been born earlier that morning. We were encouraged by the home finder to go to hospital and begin bonding with him. Initially, I had concerns about meeting his biological mom without a caseworker there. We were told she was unstable, and it would be best to only visit the baby if nurses were present. We agreed. Walking into the special care nursery was so amazing. Holding him for the first time brought me so many feelings of redemption. I had waited a long time for this. We gave him the nickname of Sprout. There was still a long way to go, but he was in our arms and that was the first step. My husband and I were anxious about meeting his biological mom. It was a pleasant surprise to see that she actually wanted to meet us. We explained to her that, as foster parents, our goal was to encourage reunification. One of the first things she asked us was if we were interested in adopting her son. She was no stranger to foster care. She was already working two other case plans for her older sons. I truly believe that first night of meeting her and us getting to know each other was a gift from God. We had so many questions, and she wanted to get to know the people who would be caring for her son. Sprout was ready to be discharged a few days later. I had expected to see his biological mom again and reassure her that we would take good care of him, but the agency had other plans. They put us in a room separate from her. The nurse brought Sprout in to us to get him bundled and settled into his car seat. We left for home, but we knew our next foster care adventure was only beginning.

We instantly fell in love with this sweet little boy. Sprout's biological mom was given a case plan which involved her visiting him on a regular basis, completing parenting classes, taking a psychological evaluation, finding and maintaining a job, and finding suitable housing for the two of them. A few weeks into her case plan she was doing so well that the caseworker increased her visits from twice a week to three times a week. I was happy that she was consistent, but so disappointed that it looked like we would lose another baby. It had not taken long for us to fall in love with him and we had begun to pray that we would be able to keep him. There is such a fine line in foster care. I found that we were caught between doing what was expected of us and what felt right. Our standards for these kids and what their biological parents are expected to provide differ greatly. For example, Sprout's biological mom thought that he should be eating Goldfish crackers and Kool-Aid for lunch at six months old. At our house he was still eating only baby food and Cheerios with only baby formula or water. If we brought it up to the caseworker, they could argue that at least she is feeding him. As foster parents, we are required to take an initial thirty-hour MAPP (Model Approach to Partnerships in Parenting) class and an additional 24 hours of training every year. Our homes are certified and safety clearances are performed once a year. There is a certain level of care we are required to provide and one would expect that standard should at least be carried over into his mother's home, but it is not.

In May of 2011 Sprout's biological mom started canceling visits or missing them altogether. He was only a few months old. I was thankful that he did not know what was going on, but I was scared for his future. I prayed that God's plan for Sprout's life would become clear. His biological mom continued to miss visits. On more than one occasion, even though the caseworker brought Sprout to his mother's home for a visit, she told the worker, "I didn't call for a visit today." She would refuse the visit and the caseworker would bring Sprout home to me.

Suddenly, as Sprout's biological mom stopped working her case plan, Sprout's paternal grandmother came into the picture. She wanted custody. Even though we were told this was a pre-adoptive placement we knew that family could still step up and request custody. My prayer life consisted of asking God for clarity on how this case would turn out, and to give me the strength to let Sprout go if it came to that. Sprout visited with his paternal grandmother three times. At one point she asked what size diapers he was in and what brand of formula he was taking. The thought of him living somewhere other than with us broke my heart. I could not imagine Sprout going home to a "mother" that did not appear to value her time with him or put his needs above her own, but I had no say in the matter.

In August of 2011, I got a call from the caseworker telling me that Sprout's paternal grandmother decided to withdraw her petition for custody. She decided he would be better off with us. She also told the caseworker that she thought it was in Sprout's best interest for her son (Sprout's biological dad) to surrender his rights so we could raise him. We were honored that she felt that way, but we knew that it was not her decision to make.

Sprout celebrated his first birthday in our care. He happened to have a visit with his mom scheduled for that day. His biological mom had tried to put together a small party for him, but no one came to this party, and she had no gift for him. She sent the caseworker home with five dollars hoping I would pick out something he would like. The caseworker told me that the "party" she had planned was the saddest thing. She wore a dress and played with him. She took some pictures, but all Sprout wanted was to get into the arms of the caseworker because he knew that meant he would come home to me. I was happy that Sprout was too young to understand what was going on around him. As far as he knew, we were his family.

Sprout's permanency hearing was scheduled for May of 2012. Sprout's biological dad was produced in court from prison. At that time he had only seen his son for three supervised hours in prison. At court, it was determined that DSS should file for termination of the biological father's parental rights. He had spoken many times of surrendering his rights, but never followed through. The county warned us that, even though the judge ordered termination, they were in no hurry because biological dad's incarceration entitled him to more services than they had been giving him.

Sprout's biological mom continued to miss visits, and in June we found out that she was expecting her fourth baby. The caseworker tried to convince us that this new baby meant that she would surrender her rights to Sprout. It was obvious that we were the only ones in a hurry to get Sprout out of foster care. We spent the summer enjoying every minute watching Sprout learn and grow. From the moment he was placed in my arms I made a mental note to enjoy him as if he were staying forever. Sprout turned eighteen months old in June of 2012. His biological mom was very inconsistent with her visits. By August they had stopped altogether. We were told by the workers that she would start to give up on Sprout, and focus more on the new baby she was having. That was the pattern that she had developed. Once she had a child removed and placed in foster care, she would get pregnant again and stop working her case plan.

In October we went back to court expecting that DSS would have already filed the Termination of Parental Rights. They had not. Later that month Sprout's biological dad surrendered his parental rights. He wrote a long letter to the county worker and told her that he would rather Sprout be raised by us because it would be wrong to take him from the only home he had ever known. We were thrilled. Our boy was half freed for adoption! As amazing as it was to walk out of court with our boy almost ours, it was bittersweet to sit in that courtroom and listen to the judge question the biological dad to see if he was really ready to surrender his rights. As he sat there handcuffed, shackled, and chained I just wanted to put my arms around him and thank him. Our hearts hurt for him, but we were so happy.

About three weeks later Sprout's biological mom surrendered as well. She was worried that CPS would take her new baby, so she was willing to sacrifice Sprout. Although I will never understand her choice I will always honor her decision. At one point she had mentioned to a worker that she knew how much we loved him. After a long two years, only two days before his second birthday, Sprout became our son. We were so elated to walk out of that courtroom and know that he would be a part of our family forever.

God has been so faithful to us. I look back now and know that if we had adopted Colby or Rose or any of the other babies earlier in our journey, we would have missed out on the amazing little boy that Sprout is. I would have also missed out on the lesson that God was trying to teach me - life is not about me and what I want. I have always related my journey through foster care back to a story I once heard:

While at the beach a mother and her daughter saw hundreds of starfish wash ashore. The little girl scrambled as she tried to throw them all back into the water one at a time so they would not die. "Don't bother dear," the mother said, "it will not make a difference because you will never be able to save all of them." As the little girl listened to what her mother said, she looked into her hand. She threw the starfish into the water and said, "It will make a difference to this one."

God sent each one of those tiny "starfish" to us before Sprout to be loved and cared for until the families He had for them were ready. God wants us to be faithful in what He calls us to do, especially in the small things. Every day as I watch this little boy grow and learn, I am reminded of how faithful God is. We are truly blessed.

In the years that have passed since we said goodbye to our other foster children, Colby has thrived in his adoptive home. We have the privilege of watching him grow up through social media. In 2008, his adoptive family was able to bring home his full biological baby sister straight from the hospital. They finalized his adoption in 2007 and her adoption three years later. Felix started school this year and we are thrilled to be able to watch him grow up through social media also. He lived with his maternal grandmother for two years. His mother is now drug-free and he is home with her. God is faithful! Rose is thriving in her adoptive home. Her adoption was finalized in 2011. God is so amazing! Colby and Rose are cousins through adoption as both of their adoptive mothers are sisters. Rose's adoption took a bit longer because of her biological mother. The county needed to prove that they made "reasonable efforts" with her biological mom because of her cognitive delays. We rejoiced with her adoptive parents when the adoption was finalized. Most of the babies that have been with us are still a part of our lives. We either see them around town, or we are able to watch them grow through pictures. It is closure for my family and me, and it proves that God's plans are exceedingly and abundantly more than we could ever ask, dream, or imagine.

2

A Christmas Surprise

It all started with an ill-timed phone call. Our lives had not even had time to recover from the sibling group of three that had just moved into our home. It felt like a struggle just to get out of bed some mornings. On that exact day, the business that we own had a very large order come in completely wrong, and it was going to cost us thousands. We were tired, overwhelmed, and had no idea our life was about to be hit by another wrecking ball. A wonderful wrecking ball, but a wrecking ball nonetheless.

"Hello?" I said as I answered the strange number that came up on my cell phone.

"Hello, this is Amy from DHS (Department of Human Services). I see the Watson children were placed with you two months ago for adoption. Mom just had another baby. Do you want her?"

To say I had never been so blindsided in all my life would have been an understatement. All I remember saying is, "Yes… (pause)…yes…(pause)…yes. We want her. I don't know where I am going to put her, but I want her."

I got off the phone and everything hit me all at once. *Where are we going to put this baby? We only have three bedrooms and they are already full! We do not have enough seats in our car! How did this woman hide another pregnancy?*

I had just said yes to a baby. Now I would have to go downstairs and tell my very stressed out husband that I had said yes to something that we were totally unprepared for.

As I walked down the stairs to my husband's office the tears started to come. As I stepped down each stair I felt like I was being battered by waves of emotion that were hitting me all at once. I was completely overwhelmed and excited all at the same time.

"Mark, we just had a baby." I said to my unsuspecting husband with a shaky voice and a huge goofy grin on my face.

"What do you mean?" he answered in a tone that was a mix of concern and confusion.

"We just had a baby." I repeated, trying to get myself to believe what I had just been told on the phone a few minutes prior.

"What does that *mean*?" he asked again.

"Honey, the kids' mom just had another baby. No one knew she was pregnant. She went to the same hospital she always does and had the baby. Both the mom and the baby tested positive for having pot in their system. The hospital should have called DHS, but they didn't. They let her take the baby home. They don't know where the baby is, but they are going to try to find her. When they do they want us to take her. They asked me if we would take her and I said yes. I couldn't say no. Did you want me to say no? I could call them back..." I rambled.

As if we did not have enough on our plates already. Just two months earlier we had moved the baby's three siblings into our home, a brother and two sisters. We also had two biological children and one adopted child before we even started the process of adopting the sibling group of three – now turned four!

We had been fostering for four years, and there had been no reason to believe we would be able to adopt any of our foster children. That is why, a year and a half prior, we had decided to go ahead and try to have another biological child. Ben, our oldest, was six years old when we had started the fostering process. He had been a big brother to four foster children that had come and gone. Several of those children had stolen our hearts, and when they left we had been crushed. Our hearts had been beaten up by

16

foster care, so we took matters into our own hands. As soon as I became pregnant, Courtney, our third foster child who was still living with us, became available for adoption. As my baby grew inside me, I also filled out adoption paperwork.

As the days quickly passed, and my c-section date approached, I got a call from a friend of mine. She was fostering a sibling group of three who we had met two years before. "The judge is finally terminating," she said. "Dad has been caught in so many lies that they are done giving him chances."

With my c-section date only a week away, and an adoption already in progress, we were not exactly looking to adopt any more children. However, we had never been able to shake the feelings we had the day we met these three foster children. We had spent all of half an hour with them, but as we walked out of my friend's door, my husband unwittingly said, "If they ever come up for adoption let us know." Those words stuck with me over the next two years. I had felt the same way. So I watched and waited from afar for this set of three beautiful children to become legally available for adoption.

In March of 2012, I gave birth to my biological daughter, Lynnlee. From the moment I found out I was pregnant with her, my war torn heart began to heal. Foster care had been hard on me. I had taken the brunt of it because I was the one who did the paperwork, dealt with the visits, talked to the social workers, lawyers, biological family, and everyone else. I had seen my foster children scream for me as they were carried into visitation rooms. I had been the one to call the police while I sat in the ER with one of my foster children as she had a rape kit done after an overnight weekend visit at her biological mom's house. As I stared at my new baby, my first legal daughter as well as biological daughter, some of the scars started to fade, and things started to feel hopeful again.

Summer blew in, and with it came our first adoption from foster care. Courtney was legally our daughter after two years of being our foster child. She adjusted to the roll of big sister to Lynnlee wonderfully, for which I was so thankful. Courtney had always been my most challenging child. I had never been one to put a lot of stock in first impressions, but when I think of my first meeting with Courtney, well, I have to say that sometimes you can judge a book by its cover.

17

The first time I met Courtney was on the day I was to pick her up from the agency and bring her home with me. I was sitting in the agency's waiting room when she bounced in with her great aunt. She was a human Ping-Pong ball. She was everywhere and into everything with too small clothes on and short dark hair. During the meeting, she was totally out of control. All I could think was, "What have I gotten myself into?" I kept expecting her great aunt or her biological mom to control her, but they did nothing. I took matters into my own hands and I scooped up that chunky eighteen-month-old that did not know me at all. I held her on my lap, and let her play with my cell phone. At the end of the meeting, I lifted her up and realized her diaper had leaked all over me. That pretty much set the tone for the next two years.

When we received the phone call for this new baby, a baby who would turn our family of eight into a family of nine, we had to accept that any plans we had made were going to fly right out the window. There we were, two biological children, one newly adopted child, three children who had just moved in two months earlier who we were in the process of adopting and getting to know, and now we were expecting a newborn that we had not even known existed.

Foster care is the epitome of "hurry up and wait." We were excited, nervous, and worried. After that first phone call, we did not hear from anyone for three or four days. No call to say they found her. No call to say they could not find her. Nothing. So we started to make plans under the assumption that eventually they would find her and bring her to us. First, I put out a cry for help on Facebook. I had just sold all of my newborn things, and I was just sick over it. Thankfully, I had a friend who was not as rash as I was when it came to getting rid of her baby supplies, and she was happy to let me use all of her (very blue) baby items.

After letting the cat out of the bag on Facebook, we had to go through the announcement phase again. A lot of the people in our lives, while very supportive, thought we had, perhaps, taken on too much by adding three more kids to our family. As social workers and police were out searching for this baby girl, we felt obligated to tell everyone who would not be finding out online. My parents, while well-meaning, had already had a hard time seeing foster care chew me up and spit me out, and were concerned that I was taking on too much.

"What about Lynnlee?" my mom asked. Lynnlee, my biological daughter, was only nine months old at the time and still nursing. Along with being so young, she had always been a very high maintenance baby. She never slept through the night, and she had a pretty good case of stranger danger towards anyone besides my husband and me.

"You don't have to take her. The other kids don't know her. You could just let someone else take her." While not spoken aloud by me, that thought had gone through my head while on the phone with the DHS worker. It had gone through my head during the first phone call, after the phone call, the morning after the phone call, and while I made plans for this new baby that would change everything. I really did not have to take her. This baby would have been a great baby for someone else to adopt. A newborn baby that would be available for adoption almost immediately is a rare thing in the foster care world. Regardless, there was just something inside me that knew she was mine. It also helped that my reserved, levelheaded husband was all for her coming to live with us. "If she is my daughters' sister, she is my daughter." It sounded so simple. However I knew this would put us into a tailspin for a while, and I was just recovering from the last major change in our lives. I kept telling myself, *"You will love this baby as much as you love Jessica and Sara,"* her biological sisters.

I have never regretted saying yes to any of the children we have fostered, not even the sister and brother sibling set that I had asked to be moved after only a week of them being in my home. The little boy had Fragile X. The social worker had told me that it mirrors autism. I had always wanted to say yes to a child with autism because I had wondered if I would be able to parent them. My experiment was short lived when he started attacking Courtney constantly. He would be standing next to her, and then, out of nowhere, bite her so hard it broke the skin. She had marks all over her body by the time he left, and I could not have been happier to see him go. It was a good learning experience for me. I always liked to think that I could handle anything, but I learned quickly that I do not have the required skills to parent a child like him.

Saying yes is always the easy part, but you never quite know what you are getting yourself into. Sometimes you have no idea what you have just said yes to. In our case, we at least knew some of the things we needed to do to prepare for this little baby girl.

19

Our first issue that had to be immediately addressed was our car situation. My husband had just quit his job to run his own business. At his prior job he had a company car. When the three siblings moved in with us, we traded in my car for a minivan that would seat all eight of us. Not a seat was spared, but we had no plans to buy a second car. We thought we would see how things went with just one. Now, with the new baby becoming the ninth member of our family, we would have to buy a second car and drive two cars everywhere that we went as a family.

I could not quite bring myself to agree to buy the new car until we had at least heard something. Around a week after we got the first call we finally received a second call. It was from a friend of a friend who worked in the county where all of this was happening. She told me that they had found the baby.

She went on to tell me that at the hospital where the baby was born, the biological mom had listed her father's address as her address. When CPS (Child Protective Services) went to the address the hospital had on file, her father, the baby's grandfather, claimed he had not seen his daughter for quite some time. I guess whoever questioned him did not believe him because they went back to his house with the police, and they questioned him again. He finally admitted that he had picked Mom and the baby up from the hospital and had driven them somewhere, but he said that he could not remember where he had dropped them off. Eventually they questioned him enough to make him tell them the whole truth. He got into his car and led them to the garage apartment where he had dropped Mom and the baby off.

From what I have been told, when the police knocked on the door the biological dad answered. His immediate response upon seeing the police was to turn to Mom and say, "Get the kid's stuff, it's time." The CPS worker who was with the police noted that the biological dad was obviously with the biological mom, which is the whole reason the court terminated his legal rights to their three older children.

After CPS took the baby, they ran her straight to the doctor. She weighed in at only four pounds and seven ounces. She was such a tiny little thing. She was taken to a foster home in the same county where the parents lived. She stayed there for a few days while a court date was scheduled and the county waited for permission from the judge to move her to our home.

After the judge gave the county permission to place the baby out of county with us the paperwork started to fly, but in all the wrong directions. I received a phone call from a lady I had never spoken to before. She told me that they had the baby and they were ready to place her with us. She said she had sent some paperwork over to my agency, but she had sent it to someone who had no authority to sign the agreement. At this point it was about five days before Christmas day. With Christmas being on a Tuesday I knew that if I did not get the new baby into our home by that Friday we would not have her for Christmas.

The county the baby was in wanted to do a "Borrowed Bed Agreement" with our agency. A "Borrowed Bed Agreement" is when an agency has a "free bed" that a county wants to fill, but the county wants to maintain control of the case and not hand it over to the agency. I called one of the people at our agency that I knew could sign the agreement, and he basically told me, "We don't do that." All I could think was, "Well, you are going to have to!" So, I called the lady back who was trying to place the baby with us and gave her the name of the person at my agency that she needed to talk to. I also asked her to email me a copy of the paperwork that she needed to have signed so that I could try to get it into the right hands.

The next morning I received a call from our agency. Basically, the county that had the baby strong-armed our agency into agreeing to the "Borrowed Bed Agreement." I was thrilled! I printed off the paperwork that needed to be signed and ran it to the agency myself to ensure the right person signed it and that it got emailed back to the county that day. When I got home I called the lady placing our new baby and let her know that I had emailed the signed agreement to her. She said she would have the foster care worker contact me in order to set up a time for us to pick up our little girl.

I was so excited, but nervous because I was pretty sure something was going to go wrong. Often it is so hard to get foster care workers to call you back. If I missed her call or did not hear from her soon enough, we would not have any extra time to try to get the baby home before Christmas. I had literally twenty-four hours in which to try to pull off a "Christmas Miracle;" and in foster care, twenty-four hours is not much time. God was going to have to step in if this was going to happen.

21

I woke up Friday morning before the Christmas weekend and found an email in my inbox. It was from the foster care worker. She had listed the names and phone number of the foster parents that were caring for our baby, and told me to give them a call to set up a time to pick up the baby that day. She told me that the foster family was expecting my call. Sounds simple enough, right? Wrong.

After reading the email, I immediately called the phone number of the foster parents. The phone line was busy. I thought to myself, *"That's odd."* I know that if I am expecting a call about one of my foster kids I make sure to keep the phone line available. I continued to call the number about every twenty minutes or so. I was not able to leave a message or anything. I got a busy signal every single time. After a couple of hours of this, I emailed the worker to see if I had the right number, and to see if she had a different number I could try. I never heard back from her.

As this was going on, my husband was getting more and more upset. He kept saying, "They are doing this on purpose. They are trying to blow us off today so they can keep her for Christmas. How selfish. She isn't their baby. She is our baby, and she should be with her family for Christmas!" It was exactly the same thing I was thinking, but was too nervous to say out loud. As if by saying it everything would immediately go wrong. My feeling that this was not going to be as easy as it should have been was turning out to be right.

However, I am nothing if not resourceful. I kept looking at the information in the email and tried to figure out how to find these people. I started searching the Internet for their names and finally found several leads. Eventually, I found their names connected to a phone number that seemed like it might be worth trying. It was not the same phone number as the one in the email from the foster care worker. I went ahead and dialed the number, and a man answered right away. I asked for the foster mom by name, and he put her on the phone. I had found a number for them that worked! I did not mention to the foster mom anything about the phone number that did not work. I just asked if she had talked to the foster care worker, and asked what time would be good for us to pick up the baby that day.

She was a seasoned foster mom, an older lady, who had adopted several of her foster children. She had a raspy smoker's voice and, like most foster moms, was full of information and opinions. She said she thought that her husband actually knew the baby's father. After listening to her, I realized that her husband knew the baby's grandfather. They both have the same name. She also told me that her kids were so sad because they were all hoping that the baby would be with them for Christmas. I could not help but sympathize with her. If I had been in her shoes, I would have hoped for the same thing. It is amazing how quickly a little one can steal your heart, and I was thankful that it sounded like this stranger on the other end of the phone had cared very well for my daughter.

After talking about pretty much everything under the sun in relation to foster care, besides asking why her phone had been busy all day, we hung up with a plan for us to pick up our tiny bundle in a few hours. By this time, a small blizzard had been laying the perfect Christmas snow on the ground, but it also made for a hazardous car trip. The baby was a little over an hour away from us, and whoever went to pick her up would be headed into the worst part of the storm. My husband and my oldest son packed up and headed out onto the snow-covered roads. I wanted to go, but I did not have anyone to watch the other kids, and my husband did not want me to go out on the bad roads by myself.

So, off they went to pick up our newest little girl. About an hour and a half later I received a picture message on my phone from my husband. He finally had the baby, and she was sleeping in a car seat behind him. We finally had our daughter! A wave of relief washed over me as I stared at that little face on my phone screen. Thankfully, my husband, our son, and the new baby arrived home with no issues from the bad roads. My husband carried in the car seat, and I peered into the blankets. She was as small as she could be and looked like, perhaps, she should have spent some more time growing in her biological mother's womb, but I assumed it was best for her to make her way out. Her little legs were so thin. As I lifted her out of her car seat I felt like I was going to break her. She continued to sleep as I held her in my arms, and I tried to get my head to catch up with my heart. This little person that I had only known for a few minutes was my daughter. Not by biology or even legally, but the legal part would come soon enough. In the meantime, our little miracle had made it home in time for Christmas. She was, by far, the best Christmas present I had ever had the pleasure of receiving.

Foster care had been nothing like we hoped it would be, and everything that we feared it would be, but God's timing had always been perfect. When we started this journey our plan was to adopt. We were going to go in, get our kids, and get out. No plans for more biological children, definitely no plans of adopting five children, but God had better plans than we ever could have dreamed. The first call we ever received was for a newborn baby boy. I said, "Yes," hung up with the worker, and then promptly got a call back letting me know the baby had been placed with a different agency.

Had our first placement been a baby who had later become available for adoption, I honestly believe we would have never decided to have our second biological child. The thought of that sucks the wind right out of me. Our life now is proof that God's plans for us are always best. If we would have been able to adopt our first placement, I know we would have been done with foster care. No Courtney, no Lynnlee, no Jessica, Sara, their brother or the baby that this story is about.

I cannot imagine my life without them. I do not want to imagine my life without them. It hurt terribly when several of our foster children were returned to their biological families. We had fallen in love with them and ended up having no say in their future or their safety. However, had that not happened, our family that we have now would not exist. To say God was there every step of the way would be an understatement. God made sure that no step was missed. He led us to every child that was supposed to be in our family. He tore down walls that are usually considered impenetrable in the foster care world. He brought us together, and He is the one that is still sustaining us as we live and thrive as a family of nine.

3

Miss Jeckle and Hyde

It was 3pm on a Friday afternoon, and I was sitting alone at my computer desk. The neighborhood kids were all playing inside their houses on this muggy, hot day. The dogs were sleeping, and my house was exceptionally silent.

The phone rang and I looked at the caller ID. My heart skipped a beat, and my hands shook as I picked up the phone wondering if this would be the moment I had been waiting for all this time.

"Congratulations! I have it in my hand!" exclaimed the voice on the other end of the phone.

It was my licensing worker. It was official. I was finally a licensed foster parent. I did not know what to say. For almost a year I had been waiting. For almost a year I had been told "two more weeks." I hardly dared to breathe. I did not want this to be some kind of dream. Finally, more to myself than the worker, I said, "Wow."

I was in shock. I had been told for days that my license was being worked on because they were in a rush to get it done. My licensing worker was scurrying to get me licensed before the weekend because they had had quite a few children come into care recently and they needed more licensed homes.

I spoke with the licensing worker for a few more minutes. I do not think the smile left my face the entire time. I was so excited. I was still sitting at my desk forty-one minutes later when the phone rang again. I looked at the caller ID, and my heart sank. Why would she be calling back except to say there had been a mistake and that I was really not licensed? I took a steadying breath and answered.

"Would you be interested in two little girls? They are as cute as buttons. One is a year and a half, and one is almost three. They've had it pretty rough. You would be their sixth home in five months. They have been bounced around from foster home to family and back several times. No one seems to want them very long, but everyone reports that they are busy, but good, little girls. Did I scare you off, or are you still interested?"

I had been licensed for forty-one minutes, and they wanted me to take kids now! I found myself saying, "Of course!" before I could even think through the information she had just told me.

"Can you be to the agency by four? We lock the doors at four, and it would be so much easier if you could get here before then."

Thirteen minutes later, I found myself walking through the doors of the Department of Human Services building. I had been in this building many times, but never as a foster parent. I was nervous as I told the receptionist why I was there. I was nervous as I rode the elevator to the correct floor. I was nervous as I walked down a hallway that seemed a mile long. I was nervous as I searched the maze of cubicles for my licensing worker. I was nervous as she introduced me to the caseworker for the girls. Then I saw their sweet little faces, and my nerves went away.

A very short time later, I was walking back out that door with two little girls. I could not believe that less than an hour and a half ago I was sitting at my computer desk listening to the silence, and now I had two little girls to love.

"Mommy, I tirsty."

My brain jumped. "Mommy?" Did this little girl I had just met minutes prior really just call me mommy? It felt so good, and yet so strange. I had noticed that she called her aunt "Mommy," too. I felt sad that she did not really know what a mommy was.

26

She had no idea that a mommy was not just any woman who took care of her, but was supposed to be one very special woman for every little girl.

The first week was extremely busy, but as we settled in, life slowed down into our new version of normal. Kara and her little sister Chastity were pretty well behaved and not "busy" at all. I was told the other foster homes and other family members could not handle the girls because of how "busy" they were. But Kara especially was not "busy." Kara wanted nothing more than to have a sippy cup of juice in her hand as she laid on the couch watching "her shows."

After three weeks of having the girls in my home, the honeymoon phase ended. Chastity was still a mellow and easy-going baby, but Kara was going to give me a run for my money. As long as things were going the way she wanted them to, life was good. However I was not going to allow her to sit on the couch all day long watching TV.

The first time I turned the TV off and asked Kara to bring me a book to read, all hell broke loose. She threw herself down so hard that when her head hit the floor it bounced. She grabbed the book her sister handed to her and ripped it from cover to cover. She then stood up and started stomping on the pages. She threw herself back onto the floor, and let out a scream that was unlike anything I had ever heard. It was as if the scream was coming from her soul - not her tiny little vocal chords. It was filled with rage, fear and hatred.

I picked her up, not to comfort her, but to stop her from hurting herself as she thrashed around. That made her even angrier. I did not know what to say, so I said nothing. She bit me. She kicked me. She scratched me. She head-butted me hard enough that I saw stars. My cute, tiny little girl had turned into this crazed monster. The screaming eventually stopped, but the rage did not. I am not sure how long it lasted, but by the time it was over I was covered in sweat, blood, and bruises. She marched off and got a drink of water from the dining room, walked back into the living room, sat down, and just as calmly as could be asked me if I could turn the TV back on.

After the girls had been with me for a few weeks I noticed that Chastity would scream and cry for no apparent reason. As I tried to figure out what was triggering her sudden outbursts of crying,

I also started to watch Kara more closely. Kara would be sitting on the floor playing with her toys, and Chastity would walk past. Kara would casually stick out her leg and trip her sister. The laughter that erupted afterwards was maniacal. She was so sneaky. She would hit her sister on the head with a toy and then quickly go back to where she was sitting. It got to the point that I could not leave the girls in the same room together without supervision. Kara was so mean and devious that even me going to the bathroom meant an injury for Chastity. I did not know what to do. I did not know how to keep Chastity safe.

I emailed our licensing worker and explained to her what was happening. I told her I was not going to disrupt the placement, but I needed help dealing with Kara. I needed to know what to do to help her, or at least how to keep Chastity safe. She tried to be helpful, but she did not have any answers. Our county's mental health department will not work with a child before the age of four, and neither would the other places she suggested.

About three months after they moved in, the girls' biological dad told me that he was going to court to try to get custody of them. He was working his case plan and doing everything they asked him to do to get the kids back. The girls' caseworker was so sure that the judge would agree to place the girls back with their parents, that she told me to have all their stuff packed and ready to go. I did all of their laundry, sorted all of their toys, and packed their little toothbrushes. Inside, I was a mess of emotions. I was more than ready to have Kara go, but I really loved her little sister and was going to miss her terribly.

Kara knew something was going on. She was a very smart three-year-old. All of her belongings were sitting in the middle of the living room. I told her that "Mommy and Daddy" were at court talking to the judge. If the judge said it was okay, then she and Chastity were going to go live with her daddy and grandma. She really did not seem to care one way or the other. She just asked if I would turn the TV on for her.

All day we sat and waited. Every time the phone rang, I would jump at the thought of it being the caseworker letting me know it was time to bring the girls to their father. Finally, the phone did ring, but it was not the news I was expecting. The judge did not make his decision on the spot. I was told that usually, if it was good news, he would tell them in court. If his answer is no, he would send a letter through the mail.

My heart sank. I was really hoping that this was the last day I would have to deal with the tantrums and rages. I was prepared in my heart to say goodbye to Chastity, and now my heart had to do a total turn around. I was told that the judge would let their parents know in a week and not to unpack all of their belongings.

For a week the girls lived out of suitcases and boxes. For a week they had to put their toys in a separate box when they were done playing with them. One week turned into two. Their case-worker said that the long wait probably meant the judge was going to say no. If that was the case, I needed to plan on having the girls for at least another three to nine months. Their case had already gone on for nine months. At the one-year mark, they could extend it for another six months if their biological mom was not doing all she needed to do.

I sat down and cried. I did not think I could handle another nine months. The girls had only been with me for four months. How would I be able to make it through another nine months with Kara? I was determined to not put the girls through another move. They had now lived with me longer than they had lived at any other place, but how could I keep my own sanity with Kara here? I did not have the answer, but I knew I had to think of something.

Meanwhile, I was turning into a person I did not like. I was angry all the time, even though I tried really hard not to show it. I was getting depressed. I began to doubt my ability to be a foster parent at all. I was sinking into a black hole, and it felt like no one noticed that I was drowning.

Kara was such an adorable little girl and she could charm the socks off anyone. I honestly felt like no one believed me when I told them how angry she was, or what her rages looked like. I cried every time she hurt Chastity. I felt like a total failure. I could not keep Chastity safe. They had come to my house to be safe and loved, yet I could not keep one safe, and I could not love the other.

I finally heard from Kara and Chastity's mom. She told me that they had just gotten their letter in the mail that day, and the judge had given custody to the girls' dad. I could not wait to get her off the phone. She kept saying how sad I must be that the girls were leaving. A small part of me was sad about Chastity, but the tears streaming down my face, were not tears of sadness. They were tears of relief. Soon I would not have to feel like I was letting

Chastity down every day. Soon I would not have to be angry all the time. Soon I could go back to my old, happy self and not have to pretend that my world was okay when it really was not. Soon I could move on with my life.

Kara overheard me talking to a friend on the phone and asked me if she was going to see "Daddy." I explained to her that the judge had finally said she could go live with her daddy and grandma. She did not seem happy at all. She really did not seem to care at all about where she was going to live.

The next morning, I knew I was in for a rough day. Kara had woken up with that look in her eyes. As I walked down the stairs, Kara scooted past me and tripped me as I was coming down. Luckily, I caught the banister and did not fall, but I did twist my ankle pretty badly. I should have known she would try something. I had thought of almost every situation in my head and had a plan of how to keep Chastity and I safe. Never once did I think she would try to trip me going down the stairs.

I took Kara by the hand and led her to the time out spot. Of course, she started raging immediately. She was slamming her head violently into the wall. Within a minute, I could see a goose egg forming on her head. I picked her up to move her away from the wall, and she bit me so hard that I had bruises and teeth marks in my skin for weeks after. She scratched me and drew blood. She hit and kicked me repeatedly. For three hours she raged, never stopping or slowing down. When it was finally over, she did her three-minute time out and ran off to play like nothing had even happened.

I tried to talk to her. I tried to explain that it was a good thing that she was going to live with her daddy. I tried to get her to tell me how she was feeling, but at three years old, she just did not have the words. I did get her to say that she was mad, but I never could get her to say what she was mad about.

Most of Kara's last day with me was spent being watched like a hawk. The more I watched her, the angrier she looked. I knew she wanted to hurt her sister, but I was determined that the last memories Chastity would have of my house were not going to be ones in which she was being hurt.

Dinnertime came and with it came another rage. Kara wanted peas for dinner, and we were having green beans. I opened a can of peas and told her that she could have peas instead. Normally, I

30

would not have done that, but I did not feel like dealing with another meltdown. It did not matter though. Just the fact that I had planned on having something else was reason enough for her. The rage began. She threw plates and knocked over chairs. She went over to the computer desk with the intention of throwing everything that was on it off. I got to her before she could. I scooped Kara up and headed upstairs.

There was more anger than I had ever seen coming out of this small child. I finally could not handle being abused anymore, so I put her in her sister's bedroom. There was nothing she could hurt in there, and not much to throw around. I closed the door, walked away, and let her rage. Chastity needed me. So I left her alone, something I had never done before. I felt guilty, but it was what I had to do. By the time she calmed down, it was time for bed. I put Chastity to bed and then Kara. I laid Kara down and covered her up. I told her goodnight. She looked up at me, and with that sweet, little voice of hers said, "I love you, Mommy." That was the first time she had ever said those words first. Every night before, I had said it first and then she would tell me that she loved me too, but she had never said it first before.

Finally, Kara was sleeping. I went up to Chastity's room. I scooped her up and cried into her pajamas. I told her everything I had been feeling for the past five months. I apologized to her for all the times that I had not been able to keep her safe. I told her I was sorry that I did not have as much time to play with her as I should have, and that I had not read her as many books as I would have liked. I apologized that I rushed them through their baths just so I could get Kara to bed and not have to deal with her any more that night. She reached up and put her arms around my neck. She squeezed hard and did not let go. She kissed my cheek, and with that I knew I was forgiven.

Kara and Chastity went to live with their father the next day. As sad as I was to see Chastity go, the relief that washed over me was undeniable. I no longer was responsible for Kara. I arrived back home, and I just stood there looking around. The house looked so different without all of their things in it. But the biggest change was in how I felt. I felt as if the weight of the world had just been lifted off of me. I felt I could breathe again for the first time. I could sit and relax and not be on guard every minute of the day. I was free.

31

My house was put on hold for a while to make sure Kara and Chastity did not come back into care. I told the agency about two weeks into my hold that even if they did come back into care I would not be able to take them back. I told the placement worker that I would take Chastity any time, but that I would not take Kara. Placement coordinators try very hard here not to split up siblings, so I knew the chances were low that Chastity would ever be placed with me again. I was sad about that, but knew that was what I had to do.

Since Kara and Chastity were returned to their biological father, I have had another sibling set come and go. They were only here a short time, but I still miss them and think about them every day. Two weeks after my second placement left, another set of siblings arrived. They are still with me. Kara and Chastity certainly baptized me by fire into life as a foster mom. They were by far the hardest placement I have had so far. My other placements have been a pure joy to have in my home. I foster because I love kids. I hope that someday I will be able to adopt a house full of kids, but in the meantime I just enjoy hearing the laughter.

4

Goodbye is Never Easy

As we sat in the hospital lounge playing various card games, the constantly ringing cell phones were a welcome relief to the painful alternation between sobs and intense fear. Most of the calls were from friends and family wishing us well, expressing their love and concern for my father, but there were a handful that came in quite obviously oblivious to our family's plight. I knew them by their area code, first one, then another. By the end of the day we had received four separate calls from the Department Placing Group asking us if we could take 12 different children. More importantly, we had received a bit of excitement and hope for our future that had otherwise been quite dark.

As many will tell you, it (almost) always starts with a phone call. Those phone calls are exciting and tend to initiate each new roller coaster ride of foster care. As we say "yes," it is like strapping into the roller coaster car, listening to the ride operator explain that we need to keep our hands and feet in the ride at all times, and then exuberantly waiting for that button to be pushed that launches us forward into the new adventure that awaits us. We were unable to say yes to any of the placement calls that day because we were out-of-state. My father had been in a very serious accident and was fighting for his life, so my siblings and I had rushed to his side. This was just the last of a series of events over the previous three weeks that included two other deaths, a serious leg injury, and a broken car. In the midst of all that crazy, we also said goodbye to our first foster children. We had naively thought that they would stay forever and had fallen madly in love with them. Now, here we were, gratefully watching my father recover, and happy to have that little bit of excitement every time the phone rang with an unfamiliar phone number.

It only took a few more days for my father to be released from the hospital, and a few more after that for my husband Jackson, son Lance, and I to make the 24-hour drive to return home. There had been a major family fight, police, and excommunication involved before we left, but who was counting? It would be an extreme understatement to say we were really looking forward to getting back to some sort of normal as we came home. We quickly learned that our life was not normal. The only thing normal about being foster parents is that nothing is ever normal.

* ◆

As I walked into the house on Tuesday, I was exhausted in every way. I knew Jackson would be at work for the evening so all I was thinking about was how I could find something easy to feed Lance before we both collapsed in bed. It was 6:05pm and the house was completely quiet - at least until 6:06. I had hardly unlocked the front door to step inside the house before my cell phone rang, to my complete surprise. With everything going on, my hobbling in an ankle boot, and trying to carry everything in the house, all I could think was, *"What now?"*

That call would forever change our lives. Her name was Tina, someone I would later come to know as my own personal placement worker because of how many children she would eventually place in our home. Tina brought us a ten-month-old boy who had been removed earlier in the day due to neglectful supervision. His parents had left him alone multiple times while they got high with their drug of choice – powder cocaine. The home was obviously not safe. As investigators came to remove the child, they found drug paraphernalia and residue throughout the house, something

34

quite common in these types of cases. The baby, David, did not appear to have family available to take him.

I tentatively agreed to parent him, called Jackson to confirm, and then called Tina again to finalize the placement agreement. As we waited for him to arrive, I ran around the house to do a bit of prep work. Thankfully, with all that had happened, I had not put away the crib and everything else I had out from the previous placement that had included a boy just slightly older than David. I sorted through the few clothing items I had, made sure the bottles were out and available, and re-checked the bedding to make sure I had cleaned and sanitized it, per regulations. Everything was as ready as it was going to be.

David was from a local county whose office is nearby, so it only took about 90 minutes for him to arrive at our doorstep. He was so sweet with his beautiful blue eyes, dimples, and happy nature. He played on the floor with Lance while the investigator talked to me a bit more about his situation and I signed the usual paperwork. Everything was so natural and fun. David was already restoring joy to our home.

Out of excitement and respect for my husband, as soon as the investigator left I packed up the kids and headed straight to meet Jackson at his workplace so he could meet our newest son. Thankfully, Jackson was able to take a quick break so we met at Walmart to shop for the bare essentials we would need for David, like formula. We spent less than 30 minutes together before we said goodbye to Daddy and headed home. That is all it took for us to be hooked on this little guy.

The ride home was not as pleasant. He screamed the entire ride, which, unfortunately, lasted nearly 40 minutes. By the time we got home, I was praying I would know what to do to help him calm down and was wondering what I had gotten myself into. The sweet natured boy had turned into a raging monster in the car and that was not pleasant. I tried to feed him a bottle, but he rejected it. I tried to rock him; he screamed more. After a 45-minute attempt I gave up and decided to place him in bed. I did not know what else to do. To my surprise, he took a big breath, sighed, rolled onto his belly, and immediately went to sleep. I think I heard him say, "Ah! Finally she understands me." From then on he was known as my little sleeper.

One of the scariest things for a new foster parent can be interacting with the biological families. Most agencies and areas have precautions that protect foster parents from interacting extensively with the family involved in the case, but there are times when interaction is hard to avoid. Court is one of those times where I have learned to embrace the opportunity to meet the parents by boldly introducing myself to them and answering their questions, rather than unsuccessfully trying to hide out in the back of the courtroom. There is a prevalent stereotype about parents of children in foster care. Generally people presume these parents are scary, drug-involved, dirty, poor, dangerous people with whom you would rather not ever come in contact. For most of my cases at least some of these things have been true. But with rare exception, I have been able to find common ground with the parents of my foster children. It started with the time I met the parents of my first foster child. The man I saw waiting outside of the visit was shaved bald, completely tattooed, missing teeth, had not showered, and dressed as if he had been working hard labor. To top it off he was smoking a cigarette. I did my best to avoid him, but as soon as I got the kids out of the car they screamed "Daddy!" and ran to him. I was forced to meet him and it changed my life. He was kind to me. He asked me questions about how the kids were doing, and I could tell it comforted him when I was able to provide him answers. It all went so well that by the end of the visit he had given me permission to cut his children's hair, something very unusual in foster care. I remember leaving that visit having fallen in love with fostering and the ability to pour into the lives of parents, not just the children. I was less fearful of the parents, but the stereotype mostly remained.

David's parents were completely different. Mom was a few months younger than I was at the time (27), and dad was in his early 30s like my husband. They were well spoken, clean, and if it were not for the apparent tears in mom's eyes you would not have been able to pick them out as parents who had just lost their child. They did not appear to be chronic cocaine users or perpetual criminals. They were just like us. Another day, another place, we could have been friends from the same circles. As it turned out, one of the parents had attended an exclusive private school in the area. The other had a career in a well-respected sector of the financial services industry. Upon first impression, they just did not fit the foster care mold. It was there an interesting friendship was sparked.

Every foster parent I know searches the Internet for information about the parents of the children in their home. In part, this is because we are nosy, but in large part, this is because the state has an obligation to protect the confidentiality of those involved in a case and therefore we ourselves have to find information about the children in our home. We want to know if the parents have a criminal history, and, if so, what it has involved. We want to see if we can find pictures of the children when they were younger. We want to know what the biological families are like. We want to know where they live.

We live in a small town where the population is less than 10,000 people. Everyone does not know everyone else, but with one grocery store, three gas stations, two nail salons, and three fast food chain locations you inevitably run into the people you do know from time to time. You can imagine my surprise when in court I heard that mom would be in drug treatment in the next town over and planned to get a job at the local Starbucks.

About two weeks into the placement we were shopping at the local large-pet supply store to accommodate the new turtle that daycare was so kind to provide for us. We were wandering around the store, taking our time to look at the fish, the birds, and the reptiles. David was sitting in the cart enjoying it all. As we walked the aisles we kept running into another family who appeared to be enjoying their visit at the store. At one point we passed each other and as they turned the corner to the next aisle I heard the dad tell the mom, "You know who that kid looked like? He looked like David!"

We immediately left the store. I had no idea who those people were or how they knew our child and I did not intend to stay around to find out. What I did know, without a doubt, was that this family recognized David and could have been anyone from a family member to a friend to the parents' drug dealer. At some point in the case I told David's mom and dad about the encounter, but I never did figure out who those people were or how they knew David. That experience did make me much more conscious about our surroundings when we had our foster children out with us, and somewhat more concerned about finding out as much as I could about their biological family.

Though not much about foster care is predictable, I have found the pattern of welcoming new children into our family tends to be very consistent. The first two weeks tend to be the most challenging for me. On top of trying to get childcare set up because I am a working mom, I also have to set up an initial doctor's appointment, Medicaid coordination phone calls, initial visits (caseworkers, lawyer, CASA (Court Appointed Special Advocate), and others), and plan for initial permanency conference and hearing dates to be set. In the mist of all these appointments, we are also trying to get to know each other as parent and child(ren). Figuring everything out can be a logistical and emotional nightmare. It is exhausting. Each time we have gone through the welcoming process we have learned new tricks to make this phase easier, like pre-filling out daycare enrollment forms with the information that stays consistent, but those first couple weeks remain a challenging period no matter what. It is always nice when things start to settle down in the third and fourth week as routines are established and everyone begins to adjust to the new family dynamics.

David adjusted very well into our home and that made the welcoming phase easier on us than some of our other cases, but he also brought us a different challenge we had not planned for or thought through prior to his arrival. It turned out he was removed three weeks before his first birthday. Lance had four parties when he turned one. I could not bear the thought of any child missing out on a first birthday party. This meant I needed to hurry up and plan a first birthday party with three weeks notice for a child I hardly knew, and, therefore, my friends and family did not know well either. I decided to have an Elmo themed party at my home the afternoon of his actual birthday with my local family and friends from church. It was a great party with festive pictures and video that I cherish to this day.

Unfortunately, David's first birthday was overshadowed by changes in his case. His mother had disappeared the week after I met her in court. I was told she was back on the streets, spending her time partying rather than participating in services. The woman I had met the week prior at court who had appeared to me to be ready to do whatever it took to get her son back had not quite been ready. She was gone. It broke my heart, but not as much as playing the roll of "Mom" in the birthday festivities knowing I was celebrating her son's birthday. David was so full of joy as he smashed

38

his own face into his personal birthday cake, and his biological mom, as I pictured it, was strung out in a crack house somewhere. I wondered if she thought about him. As a mother to a biological son, I remember how special these events were, how proud I was of him on his first birthday, and how rich our celebration was when he turned one. I could not fathom missing it. I was angry with her for choosing drugs over her son and yet my heart broke for her knowing she must have been in a dark place, at least some part of her deeply regretting her decisions.

* *

With mom gone and dad actively working his plan to get David back, the likelihood that David's paternal grandmother would get custody grew stronger. The caseworker and CASA volunteer both began trying to prepare me for his eventual move that was supported by dad (and everyone else in the case except Mom, who seemed to have given up her vote when she took to the streets). This grandmother made herself known at the very beginning of the case, but was unable to immediately take David with her upon removal because she lived out of state. When relatives live out of state there is a specific process that must be followed so that the different state agencies can work together to enable a kinship placement, otherwise known as ICPC. It can take several months to receive approval for an ICPC placement and the child to be moved. We kept David in our home for eight weeks while the state looked into whether his grandmother was fit enough to care for him, all the while falling in love with him day after day. When word came that grandmother was approved and the state was going to send him so far away our hearts broke into a million pieces. We wanted the best for him, and supported reunification, but we did not want to lose our sweet boy.

Everything changed just in time. Mom suddenly came back into the picture as if nothing had ever happened. Mom and Dad reconciled and began working their service plans together. I will never know if Mom came back because she was told David was going to be moved to a home 1,000 miles away or if she was just tired of the lifestyle she had been living. All I knew, at the time, was that she had returned and was very much engaged in the process of getting her son back. She was doing everything she could to keep her family together. It seemed to be working out for her because she managed to get a job and she appeared very happy. I was encouraged by her progress, and we began developing a true friendship.

• •

The longer David was with us the more our love for him grew. There was nothing unlikable about this little boy. He never threw tantrums and was very easy going. He slept very well and was always a pleasure to be around. He laughed and clapped and smiled and hugged. David loved his mom and made that clear when he was at visits, but he loved me too, making it clear that I was "Mom" as well. Unlike our first placement, in this situation David's parents were completely supportive of our place in his life and acknowledged it often at visits with plenty of gratitude.

When David arrived he had not yet mastered eating table food and preferred drinking from a bottle. When I questioned Dad about it he went on to tell me how they really never fed him baby food or table food before, but his favorite treat was pickles. Apparently, Dad would sit David on the kitchen floor and hand him a whole dill pickle as a snack to keep him occupied from time to time. As the foster parent, I wondered why they had not worked with him on the normal progression of food, starting with baby cereal, baby food, table food, but instead had chosen to feed him whole milk and pickles. I was also simultaneously bothered by their decision to give him whole pickles as a snack and grateful he had not choked on a chunk of pickle when his parents were not watching him. Surprisingly, even with parental drug use, drug exposure, and neglectful supervision, this was the most serious of his delays, which, as we have learned in the world of foster care, is fairly minimal.

Despite (or because of) having been fed nothing but whole milk and pickles, David was a big boy. This seemed to have led to his slower motor development. When he arrived a few weeks before his first birthday, he was just learning to crawl. We worked with him to help him build the strength and coordination he needed. Soon he began creeping along furniture and walking with our support. We delighted in his progress, and our house from time to time was full of shouts of joy when he did something new. David began letting go of the furniture and standing by himself just as mom arrived back from her hiatus. At the next visit I intended to show her how he could let go and stand, but he had other things in mind. I stood him up facing his mom, let his hands go, and he promptly took seven steps right to her as if he had been doing it for years. That moment was thrilling for us both, and I was extremely grateful we were able to share it together. She was equally as excited and shared her emotions with me. As strange as it may seem, that day we were both his "Mom." He knew it, we both knew it, and we celebrated together. I fondly look back at that memory today, even years later, as an example of a successful birth parent/foster parent relationship.

Our son Lance was quite fond of David. Lance enjoyed having David follow him around especially, because, unlike our first placement, David was young enough that he did not try to play with Lance's toys. Lance was also able to jump in and really be the big brother even though he was only three years old at the time. Two weeks after David's first birthday we received another call from Tina, our favorite placement worker, with a nine-month-old girl named Sophie. I ended up with what appeared to be twins and Lance would help me feed them each night before putting David and Sophie to bed. He would hold David while I held Sophie and we would talk like "big people" while they ate and fell asleep. It was a great bonding experience as a family, one that would have a big effect on Lance several years later.

＊＊＊＊＊＊＊＊＊＊＊＊＊＊＊＊＊＊＊＊＊＊＊＊＊＊＊＊＊＊＊＊＊＊＊＊＊＊＊

Mom and Dad continued to do well and appeared to be successfully kicking their bad habits and changing their lives. With this success, and Mom's disapproval of the kinship placement, the state decided to drop the conversation of moving David across the country. Instead, everyone began to seriously discuss reunification plans. The grandmother was able to come to our town to spend the night on occasion with David's family and the state granted overnight visits as long as she stayed to supervise. This happened monthly until the November permanency conference when the state was ready to finalize a transition plan to get David back into the apartment his parents now shared. Initially, the plan was to have an overnight-supervised visit in the beginning of December, as it had been for the previous months, an overnight visit on Christmas Eve, and then three weeks of weekend visits in January. As we began to look at the scheduled dates and finalize the plan, those few visits turned into seven weeks of weekend visits including one that began two days before Christmas and lasted through Christmas night.

Transition visits are hard on all involved and David was no exception. We would meet at the local Starbucks on Friday evenings and I had to verify the relative responsible for monitoring the visit over the weekend was present. We would spend a few minutes chatting about the new things David was doing or the experiences from the week. Each time we also talked about what David would be doing during his visit and the love his parents and the relatives had for him was apparent. The bond between his mom and I continued to strengthen and soon I was able to share my parenting tips with her, but also was able to encourage her as a mother who was struggling to overcome guilt and shame for her faults in parenting and in life. Every time we left David with his parents he would cry and reach out for us and every time they brought him back he would cry for them. He was confused and his figurative loyalties were divided.

I will never forget the first overnight visit. Leaving your child with the family that neglected or abused him, knowing there would be no "impartial" supervision and the neglect or abuse was free to occur, is one of the hardest things a foster parent has to do. You turn the child you love dearly over to people who have yet to prove that they are capable of taking care of him properly, hope they return the child to you on time, if at all, and try not to think about the fact that you are still legally responsible for whatever happens to him according to the state documents. On David's first visit, everything seemed to be going fine until Mom texted me late that Friday night, shortly after they had arrived home. She was concerned about purple spots on his gums. This was not the first time she had gotten on my case about his dental hygiene, because, as a dental hygienist she had a very high standard of oral cleanliness, but this time I had no idea what she was referring to and in the back of my mind wondered what she was trying to accuse me of. We worked out medical arrangements and Saturday she took him to the ER to be evaluated. Apparently David had caught a somewhat common virus that uncommonly affected him with an outbreak of purple mouth sores and blisters causing him to bleed with tooth brushing and caused pain while eating.

· ·

By the time the final date was set for David to return home everyone involved was ready to be done with the transition visits. They had lasted so long, and were taking a toll on everyone emotionally and physically. We had all grown close and appreciated each other for the unusual co-parenting relationship we had formed, but we were all ready to move to the next step, even if that meant losing David. His mom and dad were ready to prove themselves and have David with them full time. We were not confident that they would be able to stay healthy, and we could not help but worry that he would end up being removed again sometime in the future. However, we also knew that his parents had worked very hard to clean themselves up, they had work on their marriage, and they had gotten to a place where they had the best shot at making their family work. In the end, we were cheering for David to be back with his parents where he belonged and hoped the relationship we had built with his parents meant that we would continue to play a role in David's life long-term.

We wanted David's goodbye to be special, honoring the celebration we all really felt it was. I got the crazy idea that it would be best to invite David's parents to our home to pick him up rather than determine a neutral spot to do the hand off as we would with every other child going home. They accepted our invitation and showed up bright and early on Saturday morning to pick up David. Yes, they came to our home, something extremely unusual in typical foster care. We gave them a tour of the house and showed them where David had been eating, sleeping, and playing for the past nine months. I sincerely believed that if they were going to succeed it was important for them to have the visual image of how he lived while they were in rehab and pursued their mental health in order to get him back. At one point they turned to Lance to let him know that he would be invited to David's birthday parties. As we walked through our house we chatted some more about how we loved David and they mentioned how grateful they were that we were his foster parents. They stopped us when we got downstairs into the kitchen to ask us a serious question. Dad wanted to know if we would be his godparents so we could continue to play a significant role in his life, forever. I was extremely touched and excited at the possibility that our families would be friends for years to come, brought together by unfortunate circumstances, bonded over a special little boy, and encouraging each other toward greatness as we raised our children as brothers in Christ. It was just as perfect as I had imagined.

People always ask if it is hard to see a child go. David's was a case where the ambivalence of letting him go was as strong as it could have been. On one hand, we hated losing David. He felt like our child, our children's brother, and we had a special place in our hearts for him. On the other hand, we rejoiced with his parents, and wanted to see them succeed in raising him the way it should have been all along. In our experiences there has always also been a third, seemingly God-ordained distraction to help undoubtedly weigh the scales in favor of letting the child go, and in this case it was the flu. My husband, who never gets sick, had come down with the influenza virus and had been extremely ill for about six days. David and Sophie, our other foster child, had started running a high fever just a few days prior to David's return date and became difficult to manage (particularly when also caring for a sick dad). To top it off, God had blessed our region with 13 inches of snowfall, something that had not been seen in the area in 40 years. Life certainly lacked normalcy. So, on top of genuinely supporting the reunification plan, the promise of one less sick child to care for made us grateful that David was finally leaving to go back to live with the mother and father who biologically created him.

I was encouraged the right decision was made when frequent text message conversations with mom began. She would often text me to ask me how I handled certain behaviors David displayed (like whining after waking up if he did not immediately have a cup of milk to drink) or to let us know when he hit a developmental milestone. I enjoyed our conversations and it further confirmed to me that we had not lost David. We had gained new friends.

· ◆

When David left our home we immediately paused for bit to hug each other and celebrate life as a family of four once again. We knew we needed time to figure out what our new normal would be with David gone, though we had an idea what that would be like after having spent seven weekends with him away. Our hearts were sad, but there was also the relief of knowing that the transition period was finally over without having to say goodbye forever. We placed our name on the list of homes with open placements the following Monday, but it took three weeks to get the call for our next adventure. Two weeks after that we were onto yet another adventure as we said goodbye to those children and hello to our new ones on the same day. Life certainly was back to our version of normal.

Calls, emails, and texts from David's parents began to trail off. As far as we knew, we were still waiting for a baptism date so we could officially become his godparents, but we were allowing them their space to bond as a family without our constant involvement. I had the opportunity to take Lance and our newest daughter, Sophie, to California for a relative's baby shower. Our foster children stayed behind with my husband, Jackson, because we had not had them long enough to receive approval to go out of state, which gave me the opportunity to be a mom of two for a weekend. We were having a great time with family and friends, and I was reveling in the ability to share my daughter with the people she had never met.

I was in a strange mood at the baby shower for the friend. On one hand, I was excited for everyone to meet Sophie and see Lance. On the other hand, I had this feeling of being left out. I felt left out of the party, the lives of my friends and family, of the celebration of my being a new parent six times over by this point, and of the support traditional parents would receive if they lost a child. Truth be told, I was ready to go back to the crazy world of foster care; at least then I would feel at home.

And then there it was again, the call. We were not on the list to receive new placements because our home was full. Furthermore, I was out of town. What came next broke my heart more than losing any of my foster children had up to this point.

Tina wanted to talk to me immediately because she knew we had previously had David in our home and he was once again in need of a foster home. My knees buckled and I remember rushing outside in a panic. My world was spinning, the party attendees were wondering what was wrong, and I was struggling to keep my composure. One of my babies was in foster care and I could not immediately scoop him up because I was far, far from home. I was furious at David's mom and dad. Apparently David's mom had disappeared to the streets again and his dad was arrested for drunk driving while David was in the car. One of Jackson's friends had actually arrested David's dad and reported to us that during the arrest Dad said, "Fine. Take him. I don't want him anyway." My heart was broken and I was so confused as to how the situation could have taken such a turn.

In the end we were not able to take David though we did everything we possibly could to get him to our home. All spots in our home were full when they called and we were not able to immediately move the children who had just come to live with us, though we would have if it were possible. Our license was limited to four children, and, though we begged to get them to extend it to allow for five, the reality was that the approval process took weeks and expedition was certainly not possible on a Saturday when the approving supervisor was not going to be around. I tried. I cried. I felt so incredibly helpless.

* *

After about ten days David went to live with his grandmother out of state. Because the arrest had happened during a period of time called "monitored return," where the case is still open and CPS is still involved in monitoring parental progress, David's parents almost automatically lost custody, permanently. Before long, David was placed under permanent guardianship of his grandmother, left for her to raise him to adulthood. A Facebook account was created for everyone who knew David to be able to keep in touch with him, but it was only updated a few times and then became stagnant. I tried to reach out to the grandmother letting her know we would always be available to her and to David, but never heard a response. It was clear to me that after everything that had happened we had lost David after all.

Several months after this incident was over, Lance asked me when David's birthday party would be. After all, David's parents promised that we would be able to see him again at his birthday and apparently Lance was really looking forward to being able to see his little brother again. The request caught me off guard, not only because I did not want to hurt my sweet son's feelings, but also because I was shocked that I had not communicated to him that the situation with David had changed. Maybe it was an oversight or maybe I did not know how to explain this complex situation to my four-year-old, but in hindsight it was a huge mistake. Lance was devastated when I told him we probably would not see David again. Over the next two years Lance occasionally reminded us how much he loved David, his "favorite". To this day I have no response to really help Lance feel better about losing David. On occasion I have searched online to see what his parents were up to and if I could find anything that would tell us how David is doing with his grandmother. I found out Mom and Dad divorced shortly after David left and neither seemed to be able to stay out of trouble for long. I have learned mug shots are available online and people can look quite different in those photos than they do in court.

One night I went on a run in the evening after my children were all in bed. When I arrived home I sat in front of the television to relax and re-hydrate. The local news was playing in the background, but I was not really paying attention as I took my shoes off and caught up with my husband in the other room. Then my world stopped. I had to rewind the news story to hear it again, then again to share with my husband, then again just to make sure I heard it right the first three times. The anchor told of a young woman who inexplicably led local suburban police on a wild pursuit. There was disagreement from eyewitness accounts on exactly how it all happened, but, in the end, the woman was shot in the head by police as she drove her car toward a police officer on the side of a major highway in a major city. Then they shared her name; it was David's mom. My one time friend and co-parent was now dead.

Foster parents have limited support from society at large, especially when it comes to the emotional impact of what we do on a regular basis. With David's mom's death I felt completely alone and unable to find someone to commiserate with. This was my friend for whom I grieved. Unlike friends from different circumstances, I had to learn about her death through the news. I read news reports and comments from readers online and found myself fiercely conflicted, wanting to stand up to those who said she was nothing but a druggie who got what she deserved, but also strongly wanting to correct those who came to her defense calling her a loving mother. I personally knew better than both of those camps. She had so much promise and potential, and life could have been much different for her. I wish she did not have to die. I also knew the facts of the relationship with her child and did not want to allow others to paint her as a saintly mother after what she had done to my baby. I strongly considered searching for and attending the funeral services, but worried that seeing her memorial in person would either cause me even more internal conflict, or lead me to find I was unwelcome because of the nature of the relationship I had with her.

It has been two years since David left our home. Since then we have had 21 more foster children, and have completed Sophie's adoption. There have been nine more goodbyes, all with their own circumstances, only one having ended successfully in reunification that is expected to last. David still has a place in our hearts and there has always been a desire to reunite with him and his family. After his mother's death, I searched online and found a picture of David at three-years-old, playing in the snow, a happy little boy. It gave me the opportunity to reach back out to David's family, sending my condolences but also letting them know we are still available for David if he ever needs us.

Foster parents often hear, "I don't know how you do it." What I have learned is that foster care is hard. It is an unbelievable roller coaster of events and emotions that is completely unpredictable. It breaks our hearts and makes us grow. We live our lives never really being able to know what will happen next. Even when it seems the story has been written, and chapter closed, we have been taught to expect the unexpected. We have also learned that it is completely worth it. We can confidently say our lives are better for having known David, having known his parents, and having walked this road.

5

Our Brown-Eyed Princess

"Mary told me to call you. I have a little girl," said the voice on the other end of the phone.

"This is it! A daughter!" My heart squealed in delight.

The caller went on to say that the little girl was twelve months old, and they would like us to meet her first. That was new to my husband and me. Usually our foster children just show up on our front steps. Later that week, we arranged a sitter and drove to the Social Services office to meet our new daughter. My very first thought was, "She's really big for twelve months." She was actually 20 months old and her name was Claire. Her developmental age was at about a twelve-month level. We got down on the floor with her and watched as she toddled a little unsteadily. We watched as she put every tiny thing she found into her mouth. We watched as this little girl drank two sippy cups in a matter of minutes. We watched as she spit up a half dozen times in 30 minutes. Claire came to us without missing a beat. She cuddled into our laps and we melted. We talked to her great aunt for a little while.

49

She had been caring for this sweet little girl and had no choice but to put her in foster care. Claire's birth mother refused to care for her, and because of her own health problems, this great aunt was unable to care for Claire on her own. After talking with the great aunt, we were given a date by the social worker for Claire to be transferred into our care. I was so excited, but had to wait six long days for the transfer to happen.

My Facebook profile page featured a balloon with a number each day, counting down the days until my little girl would move in with us. Finally it came. "Today is the Day!" my Facebook profile picture read. We had to wait until my husband was off of work and Claire's great aunt could meet us. She arrived with a truck full of stuff. This is an oddity in the world of foster care. Most of the time, children land on our doorstep with only the clothes their backs. Not Claire. Her great aunt had loaded up every single thing that Claire owned. Claire's crib, her toys, clothes, rocking chair, and even her baby spoons were all transferred into our cars. It was overwhelming. However, it was very much appreciated. We, thankfully, had brought two vehicles and they were both loaded down with her belongings, Claire, and our other four children.

When we agreed to take Claire as a foster child, we thought our darling foster son, Michael, was leaving to live with his grandparents. That is why we got the call for Claire. We were only licensed for one foster child along with our three biological boys. So for about a week we had five kids, then we said goodbye to Michael. I was having so much fun playing with a girl. Getting her dressed in the morning in adorable little dresses and hair bows helped me cope with the sadness of Michael leaving. We settled into a family with four children. A few weeks after he had left, Michael was returned to us. His placement had fallen apart. I was a mother to five children, two of which were under two years old!

While I was getting used to having two toddlers, it became obvious that Claire was behind in her development. She was very unsteady on her feet. She did not speak. In fact the very first night in our home my husband jokingly said, "Say dada." She responded "Dada." We all laughed. At the time, I had no idea that was the first and last time I would hear her talk. Her eye contact was minimal. We went to the doctor and came home with four prescriptions and three referrals to specialists. If you have ever dealt with specialists, you know the wait can be torturously long. Our wait was no exception. Claire had in home therapies scheduled twice a week. It seemed each week that she was slipping further and further behind. She began to stare into space more often. She was about twelve months old developmentally when she came to us. Within a few months, the therapists gauged her at about eight months. Obviously, the fact that she was going backwards in her development instead of progressing was concerning all of us. Finally the time arrived for the first specialist.

Claire's medical background folder was thicker at 22-months-old than a lot of grown adults. Her main issue was her time in her mother's womb and her birth. Claire's birth mother, Theresa, was only 16 years old when she gave birth to Claire. Her birth father, Tommy, was only 17 years old. Theresa had no prenatal care, she was a high school dropout, and had an STD (Sexually Transmitted Disease). She did not realize she was going into labor when she ended up giving birth suddenly and violently in the toilet at home. From the records, it seems that she was confused as to what to do. She called for her sister-in-law to help. She did not take Claire out of the toilet until the sister-in-law arrived, about three minutes later. Claire was born prematurely. The doctors guessed that she was at about 28 weeks gestation. There is speculation that she could have been anywhere from 24 to 28 weeks. She weighed in at a whopping two pounds, six ounces. She remained in the NICU (Neonatal Intensive Care Unit) for six weeks.

Around the time Claire turned one month old, the doctors noticed a rash on her back. The STD that Theresa had been infected with had transferred to her daughter. This probably happened in utero, but could have happened during the birth. By the time Claire was one month old she had defied death twice. Her early traumatic birth and this horrid infection both should have taken her life. While in the NICU the doctors and nurses became very concerned about Theresa and Tommy's involvement with their daughter's care. A safety plan was put in place by the hospital social worker. Claire was to be discharged to Tommy's mother. At six weeks old, Claire left the hospital. The arrangement lasted for two days. Tommy's mother called and said she could not care for Claire. Claire then officially became a foster child.

The county found a home for Claire, and because Theresa was getting into so much trouble, they placed her in foster care as well because she too was a minor. For a year Claire and Theresa lived with a foster family. During that time, Claire was developing normally and was a chunky little girl. Around her first birthday, she began having issues with a recurring fever. The foster mother brushed it off as being related to teething. When Claire was finally taken to the hospital, there were major concerns for her health. She was lethargic and dehydrated. The ER doctors sent her home once she had something to drink and seemed to perk up. This ended up being a huge mistake.

After 13 months in the foster home, Theresa began to beg her Aunt Beatrice to take her back in along with Claire. Aunt Beatrice and her husband, who had custody of Theresa and her little sister Lynn, began the process of becoming a foster family. They did all of the classes and background checks. They were thrilled the family would be together again. Theresa and Claire moved back in with Aunt Beatrice before school started that August.

A few short months later, Theresa turned 18 years old. She promptly packed her bags and left her aunt's house leaving behind photos, mementos, her little sister, and most shockingly of all her daughter. She simply left. Great Aunt Beatrice was under the assumption that Theresa was planning on caring for Claire. Aunt Beatrice had a brain injury that left her unable to take care of Claire on her own. She did not want Lynn to be responsible for her sister's child at only 14 years old. Aunt Beatrice made the hard decision to put Claire in foster care where she could be cared for properly. That is how Claire entered our lives.

When the wait for the specialist appointments was finally over, Claire had an MRI and an EEG done. The blank stare that we kept noticing turned out to be silent seizures. Unknown by anyone, Claire had been having seizures nearly every 15 minutes. No wonder her development was backsliding. She was given a prescription and a follow up appointment was scheduled for a few months later. According to Aunt Beatrice, Claire had always had reflux. Her records showed a scope that a doctor had performed when she was younger. It showed no medical reason why Claire was throwing up all the time. The throwing up was very hard on us. When I say she would throw up, I am not talking about spit-up. Claire could not keep anything down. She would even gag herself. It was constant. She even threw up in her sleep. I put bibs on her and I always had extra clothing with us. Regardless, it became very hard to go anywhere. People would stare and then say, "She's spitting up." We knew she was and there was not anything we could do to stop the constant throwing up. Her clothes were soaking wet all of the time. I had to change her bedding every single morning. This steadily got worse after the seizure diagnosis.

We made it back to the neurologist and had another scan. I was concerned that her seizures were changing. She had begun dropping her head repeatedly while at home with us. At first I thought we were mistaken, I then realized she would fall to the floor if this happened while she was standing. Another EEG and MRI confirmed my concerns. Her seizures had changed to Atonic (or Drop) Seizures. Claire did not twitch like one would imagine during a seizure. Instead her whole body would just drop. If she was restrained, in her high chair or swing, it was barely noticeable. Her head would just drop down. However, if she was standing, she would collapse to the floor. It was heartbreaking to watch. The seizures did not seem to hurt her, but sometimes they appeared to make her cry. Other times they seemed to wear her out and she would fall asleep. The neurologist discovered a blank spot in her brain. A spot that should light up during a scan only glimmered. She had brain damage. We did not know the extent of the brain damage until we saw a developmental pediatrician. At that time we were hoping for a diagnosis of Autism. The Doctor confirmed that she did not have Autism. Her brain damage was causing her delays and regression. As he spoke, the doctor's outlook for Claire's life was bleak. I will never forget the night after that appointment. I came home and waited for my husband. When he arrived home I quickly left. I needed to be by myself. I needed to grieve. I sobbed over what had been done to Claire. The fact that this could have been prevented had me sick to my stomach and angrier than I had ever been in my life.

Earlier at the appointment, the doctors had made somewhat of a timeline of how all of this may have happened. When the STD that was transferred to Claire then flared at her one-year mark, she was not cared for properly. Because of this, the virus attacked her brain. There it lived while destroying her Temporal Lobe. That is why she was able to speak that one time, but had not been able to since. Speech and language are stored in the Temporal Lobe. My anger was blurring my vision along with my tears as the doctor described this to me. It could have been prevented. Her birth

53

mother chose not to inform anyone of her STD and then passed this virus to her child. Claire would never run with other children. She would not be able to dance at her prom. She would not enjoy getting a pedicure or shopping with me. I grieved for what I had lost in a daughter and what had been taken from her. I bought ingredients for my favorite comfort food. Then I bought a plant. I gave myself one night to feel sorry for myself - to make it all about me. Then when the sun rose, I transferred the plant into a new pot. It symbolized Claire's life, a new home, and a new life. I would fight for her!

I called Social Services and told Claire's social worker exactly what was on my mind. She kept insisting, "We will let this play out." I ended up finding out that Claire's biological mom was pregnant again. This complicated everything. The child protective services workers wanted to prove the pregnancy before they could move forward with Claire's case. Theresa, Claire's biological mom, had gone missing. No one could find her, she would not answer the phone, and she refused to show up for meetings with the social worker. Claire's birth parents had not been to one visitation and regularly missed important meetings. They did not care. I was ready to move forward and get Claire the permanency she needed. Medicaid would only cover so much, and she needed to be on our insurance. I was sick and tired of playing nice and waiting. Our social worker had never done an adoption before. She had never done a termination of parental rights. She did not want to move too fast. However, I knew the law.

Claire had not seen her birth parents in over six months, and I knew the case could move forward. I went over our social worker's head. I called Claire's Guardian Ad Litem. He was supposed to be her voice in court and advocate for what was in the best interest of the child in the courtroom. Though I had never met him before, I invited him to our home and explained everything about the case to him. He did know a little bit about Claire and her birth parents. He agreed it was time to move forward. I will never know exactly what happened in the meeting he had with Claire's social worker, but within two weeks of our meeting Claire had a new social worker. She was already the foster care worker of our other foster son. We knew her and liked her a lot. She got the proverbial ball rolling. A court date was finally set.

Court is a big deal in the foster care world. Families can be formed or your world can be turned upside down all in one room. I was not as nervous about Claire's case as I had been about Michael's. Being in a courtroom did make me a bit nervous though. As I arrived that morning, I ran into our social worker. "I think Claire's case is getting rescheduled," she said. Unfortunately, that was what happened. I turned around and picked up all of my kids from their babysitters. The court system can be so frustrating! The next court date was scheduled for later that month. Claire's birth parents never showed up to the second scheduled hearing. The case was rescheduled again so that an official summons could be given for them to appear in court. I was beyond livid. The judge was very understanding and commended me on what we were doing. Finally, the court date came a third time. I was nervous, as I always was. Our case was called. I knew her birth parents were sitting right behind me. Claire's social worker had picked them up to make sure they would be there.

The case was read. DSS (The Department of Social Services) had their testimony ready. I had given them every doctor's note I had along with the specialists' and therapists' reports. At that point Claire had one pediatrician, three therapists, and ten specialists. DSS testified to all of Claire's issues and developmental problems. Theresa and Tommy had not seen Claire in 11 months. They knew nothing of these devastating issues. Theresa stood there and picked her fingernails while all of these issues were being read. She shed no tears, and did not appear to have even a bit of remorse. She just stood there picking her nails. I already knew all of the medical issues and hearing it aloud made me tear up. I could not believe that Claire's biological mom just stood there scrapping polish off her nails. In that moment, I could have punched her right in the face without a second thought. The judge had the same look in her eye. She accepted DSS's plan to terminate the parental rights of Claire's biological parents. Theresa and Tommy were given a lawyer and another court date was scheduled.

During the wait for the next scheduled court hearing, I was informed that Theresa had finally gone to the doctor for a prenatal check up. At this appointment she found out that she was 27 weeks pregnant, having twin boys, three centimeters dilated, and in early labor. She was admitted to the hospital and put on bed rest to help keep the boys from being born as long as possible.

Later that day, I found myself searching for Theresa on Facebook. I found her profile and immediately regretted it. Her status updates mainly consisted of her complaining about not being able to have her baby shower. She did not ask for prayers for her tiny boys or even express concern for them. I called the hospital. I spoke to a nurse and made sure that they knew about the STD Theresa had. She, of course, had not told them.

The boys were born at 29 weeks gestation. They weighed a little over three pounds each at the time of their birth. The hospital had plans in place to alert officials to take the boys if needed. We were offered the option of taking them and turned it down. Claire needed all of our attention. The boys were finally sent home with Claire's biological mom after a month long stay in the NICU. They both have medical issues.

In between all of Claire's court dates and doctors' appointments, I still had four other children to parent. My life was very busy! Home schooling and endless appointments consumed most of my days. We were elated when our son's adoption was finalized. We were still waiting for Claire's last court hearing. I felt like I was constantly holding my breath. I was ready to fill my lungs with fresh air. Theresa had begun to message me through Facebook. She would ask if she would be able to see Claire. She claimed she was sad that her daughter "was taken away." She never seemed to remember that she walked out on Claire. I tried to be mature and told her to speak to Claire's social worker. She continued to ask me questions and badger me. Finally, I had to block her. She would take no responsibility and I could only hold a civil tongue for so long.

Finally, the termination trial date arrived. We walked into the courtroom, but Theresa and Tommy were not there. I was irate. I was scared court would be delayed again. Theresa and Tommy's court appointed lawyers were there. I breathed a sigh of relief because I assumed we would be able to go ahead with the trial as long as their lawyers were present. Ironically, Theresa and Tommy strolled into the courtroom 15 minutes into the proceedings. The judge asked them what they wanted to do. Theresa replied that she thought she could take care of Claire, but agreed that she needed to stay with us. I had to hold my tongue. She spoke as if she had Claire's best interest in mind. Tommy, on the other hand, said he wanted to maintain custody. Fourteen months had gone

56

by since he had laid eyes on Claire. He could have asked at any time to see her, but he had not. The judge took this chance to rip into them. She asked him to name one therapy, one doctor, one specialist, a medicine, or anything about her conditions. He could not name a single one. She asked him how much money he made and how he planned to support Claire. His only reply was, "I get paid under the table." It was all I could do to not laugh out loud. Even his lawyer rolled her eyes. The judge gave her ruling, something I am sure she had decided months ago. Theresa and Tommy's parental rights were terminated. They were no longer Claire's parents. She was free for adoption.

We breathed a sigh of relief. We would be able to adopt Claire. I could not wait until I had the papers in my hands. I was so excited to be able to put her on our insurance plan. I would never again have to hear "We do not accept Medicaid." That had always translated into, "We can't help you, since you're not her 'real' mother."

Within two weeks we were in the specialist office getting our referral to the feeding clinic that we had been denied access to because of the insurance that Claire had been on while she was a foster child. We were getting information on clinical trials that she was not allowed to enter into as a foster child. In the end, an appointment for a feeding tube was made. Finally the vomiting was going to stop! That alone would greatly improve her quality of life. We were thrilled.

On July 10th, Claire and I got up long before the sun came up and drove to the far away hospital for her surgery. It took longer than expected, but they were able to get it done. From that moment on, she no longer threw up. She was weak and tired and looked so very small in recovery. I sat next to her bedside. Her crib was fitted so she could not climb out. It all looked so sterile. I sat there watching her slowly come back into consciousness. She immediately tried to sit up which caused her great pain. After 24 long hours, I begged the nurses to let her have something to drink. At home she had always carried her cup around with her and she looked a little lost without it. She had been hospitalized for dehydration three times at her previous foster home. I made sure she had liquid whenever she wanted it. I knew she would be thirsty. The nurse came in with a tiny syringe of water, about 10mls. Claire literally sucked the syringe bulb down without the nurse having to press it, and then she cried a tearless cry. It was beyond pitiful.

I could not help but think of Claire's biological mother and immediately I was filled with rage. Her daughter, her flesh and blood, was lying in a hospital, crying about being thirsty. She had a hole in her stomach and had to receive food through a tube. All because her biological mom did not tell anyone about an STD she had when she was pregnant with Claire. Images of when Claire had turned three years old came to me as the waves of anger continued. On her third birthday, Claire had a cupcake that would be the last treat she would have for the foreseeable future. I am not a violent person, but Theresa's lack of empathy or concern for her daughter made my blood boil. I know without a doubt, had I seen her that day, I would have put her through a wall. Then, as I always do, I calmed down. I thanked God for bringing my daughter through the surgery. We now had hope that Claire would begin to pack on some healthy weight and start to move forward.

Claire was released from the hospital just as rush hour hit. It took us nearly four hours to get home and settled. Our dear friends made sure we had plenty of food and desserts. That night Claire slept in the new swing we had bought for her for after the surgery. She slept through the whole night. Her feeding tube machine, that I later named "Meeper," woke me up three times that night. It would beep when it was empty, when it had a kink, and, just for fun, when it wanted to remind me what a newborn was like. I have a love/hate relationship with "Meeper." At her first post-op appointment my tiny girl had gained 1.5 pounds! At six weeks post-op, Claire has gained nearly five pounds.

One day I was going about my own business when I got an email from Aunt Beatrice. We have kept in steady communication and she and Lynn are a part of our lives. The email was to inform me that Theresa was pregnant, yet again. She was about 20 weeks along, but had not been to the doctor. I called Mary, our social worker. I felt so bad for her. Mary had just gotten back from a three-week medical leave. I was the first to call her phone that day. She just sighed. I wanted to throw up. It made my stomach turn to know she was, once again, passing her STD to another child. Then I learned "she was big for 20 weeks." She was refusing to go to any doctor appointments. Late one night, I could not sleep, so I hopped on the computer. There was another email from Aunt

Beatrice. Theresa had given birth at 28 weeks along. She had given birth to twin baby girls, both right around two pounds. Once again, she had received no prenatal care. I cried. I sobbed. I screamed at the injustice of it all. I fumed at the thought of my friends that struggle to even get pregnant, or to carry babies to term, when this ridiculous teenager kept getting pregnant over and over. Like Claire's younger brothers, the twins were allowed to go home with Claire's biological mom. I am still waiting for the day that I receive the official call asking us if we will foster them. I hope it happens before something terrible happens to any of the children that have been left in her care.

As for Claire, she is blossoming. She is a miracle of modern science. The surgery to insert the feeding tube has been nothing short of a miracle. Her coloring looks so much better. She is no longer pale with purple rings around her eyes. Her hair is starting to come back as well. She had lost so much of it when she was not getting the nutrition that she needed because of the throwing up. Her eyes light up more. She notices people and responds when her name is called. She kicks her feet happily when she's enjoying attention from someone, but she still has her bad days. Her seizures still bother her. Sometimes the best she can do is sit up for a few hours before falling asleep. Sometimes they make her stumble into walls and she bruises her forehead, but her good days are starting to outnumber the bad days. The days when she giggles and makes eye contact and sings along to the radio in her own way make all of this worth it. The days when she runs across the grass, because it does not overwhelm her anymore, are the days we live for. We simply survive the bad ones. We pray she will join us in our environment, but we are content to be with her in her place for now. Claire's world is simpler than ours. She needs very little to be happy. If you give her an extra tickle, her eyes light up. If you put a small amount of liquid in a cup for her, she thinks she is having the best day ever. I cannot wait to watch her grow up and see where her world and our world will take her. We know she will probably always be with us and that she will not be able to live on her own and that is okay with us.

Claire is our long awaited and cherished princess. I would say, "We wouldn't have it any other way," but that is not true. I would love for her to enjoy the things that a typical three-year-old likes. I would love to see her playing with her cousin who is only four months older than her. I would love to hear her voice. I would love to know what she is thinking.

Regardless of the things she is not capable of right now, her smile can light up a room. Her victories, no matter how small, remind me daily of why we do what we do. This is why we risked our hearts, our families, and our sanity. We do it to help the helpless and to be a voice for those innocent children who are not being heard. We do it because sometimes you get to look into the beautiful brown eyes of a baby girl and you know, that she knows, she is home.

6

Beautiful Transformations

Four years ago my husband Michael, our twins Jon and Megan, and I began the most incredible adventure of our lives – we became a foster care home to medically fragile infants. We have been blessed to love ten precious babies whose transformations have amazed us.

We received our first foster blessing in July of 2009. Jaden was born weighing slightly over two pounds, was addicted to drugs, and both of his parents were incarcerated. He had heart problems and peripheral vision challenges. I visited him in the hospital for a couple of days before he was discharged to us. This gave me my first taste of special precautions because he was on "blackout" while in the hospital – only people on a private list were allowed to visit or call. Jaden was barely four pounds when he came home to us and just beautiful. Jon and Megan had been three months premature so this was familiar territory for me. Over the next two months, his transformation was remarkable.

Jaden went from being a tiny, scrawny preemie to a chunky little guy who started smiling shortly before he left us. He went from fitting in my son's football helmet and being barely longer than a ruler to thriving because of love, prayer, and formula changes. We witnessed answered prayers when Jaden's heart was deemed fully healed and his vision improved. During the course of two months, Jaden's social worker quit, and his dad was released from jail. Ultimately his grandma was the one who took custody of him. She already had a few of his siblings, and was heavily involved in a "Grandparents Raising Grandchildren" support group.

A few weeks after Jaden began his new life with his grandma and siblings, I received a phone call which resulted in two-day-old Zane temporarily joining our family. He was badly bruised from his delivery and tested positive for methamphetamines, but otherwise was healthy. Zane became our "holiday baby," and blessed us with his cute self for Halloween, Thanksgiving, Christmas, and New Year's. Friends dubbed him the Michelin baby because he was adorably chunky! He was our first experience with paternity testing. Up until the results were revealed, his biological mom and "biological dad" came to regular visits. Once the tests confirmed "biological dad" was not his biological father, neither of them ever came for a visit again. Zane was a good-natured baby, very sweet and cuddly. After being with us for eleven wonderful weeks, Zane was adopted by his maternal grandparents. Zane went from a black, blue, and green newborn to a roly-poly almost three-month-old who always smiled at us - another fabulous transformation.

Sarah, our third foster blessing, arrived on the scene next and was our first baby girl. She was also born addicted to methamphetamines and needed a few extra days in the hospital. While she was in the hospital I paid regular visits to her. It was during one of these visits that I unintentionally met Sarah's biological mom, step-grandma, and grandpa. Still being a relatively new foster mommy, I was apprehensive about meeting the baby's biological family before Sarah was officially discharged into my care, but I immediately liked the three of them. Due to Sarah's situation, we were able to have an open door policy and let Sarah's extended family visit her at our home. Sometimes only Sarah's mom would come, other times step-grandma and grandpa would visit, or maternal grandma and an aunt would stop by. It was obvious that this little girl was loved and it was beautiful to see. Everyone knew where all the supplies were and felt comfortable feeding, changing, and bathing sweet Sarah. Sarah's grandparents had an affinity for pizza so that was their dinner of choice, which they brought over a few times to share with us. Michael and I had some great conversations with Sarah's mom during a few of the evenings she visited her daughter.

Three quick weeks later, Sarah's mom entered rehab where she was allowed to keep her daughter so we said our goodbyes. Luckily, Sarah's grandparents saw the writing on the wall due to their daughter's drug history, and did what was necessary should Sarah's mom ever test dirty again. She tested positive not long after entering rehab and they ended up formally adopting their beloved granddaughter.

After Sarah left, a sweet little boy named Jason, unbeknownst to us, would be the most phenomenal transformation yet. He had been hospitalized off and on throughout his seven months of life, and had recently been diagnosed with HIV, failure to thrive, and received feedings by NG tube 22 hours a day. His biological mom was a self-professed gypsy, homeless, and traveled from state to state. Once she realized that not only was her son HIV+, but she was as well, she signed away her rights knowing she did not have the ability to properly care for Jason. I was able to bond with Jason in the hospital for a few days and learned how to care for him; how to do the feedings, all about the equipment for him to receive his feeds, the recipe for his nutrition, and all about his HIV cocktail. We immediately noticed that this precious boy did not have any light in his eyes. They were dull and he did not appear to smile at all. He had a pacifier that he sucked on and knew what a TV was, but that was it. Jason would not reach up to be picked up or held, he was just *there*. But God had great plans for him.

My family loved Jason, prayed for him, played with him, snuggled him, gave him his medications, provided stimulation, blended up his formula concoction for the pump, and watched in amazement as the transformation began. That adorable baby shed his caterpillar skin and the most gorgeous butterfly emerged right before our eyes. He was happy, his blue eyes sparkled, and he played with toys. He ripped out his NG tube and the child that refused all food and drink ate real food and guzzled his bottles!

63

He grew, he started therapy, his HIV was no longer detectable in his bloodstream, he learned to clap, and we clapped for him when a family said "Yes" to adopting him! They met him, visited him, and had an overnight visit. Seven weeks after we met him, Jason started his happily ever after with his forever family - which now includes a biological half-brother as well (who tested negative for HIV)!

At this point, after loving on four foster babies, my husband Michael, asked me to agree to take a break from fostering, which I did, begrudgingly. Jason left on a Wednesday. That Friday I received a call. After all, two days constitutes a "break," right?! Noah was seven weeks old, had suffered over 36 fractured bones in his short life, had three brain hemorrhages, was deaf-blind, and wore a special harness to help his new femoral fractures heal. They asked if we would we take him. My "Yes!" began a journey in which God allowed us to witness miracle after miracle over the next 50 life-changing weeks.

For the first month, Noah was on pain medication around the clock. He had multiple doctor appointments and x-rays to monitor his legs. Noah would cry if he was not being held. He could not hear or see you, and lying down put more pressure on his fractures, so he was held *a lot*. Around the time Noah was allowed to be harness free, his vision and hearing slowly started to return. The neurologist told us he should be in a vegetative state, but he was not. He was loved, cherished, growing, trusting our safe touches, learning there would not be pain at our house, and milestones were starting to be met. Unfortunately for Noah, there were visits with his biological mom and dad. His biological mom shared that she was pregnant, again – with her seventh child, and asked me to adopt her unborn baby. I thanked her for the unbelievable opportunity, but declined. Eventually she went to jail (after the plan of taking the blame for Noah's injuries, claiming post-partum depression, receiving counseling and having three of her children returned to her failed). The newest baby that she gave birth to was adopted by an unrelated family, but Noah's biological dad continued to have visits with Noah. Noah was not himself after each of these visits. He had meltdowns every time he returned home after a visit. Noah had spent the first two weeks in the hospital after he was born. He was then hospitalized at six weeks old for the femoral fractures. He came to live with us at seven weeks old. Despite being so young, he remembered. Whether it was his biological dad's voice or just the way he touched him, Noah remembered who had been there when he was being hurt during those first six weeks of his life. It was heartbreaking.

There was court date after court date. "He said" and "She said" were the only consistent things that happened in court. Discoveries were made that Noah's biological dad and Noah's paternal grandma were stalking people. Meanwhile, Noah was defying the odds. His bones healed. His vision and hearing were completely restored. He was thriving. Month after month, he accomplished the impossible. He had the cutest smile ever. He learned to roll, to sit, to stand, and to crawl – fast, really fast. He would see us coming and would crawl as quickly as he could around a corner laughing hysterically. He would pass gas and then laugh at himself. He thought balls were the best. Jon was his buddy. Their favorite activity was playing with water. We bought Noah a little pool for the backyard. His face alighted with glee while Jon filled up containers and poured water on Noah. He adored every second. Noah was fully immersed in our family life. Everyone who met him adored him.

Although we were licensed for two, because of my biological daughter's special needs due to her premature birth, and taking medically fragile children, we have always said yes to just one baby at a time. However, we received a call from Jason's placement worker with a unique situation. There was a baby girl who needed a home for just a few days. The foster family she would ultimately go to was sick with the flu. They asked if we would take the medically fragile baby girl until the new family was healthy. I called Michael while the placement worker was on hold and he said yes. A few hours later, the placement worker brought over Leilani who was three months old and being cared for by hospice. Half of her brain had disintegrated in utero and she was not expected to be born alive. Even though she was born alive she was not expected to live more than a few days. Three months later, she was still alive. The hospice nurses had an appointment set up with Leilani's biological mom. When they arrived at the family's home, nobody answered the door. The hospice workers called the biological mom on her cell phone. She and her toddler were at the store. Where was Leilani? Home alone! A baby who had seizures

65

and needed extra medication after a seizure lasting longer than 15 seconds was alone in an empty house. This family was from a different country. They knew minimal English. The husband was a truck driver. The toddler had special needs also. Mom, I was told, did not want to bond with the baby so she would prop the baby's bottle up, which resulted in numerous aspiration issues.

As soon as Leilani was brought to my house, I immediately removed her from her car seat and snuggled her. The placement worker's assistant told her co-worker, "She's going to be loved here." Yes, she was. Due to her unique circumstances, I had a few conversations with nurses on the phone. One told me never to call 911. The doctors or hospitals could not put her on any higher dosages of medications than she was already on. They would rather her die in my arms than alone in the hospital. I completely agreed. It was assumed that she would die from seizing or aspiration. My kids did amazing every time Leilani would start to seize, they immediately looked at the clock and timed the seizure. More times than not, the extra seizure medication and morphine had to be given. It was so sad.

The day after Leilani arrived, I called our incredible church and asked for a special baby dedication and described our unusual situation. The next morning, Noah, Leilani, and I arrived at church where a pastor, a bunch of staff, and a photographer blessed us with the most memorable baby dedication ever for this precious blessing who was not going to be in this world long. After six days of loving Leilani, she joined her new foster family. The new foster family's mom was good friends with Jason's mom so the day I brought Leilani to her new home, Jason and Noah played together and Jason's mom took a picture of me with "my" three babies. That is one of my most prized photographs. Ultimately, Leilani was returned to her biological mom and we have not heard from her since.

Our sweet Noah, who was still with us, turned one year old and enjoyed his block birthday cake, toys, clothes, and, of course, the boxes everything came in. The courts terminated his parents' parental rights and the social workers began looking for a home for a one-year-old with cerebral palsy. We waited and, thankfully, God revealed the most perfect forever family for Noah. He would have a mom, dad, brothers and sisters. After his new mom and dad met him and decided to go ahead with the adoption, we loaded up their minivan with all of Noah's favorite toys, stuffed animals, games, books, and blankets. The next day when Noah started having visits to slowly transition him to his happily ever after home, familiar things surrounded him. The visits went flawlessly. He loved his new family. We had a book that had pictures of us and pictures of them he looked at a dozen times a day. Almost a year after we brought home a broken, battered and bruised seven-week-old, we said goodbye to the most incredible experience of our lives.

We always leave it up to the forever families as to how much communication they want to have. We have never heard from Jaden or Zane, we have heard a few times from Sarah, and regularly with Jason. Noah's new mommy texted me a picture the day I found out my dad had cancer, again on the day we were on the road trip to his funeral, and other key moments of my life when a precious picture of Noah could not have come at a better time. A year later, we were invited to his official adoption party. Noah looked at us like, "I recognize you, but I don't remember from where." He and Jon were fast buddies again. They shared a dessert plate, they wrestled, and they laughed together. It was beautiful to see the bond was still there.

Since Michael never quite received the "break" he asked for, he realized he needed to be a little more specific and requested a 30 day baby break after Noah left. Thirty-one days later, we received a call for Sawyer.

Sawyer was removed from his mom and dad due to domestic violence and because his biological mom was unable and/or unwilling to obtain a restraining order. We brought him home and settled in with a very handsome, super sweet, curly haired, rosy-cheeked little boy. He came to us with a pacifier. A month later, his biological mom, pregnant again, asked for the pacifier to be returned to her because she wanted it for the new baby! Sawyer was her sixth baby. The other five had been previously removed from her care. All six babies shared the same pacifier, and now that she was pregnant with baby number seven, she wanted the new baby to use *the same pacifier* all the other children had used as well! Sawyer's mom was allowed to come to doctor visits, but always ran out of the room before he was to receive a shot. She claimed she had been able hear his sibling cry after a shot once while standing outside the building when that child was on the third floor.

It was during our amazing time with Sawyer that I was told my dad had Stage Four cancer. I made arrangements to visit him and notified Sawyer's social worker that they needed to find another placement for him, because it would not be long after my visit that I would need to go across state lines again for my dad's funeral. We are an emergency placement home, but always kept the babies until their forever families were found, until this situation occurred. We had been caring for Sawyer for three months. It was the week I was going to leave when it truly dawned on the social worker that she needed to find a home for this sweetie who adored giraffes, and fittingly enough, made the most adorable giraffe at Halloween. What complicated the situation was that we were just told that week by the neurologist that Sawyer would need skull reconstruction surgery because his cranial soft spots had fused too early. I was praying for a family for Sawyer that he could meet and bond with over time. It ended up that the new family met him and took him home the same night – less than 12 hours before my flight. This is another family who has kept in contact with me. They still have Sawyer, although through a series of bizarre events, he is not yet free for adoption. They also have Sawyer's baby brother now, and Sawyer never ended up needing the skull surgery – praise God!

During the time of my dad's sickness and passing away, I became responsible for my grandma who was diagnosed with dementia. I was not sure if I would be taking any future placements. I was now visiting my grandma on a daily basis, and we typically took medically fragile babies. But in February, I was called about a very special baby named Adam. He had been born dead. He was gray at birth, his liver and kidneys had started to shut down, and his APGAR was 0. He was born positive for multiple drugs, had a brain hemorrhage, and had open-heart surgery when he was less than a month old. His internal organs were flipped flopped, his bowel was at risk for twisting, and he needed surgery down the road on his private parts. Was I willing to bring a baby born with a broken heart home for Valentine's Day? Little did I know then how much this special baby would heal *my* heart over the coming months, or how abundantly this little guy would bless *us*.

Adam just loved life. He loved people. He loved their faces, and he was always smiling. Despite how he started life, or maybe because of it, every day was a blast. Adam's biological mom's rights were terminated relatively quickly, and soon his social worker was looking for a family who would look past the scars and diagnoses to see him for the smiley, loveable boy he was. Just like Noah, Adam hit the jackpot – a dad and mom who home schooled his soon to be brothers and sisters. His forever family lived several hours away, but through a creative vacation schedule, they all met Adam, returned a couple days later, joined us for Jon and Megan's 12th birthday party, spent the night, and started their happily ever after the following day.

The day Adam left, Noah's new daddy stopped by (on Noah's birthday) to show me pictures and videos of "my" sweet Noah doing amazing things. He was talking, eating, walking, swimming, and more. Once again, God let Noah's mommy know exactly when I needed a "pick me up."

We took another "baby break" after Adam's departure. The next phone call was for a newborn baby, a two-day-old, who was our first safe surrender. The biological mom gave birth, signed away her rights, and left the hospital. The baby had not even been given a name. I called our pastor and asked him to name this precious little one. He humbly declined citing he could not make such a monumental decision for us. So we called him Matthew – he was a "gift of yah(weh)," and would be for whomever would be his forever family. Six short days later, we were informed a family was chosen and they would come to our house later that afternoon. Coincidentally, they recognized me from the times I had talked to the graduating classes of foster parents, and they remembered Adam!

During Matthew's transition into his new home, I received a call from the placement worker about a very unique baby girl named Naomi. Because we had Matthew, I declined, but once Matthew moved in with his new mommy and daddy, I felt led to call the placement worker and inquire about Naomi's status. I was told she would be moving to a home for babies with *extreme* medically fragile needs. A few days later, however, I was called again asking if I still might be interested since that home took a new placement over the weekend and Naomi once again needed a home. Naomi had a very rare syndrome that less than 1,000 girls in the United States have. She was missing part of her brain called the corpus callosum, she had uncontrolled seizures, a cleft lip and palate, eye issues (scarring, lesions, and cortical visual impairment), and was at high risk for aspiration. She just had a G-tube put in, and Naomi was very delayed. Naomi's biological mom and dad struggled with domestic violence, and her biological dad made an extreme choice which led to Naomi and her older sister being officially removed from their parents' care. The plan was for Naomi's biological mom to be reunified with her girls after she completed specific requirements CPS (Child Protective Services) had given her.

Naomi eventually received a MIC-KEY button vs. a G-Tube for her feedings. She had cleft lip surgery which, in addition to repairing the huge gap between her lip and nose, gave her a left nostril and dramatically changed her appearance after months of special retainers, weekly dentist visits, and taping to help minimize the once 18 mm gap in her upper gum. Naomi met with a fantastic doctor who specialized in children with brain malformations who, after a four-day hospitalization in a nearby city with a continuous video EEG, prescribed a new medication and gave Naomi additional diagnoses. For a week or two, the new medication stopped the clusters of epileptic spasms this sweet, profoundly delayed little girl was experiencing. Unfortunately the seizures returned, although the new medication did begin to restructure Naomi's brain. The specialist then put Naomi on a steroid with an additional medication for evening time for three months.

We loved on Naomi for 46 sensational weeks, and her visual transformation was stunning. We were complimented daily on how beautiful she was. Naomi recently celebrated her first birthday with a gorgeous outfit, a special birthday cake we helped her play with, presents, hugs, and kisses. Her biological dad was incarcerated for the majority of her time with us. Naomi's biological mom gave birth to a baby boy after Naomi had been with us for 44 weeks. Part of the reunification plan to get her girls back was for mom to stay away from dad (which obviously did not happen considering he was the father of the new baby), obtain a restraining order, and take parenting and domestic violence classes. Naomi's social worker, after making more mistakes in this case than my other nine babies' workers did combined, turned the case over to a new social worker. Naomi had a new social worker supervisor as well as a new family service worker. Naomi's biological mom had been trying to run the show the entire time we had Naomi in our home. The former social worker tried, belatedly, to enforce boundaries and put Naomi's biological mom in a "nice, tidy box." Despite all the drama from the biological family, I just loved on this chunky princess who could not see, hear, swallow or move other than seizing and stretching. For months she cried between two to six hours a day, but, thankfully, those episodes were over. Every day was truly extraordinary with her. By the time she was reunified with her biological mom, Naomi had had 89 doctor appointments, 84 visits with her biological mom, 3 hospital stays, 2 ER visits, 33 therapy appointments, had been on 14 medications and received over a dozen medical diagnoses.

We have witnessed remarkable transformations over the past four years. Being a foster mommy to medically fragile babies, loving on the "orphan" and the "least of these" is my passion. It is where my heart is. Not only have we witnessed answered prayers and phenomenal transformations of these ten treasured babies, but my family has been dramatically transformed as well. Our lives will never be the same. We will never be the same. Foster care has changed us, and we are so grateful it has!

7

It's Not If...

I was a nervous wreck. Somehow everything about this felt wrong, but I had already signed all that paperwork. It was a Sunday morning, and Velma needed me. One of the workers gave me a puzzled look as she was getting ready to leave. She asked me if something was wrong. I mumbled an answer under my breath, but all I could think was, "You just left a 40-pound, five-year-old 'infant' with me. What am I going to do next?!"

Over the next few days I quickly figured out what I had been called to do. I had to undo five years of medical neglect. Velma needed a massive amount of dental work. She needed to see a neurologist. She needed seizure medication. She needed vaccines. She needed physical therapy, occupational therapy, and speech therapy. When the intake worker told me that Velma was crying for her mommy, she neglected to tell me that "mommy" was one of only about two dozen words that Velma could speak in total. There was a lot to be done.

I went into mama bear mode! Appointments were made. Doctors were seen. There were even a couple of hospital stays thrown in for good measure. Over time, Velma stabilized. Her seizures became a little more manageable, and her birth mom, Alice, worked her case plan. Every single visit was attended. Alice took her classes and did everything CPS (Child Protective Services) asked of her. Nine months later we went to court and Alice regained custody of Velma. I cheered. It seemed to me that "foster care" had worked, and I was happy to have been a part of it.

Ten days later, I got a call that I honestly never expected. Velma's pediatrician called to tell me that Alice had just abused Velma in her waiting room. Staying as calm as I could, I told the doctor that she needed to call the abuse hotline. I gave her the phone number for Velma's previous caseworker, but I told her that she had to call the hotline too.

Velma came back to live with me the very next day. This is when the goal of this case should have changed. This is when the aunt and uncle that came forward to take Velma the first time around should have been considered. However, this was foster care, and very rarely does foster care make sense.

Velma's case continued to move forward with the goal being reunification with her mom. Time passed, and I got used to being mom to a mega family. Papi Alan and I were busy raising six kids at this time; two biological sons, one adopted son, Velma, and two little foster additions, Jake and Sofia, that we got the summer after Velma came the first time. Parenting six kids was no easy chore, especially when one of them had the level of special needs that Velma did, but we managed. Despite the many challenges, we were happy.

About 17 months into Velma's case, the judge ordered that unsupervised weekend visits would start. As uncomfortable as I was with this, I was just the foster mom, and that meant I had to comply. Arrangements were made, and the first visit was scheduled. Velma was to be dropped off at her mom's house on Friday evening at 6pm, and I was to pick her back up on Sunday at 6pm.

You would think that, as foster parents, our most important task would be loving the kids, and it should be! As far as the State is concerned, documentation seems to be at the top of their list. Taking a cue from their priorities, I decided that I would not initially risk doing drop-off for an unsupervised visit by myself. I wanted someone else to witness me passing along all of the instructions Alice would need to care for her daughter. Alice had never been in a place where she met all of Velma's needs before, and I wanted to make sure she now understood all that was required; the medications, the guidelines to follow if Velma had a seizure, and how to put on and take off Velma's leg braces. I was more nervous now that physical abuse had been brought to the picture, so to speak. I wanted all bases covered! I brought Christy, the caseworker from our licensing agency, with me to document everything. Her official files would show that I covered everything with Alice. If Velma's needs were not met, it would not come back on me with anyone claiming I never passed on the necessary information.

Drop-off was awkward, and I was nervous. Velma had never been to this home before because Alice moved shortly after Velma came into care the second time. Due to Velma's extreme developmental delays, there was no way I could explain what was going on. She rode silently in the back of my car as we drove to her mom's house.

Once there, Velma was thrilled to see her mommy. I went over all the details with Alice. Christy documented everything and made sure Alice understood. I took a deep breath and went home to a much easier weekend than I was used to. It was nice to not have to change diapers for a few days!

Pick up on Sunday evening was reasonably uneventful. I had decided that I could handle this part on my own. When I got there, Velma did not want to leave. She threw a fit, but I just scooped her up and put her in my car as if this was all normal. Foster care is so difficult for the children. Neuro-typical children do not understand why they have to go back and forth like this, so you can imagine how difficult it was for Velma. She quickly settled down and did need a bit of redirection for the next few days, but it was not as bad as I thought it was going to be.

The next Friday I did drop-off by myself. It was simple and quick. Velma was happy to see her mommy, and I was looking forward to a less complicated weekend. I was not thrilled with the idea of these visits, but it made the most sense to at least enjoy them if they had to happen.

The pick up on Sunday was strange. I could not put my finger on it, but something did not feel quite right. Alice had Velma sitting out in the backseat of her truck when I arrived. Velma had a fast food bag in her lap. Alice gave me no explanation for why Velma was in the truck and not inside the house. Maybe Alice had been out and about with Velma that afternoon. Maybe she did not want to try to navigate getting Velma out of the truck and into the house. Maybe Velma had been crying and Alice did not know what to do. Either way, it just seemed strange.

Velma took one look at me and started screaming. She threw herself over and tried to avoid getting out of the truck. She yelled, "No!" and "Mommy!" at the top of her lungs. She did not want to come home with me at all. There was nothing I could do about this to make it easier for Velma. I could not talk to her. I could not explain that she would come back next week. All I could do was pick her up and wrestle her in to my car. Because I had been mothering Velma for nearly 18 months by this time, Velma knew I meant business. She stopped trying to fight me and she calmed down for the most part. But boy was she mad! Alice seemed oblivious to it all. I just said goodbye and told her that she would see her next week.

Once home, it was bath time. Velma needed assistance with all personal grooming. She could sometimes undress herself, but often I had to assist. That night, as I took off her t-shirt, I immediately noticed some marks on the tops of her shoulders that raised alarm. These were not normal marks that could have appeared due to normal activity. Velma had ambulatory issues. She could walk around inside a home well enough, but for community distances she required a walker. It is not like Alice had taken Velma to a park or playground, and Velma got these marks doing things average children do. No...these marks were different.

One mark was blue and was about the size of a dime. The other was an inch-long scratch. Both were right on top of her shoulders. Immediately I went into analytical mode. I called our agency on-call number. I took pictures. I tried not to freak out. No one can prepare you for moments like this though. Nothing in training tells you how to handle these types of events. Was I overreacting? Did Velma's mom hurt her? Did Velma somehow do this to herself? Everything was an unknown because Velma was pretty much nonverbal.

Eventually it was decided that I needed to report these marks to the official State abuse hotline. I was also instructed to take Velma to the doctor. The very next day Velma and I were back in the pediatrician's office - the same pediatrician's office where Velma had been abused by her mother just nine months prior. The pediatrician took one look at the marks and said they were caused by abuse. She too called the State hotline and reported it.

A special court hearing was called that week. Velma's lawyers met with Alice and her lawyer. Unsupervised visits were stopped while an investigation was officially started, and *that* is when my life was turned upside down.

Alice's lawyer looked at the judge and said, "Maybe the foster mom abused Velma."

* *

Several days later an investigator made a surprise visit to my home. As is the way of the system, if someone makes an allegation, the system is required to investigate. Even though I was the one that reported the abuse, I was now on the line to defend myself against it. Everything that had ever run through my mind about investigations had never prepared me for this. I was not nervous though. I knew I had done nothing wrong.

A surprise investigator showed up during nap time. Jake and Sofia, my other foster children, were asleep. Papi Alan and our oldest son were both at work. Our youngest "forever" kids (a term I use to describe my biological and adopted children) were over at a friend's house playing. The investigator asked me a ton of questions. I had to explain in detail how we discipline. I had to explain in great detail what it is like to care for a child like Velma. She set an appointment for later that week to meet with all of the children. Because this was a physical abuse case, every person in the house had to be interviewed. I spent the next couple of days trying to stay calm and not coach the children. I told all of the children they should tell the truth. Our "forever" kids, Alex, Patrick and Michael, were to tell the interviewer that we have used corporal punishment on them. They were not to lie. I was not worried about Jake and Sofia at the time. They were young and rarely needed redirection. I figured the interviews would be little more than a formality and this craziness would be over.

The interviews started on a Friday night at 6pm. The investigator took each one of the bigger kids upstairs to our playroom to talk with them separately. One by one Alex, Patrick, and Michael told the investigator that yes, they have been spanked before but no, we had never laid a hand on any foster children. They said that most of the time our method of redirection involves sending the offending child to stand in the corner for a minute or two. They each told the investigator that it is never necessary to "punish" Velma, and no one has ever hurt her in our home.

The investigator spoke with Jake and Sofia together. Jake was three years old at the time and Sofia was four. I seriously did not think the investigator would even be able to get any kind of answer from those two kids. When they came to us, a year prior to this situation, they did not speak any English. And even though it had been almost exactly 12 months to the day, neither child had the ability to answer open-ended questions well. I do not know what the investigator asked them. I do not even know what they really answered. But as the investigator came down the stairs when she was finished, I could tell things were not good. Apparently the two littlest children said something along the lines of, "We pop them." With a puzzled look on my face I told the investigator that they had used the word "pop" when they first came to live with us to explain if they bumped into something, but besides that I really did not know what to say at all.

The investigator did share that all the big kids said the same thing, "We do not spank the foster kids." She said herself that she believed us, but because this was a physical abuse case, she would have to report all of the findings and this could get more complicated.

Little did I know how complicated it would get! Seven days later all three of my foster children were removed from my home. I was instructed to pack a bag with about two weeks' worth of clothes inside for each child. As I placed the children in the social worker's car, Sofia looked up at me and said softly to her brother, "Mama Becky is crying." As they drove away I did not know if I would ever see them again. My husband and I were now in the middle of a full-blown investigation against us…all because I reported abuse that happened to Velma at the hands of her biological family.

In foster parent training, most everyone is taught it is not *if* you are going to get investigated, but *when*. I remember being told to take safety precautions. We were taught to be careful of letting husbands be alone with any pre-teen or teenaged girls. We were always to document any bruises or injuries. I remember bits and pieces from the trainings, but I also remember everyone saying it is just a part of fostering. If you tell the truth, typically nothing bad will ever happen to your family. I remember being told that investigators expect it and usually work things quickly when foster families are investigated.

I now have a lot more empathy for the biological families that are ripped apart when CPS (Child Protective Services) comes knocking. Yes, most of the time removals are necessary to protect the children. In this case I fully understood why it happened because it is the system's job to protect children. Even though everyone told the truth, and even though what Jake and Sofia said to the investigator did not really make sense, I understood that the system was trying to act in the best interests of the children. The hardest part of the investigation was the way CPS literally shut me out. They did not keep me informed about anything. Immediately I felt like the enemy, and I had to simply sit back and wait for them to investigate. There was not a single thing I could do to help my case. It was so difficult.

I was not told what Jake and Sofia said when they were taken to an office to be interviewed a second time. Papi Alan was required to come to the CPS office to be interviewed a second time where he was questioned extensively about me. I did not know how many other people the investigators spoke with. I did not know anything about the investigation itself. All I knew is that my foster children, who I loved very much, were taken from me.

I was simply told to wait, and that if there was any doubt at all I would never pass a background check again. Even if "the system" could not prove that I abused Velma, my official records would say RTB or "Reason To Believe" I abused a child. I was told not to follow up with the investigator's office via phone calls or emails because it was considered harassing them. Even my licensing agency could not do much to help me.

Christy, our agency caseworker, said that she submitted six months of notes supporting our methods of discipline. Her notes documented that Jake and Sofia needed little redirection and when they did all we needed to do was send them to look in the corner. The children never told Christy anything about "pops."

The CPS worker in charge of our case believed us when we said that we had never abused the children. Her notes documented things in our favor. Also, the therapist that Sofia was seeing said that we had never abused the children. Everyone I talked to said not to worry. Still, our foster children were taken from us, and we were told nothing. For 39 days we knew nothing. We just had to wait.

The waiting was beyond excruciating. An out-of-state vacation that we had jumped through many, many hoops to take Jake and Sofia with us on was suddenly hijacked. Jake and Sophia had been looking forward to visiting Granny and Papa, and I could not even explain to them why they did not get to go now. I was not allowed to have any contact with the respite provider they had been moved to.

For an entire year I had made only one promise to Jake and Sofia. I had promised them that if they had to leave me, they would get to take all of their things. This investigation made a liar out of me. All of the children's belongings sat up on their beds, sorted by child, in case we were told that they were not coming back. Christy, as wonderful as she was, did not make it a priority to get their clothes and toys from my house to the respite provider's. As far as Jake and Sofia knew, they had just lost everything they owned too. I felt awful every time I walked past their bedroom door.

And, just like that, in 39 days it was over. Christy simply called me on the phone and said it was over. No fanfare. No explanation. It was just over. No disciplinary action needed. No citations. It was just over. We were completely cleared of any wrongdoing.

The system continued to move slowly. No one knew for sure if they were going to return the children to us or not. I was not even sure if I wanted them to come back. I was hurt. I was scared. My character had been attacked in ways I had never imagined. I was not sure if I wanted to put my family back in the position of being hurt that way ever again.

Papi Alan and I prayed a lot. The system decided that they did indeed want the children returned to our home. As much as it scared us, we both agreed that we would see these cases to their ends. Fifty days after being removed from our home, Velma came back. Five days after that, Jake and Sofia came home too.

In training it is commonly said that if you tell the truth and have nothing to hide, you will be just fine. What they do not tell you is that before everything is "fine," they will possibly remove your foster kids, make you feel like a criminal, and keep you in the dark until they decide how to rule in the case. In the end, our names were cleared, but the emotional toll it took on our family was monstrous.

It was enough to make us question ever fostering again.

Foster care is a system that often sucks people in and spits them back out. For families like ours there is only one reason we decide to stick around, the children. With or without us, kids who are neglected and abused are at the mercy of the system. Even if we had decided to give up, children would still come into care. Ultimately, we decided to continue fostering because when it comes down to it, the kids are worth it!

Velma eventually got to move in with her aunt and uncle. It was satisfying to see her case all the way to the end. It was difficult when Jake and Sofia came back because they never understood why they were taken from us in the first place. But despite every-thing we went through, we keep going because the kids who are stuck in the system deserve to have good families who will love them and take good care of them! They are worth it!

Broken Dreams

As I laid flat on my back with the laptop on my stomach, I searched through hundreds of photo listings on www.adoptuskids.org. Looking at and praying over the precious, seemingly unwanted faces for hours had become a prayer habit of mine. I am not even sure how it became a habit. One random fall day each year I would find myself spending an entire afternoon looking at each photo listed on that website. As I clicked on each photo and read each profile I prayed a simple prayer, *"Father, please bring* (insert the child's name) *the family they need and deserve for Christmas this year."* Over the course of eight years I had clicked on many photos of children I could and would envision in my arms. I cried tears of heartache when, year after year, the same wheelchair held the same child in a photo. I sobbed when the face of an angelic toddler grew into the sad face of a child I knew was broken, or when I remembered the name of a child just by seeing the face. I felt attached to their photos, and then I turned off the computer and went about my life. I happily left all of the "hard to place" orphans in cyberspace as I parented my firstborn son, missed my baby in Heaven, and was working hard to help reunify our fifth and sixth foster care placements with their mother. Until, on a late September day, I clicked on the photo of two children that jumped off the screen and into my heart.

From the moment their photo filled my laptop screen, I knew they would be ours. I stared at it for a split second and casually called for my husband, Jon, to come and see the cute little boys. He looked at them and told me to email an inquiry. My four-year-old Ruben came running over to be nosy and casually asked if they were his brothers. I looked up at Jon and laughed. Jon would later recount how he never imagined that we would actually receive a reply, or that I would actually want to move forward. He would also, regretfully, not tell me until far too late that he only said "yes" when it came down to it because he thought that was what I wanted. He wanted me to be happy. I wish I could write him a letter in the past and tell him I already was.

We got an email reply that same afternoon saying that they would be closing the children to family profile submissions soon as they had a staffing already planned to choose a family. It was in that moment that I became a raving lunatic on a mission. A year ago I would have said it was because God needed to humble both Jon and me right down to our faces on the ground. Eighteen months ago I would have said it was because the Holy Spirit was moving my heart to follow a calling from God. At the moment I am writing this I will say that it was because I am certifiably insane, and no one was going to tell me "no" without any resistance from my stubborn nature. There is no way to know what drove me to become so determined to make these boys ours, but I could not imagine doing anything else more important at the time. So many things just fell into place so perfectly that it is hard for me to imagine that the Holy Spirit was not paving the way by hand. So many things have fallen apart since then that it is hard for me to imagine that the Holy Spirit had anything to do with it at all.

I started calling our county's Department of Human Services (DHS). From our experiences thus far we had come to wonder if the children of our county might be better off homeless under a bridge in a large city than subjected to the nearly unbelievable shortcomings of the child protection agency here in our small town. The few people I got through to had no idea what I was ask-

84

ing for, and the person to whom I was supposed to speak was unavailable. She was not ever available, it seemed. I emailed the adoption advocate for the boys nearly every day for almost a week, as if my persistence alone would prove that we were the ones who wanted those boys the most. Finally, the adoption advocate emailed me back and said that Friday would be the last day to submit a profile to be considered for the boys. My tears flowed and I prayed for an angel of mercy.

My phone rang later that Wednesday afternoon, it was a young woman named Meredith. She was calling to ask if she could stop by the following morning in order to update our licensing home study. It was the first moment in which I was convinced that we were bringing the boys home.

When Meredith came the next day I begged her to give us a copy of our home study because we were absolutely certain that we were meant to go get these boys. I did nothing to hide my tears as I explained to her that I had never even intended on adopting from foster care, especially not so soon into our time as a foster family. I pleaded with her saying that if she had any kind of faith, she would give me a copy of our soon-expiring home study. It took me about ten minutes to copy all of those papers. The minute that Meredith left, I began a frenzied attempt to put together an adoption profile, which was something I thought we were supposed to do.

Two years earlier we had been given an opportunity to adopt a baby girl through private newborn adoption via a friend who was friends with a couple helping a biological mom make an adoption plan. We had to make a profile. That mother ended up parenting her baby girl, but we went through the initial motions of private adoption. It was yet another moment, in hindsight, that would become for us a hallmark of the Holy Spirit on our story. No other families had made or submitted any paperwork or pictures besides the standard approved state home study. I am almost certain that no other families wrote a letter to the placement team to let them know they were being prayed for as they faced such an important decision. I spent an embarrassing amount of money to express overnight my certified, signature confirmation, and incredibly elementary appearing envelope of hope and determination to the agency in charge of my boys who had been languishing in foster care. I emailed the adoption advocate to let her know our home study was on the way and asked how long it would take to hear something back. Two weeks was the answer I was given.

The next day we received a phone call asking us to participate in an official phone conference with the team of workers, supervisors, and the foster parent, Carla, within the next few weeks. We had been chosen. The boys were ours if we wanted them. The purpose of the conference call was to disclose as much information as possible on the two boys, three-year-old Micah and four-year-old Martin. In hindsight, there are a thousand questions I know we should have asked, but I believe everyone knows what is said about hindsight. We were bombarded with lots of diagnoses with which Martin had been labeled, such as pervasive developmental disorder, sensory processing disorder, and some developmental delays. According to the agency, these diagnoses were given by two physicians, but not agreed upon by the school he attended. This was something that, had we known then what we know now, would have been a red-flag for us. We were told absolutely nothing was significant with Micah, other than he may be slightly behind his peers. In addition, Carla told us that Martin was self-injurious, such as head butting the floor and punching himself in the side of his head. We were told he was very oppositional, but not aggressive, and had to take medication for reflux. She said, "Tiresome, but manageable."

Two weeks later, we met the boys. Carla allowed us to come right to her house that afternoon. When the door was opened for us I saw the boys, and I had a similar emotion to the first time Ruben was placed on my chest after birth. It was familiarity, yet still like facing a stranger. Overwhelming feelings of love and fear intermingled as well as peace, knowing that this was exactly what I had been waiting for.

The minute we all got through the door, Jon said "hi" to the boys, and Martin ran into his arms and wrapped himself around Jon like he just knew we were his family. This should have been the second red flag. No typical children will propel themselves straight into the arms of a complete stranger they have only heard about in vague terms, or bury their face into the neck of a man who just walked through the door of their home. We just thought it was a sweet connection we had already been given. Carla did tell us that Martin never met a stranger, but how was I to know that this was concerning?

Throughout the visits over the next several months, there were dozens of "little red flags," every single one of which I noticed and pretended like I did not. It was pointed out to us that the chewing we saw Martin doing was, in fact, him "bringing up food" (vomit) to chew on. The journaling notes I have from the first visit document how Martin slapped Jon, when we had been told prior that he was not aggressive. One of the boys peed on me while sitting in my lap and pretended he did not notice. Jon recalls noting that the food cabinets in the foster home had locks on them, but nothing was said to us about food issues other than Martin having a food pre-occupation and the desire to drink or eat much faster than he should. I recall our final visit before they came home, two nights in a hotel, when I realized these boys were possibly more than they appeared. Aggressiveness with each other, pushy, no personal boundaries, ignoring most directions given, and nonstop chattering were all things I noticed, yet pushed to the back of my mind.

At a visit we had at the mall I recall having to grab Micah by the back of his neck just to get his attention. He was chattering on so intensely about himself that he could not see the things he was about to run into – even though he was looking straight ahead. In that moment I turned to Jon and said, "You do realize that this just gets worse, right? They are doing their best to impress us right now, and it is still a lot of work. This does not get better once we bring them home." I do not remember if he replied anything at all, but he did not ask to back out or take more time getting to know them.

One of the Christmas gifts we had given them was broken before we even took them back to their foster home. Martin ate the lip-gloss Carla had put in the bag of things to fill his stocking. Martin also did not sleep very much at all during that stay, but we attributed it to being in a hotel and being Christmas time. Micah talked mostly about himself, constantly asked us to do things for him that we knew he could do himself, asked many dumb questions, and complained a lot about little things. Martin managed to completely tear the sole off of his shoe and we had to go buy him a new pair. One thing I do not remember noticing was their incredibly disgusting eating habits. I have often wondered why I did not notice that, because gobbling and open mouthed chewing are both intolerable to me. Both Jon and I did notice that Carla's teenage son had no table manners whatsoever, to the point that

Jon was disgusted, and Jon does not usually care about such things. All of that said, I was just thrilled beyond measure to see all three of my boys together, wearing matching shirts, playing at the park, working together at the museum, and laughing over silliness. They were seemingly a dream come true.

I had always wanted three biological boys close together, followed by an adopted baby girl years later. It was much closer to the original dream I had than our secondary plan of just strictly fostering until we could adopt a newborn baby girl. At the same time as we were dealing with all of the paperwork craziness that comes with an adoption, we were still fostering. When we found the boys we had a two-year-old little girl and her nearly one-year-old brother. They were reunited with their mother just one day before we left for our second visit with the boys. Then, just under two weeks later, we took a sixteen-year-old girl for two days, and the day after she left we got a call for a drug-addicted newborn who was being discharged from the hospital. Carla nearly flipped out on me when I texted her that we were getting a baby. Apparently another family who had been committed to taking in Martin and Micah were placed with a newborn baby as well, then decided they could not handle three at a time. I assured Carla that the boys were mine and the baby was just a temporary placement, as we had been very good at supporting reunification. I did not want four boys!

One of the things that I look back and wish I had thought more about was how often Carla sent me random texts, awful things the boys were doing and then asked, "Are you sure you want *these* boys?" or "Guess what *your* middle child just did…" Nearly every text I got from her was something negative about them, or a photo of their naked bums in the bathtub, or them in a time out or pouting. I thought maybe it was her way of testing our level of commitment to them, as she had made it seem to us that she had quite the say in what happened to them. She could speak up against them coming here at any time. That fact was also something that kept us from discussing adoption with the boys. Carla did not wish for us to speak about adoption, allow Ruben to call them "brothers," or bring it up for discussion with her in front of them. As far as she let us know she only called us "Mom and Dad" to them, but without explaining that it was because we were going to BE their mom and dad. I asked her about possibly seeking out play therapy for them prior to the move, to allow them to work through the feelings about it all, but she told me that play therapy was a joke. She told me that kids their age did not have a good understanding of what was going on. We would just have to work it out after they moved in with us, as they brought it up. I was a mom of only five years, a foster mom for just over one year at that point, and she was a veteran foster mom of over 50 children over nearly 20 years. What could I say to refute her experience or the fact that she was still their current caregiver?

Truth be told, nothing about our story has ever made sense or been easy, aside from the initial act of being chosen as the best family for Martin and Micah. We were not adoption minded towards older children. We got a copy of the home study the day before we needed it, when it was not something even allowed. It only took a record breaking four months to move the kids to our home, when we were told it should take six months to one year. Our ability to ignore the many red flags that could have kept us from wanting to commit to the boys makes no sense. These were the things that make me believe it was God's hand guiding us. Then the boys came home.

My sister, Leigh, came with me to pick the boys up. We loaded up for a whirlwind day of driving, a quick sleep at Carla's house, and early morning trip back to our home with four boys. The morning we left to come home we packed up the boys' things which were in two big moving boxes with clothes and several garbage bags of toys. The boys had lived there for three years and did not have a suitcase or duffle bag. They also did not have photo books, keepsakes (aside from some school papers), or anything that had come from their biological family. The last and final red flag we had before bringing our beautiful boys home was the goodbye. Carla helped us get them and their things into the SUV, handed us some goody bags with snacks and busy items, and said, "You guys behave for Mama." The boys never said another unprompted word about her for almost two months. I had to lie to her and say that they missed her, but they never really talked about her other than my prodding to get them to talk about their feelings. Martin picked up on that and began a short lived test to see if he could use "miss her" as a means of manipulation when he wanted something, but otherwise they expressed no deep sorrow at losing the only "Mom" they remembered having. The first time I recall Micah bringing her up was when he was asking me if he could call her and tell her he was staying with us forever. I had mentioned to her one time that Micah would love to talk to her and tell her about school, but she never replied that she would call him. One can only imagine what it must feel like to be a child sent away, and the person you relied on the most does not bother to call. I probably should have pushed the issue for her to call more.

We tried to settle into life with the boys the best we could. At first, things seemed routinely difficult, like one would expect out of such a situation. Micah was a master of tantrums. Martin was a master of manipulation. Ruben was amazingly patient and giving, but he even struggled with losing all of my attention to the boys and their adjustment. It was not completely overwhelming, though, because both boys were required by their original foster agency to be enrolled in school immediately upon getting here. At first I balked at this requirement, but I now see that it was a blessing in disguise. It gave me precious time with Ruben, time to rest with my foster baby, and allowed me to have a focused enough mind to notice that something was amiss with Jon.

Jon had found a mass on his throat shortly after our Christmas visit with the boys and had to have surgery to remove what turned out to be a tumor on his thyroid. An original biopsy showed no cancer, but after they removed the mass, they found cancerous cells at the center. The second surgery to remove the entire thyroid was scheduled four months later after he had healed from the first. The boys were already home at this point, and despite our attempts to control the situation things just kept getting worse and worse with their behaviors. Jon has never done well with screaming, and screaming is what Martin did for the majority of each afternoon and on weekends when he was home from school. Screaming, kicking, destroying things, biting Micah, refusing to cooperate, and then acting like a completely perfect angel when anyone else came around. The screaming in particular created anger and anxiety in Jon. So when he became less and less available, I figured it was because of the screaming and crying. Once that surgery came around, I was a mess. I was terrified of losing Jon, overwhelmed by the boys, wrapped up in the drama of the new baby's foster case, and most certainly not the supportive wife I could have and should have been.

90

The night of Jon's surgery, after having had to leave him alone once he was out of recovery and in a room, I had a babysitter come over so I could go back to visit. I had not originally planned on it, so Jon was not expecting me. I got him some soup and a milkshake. When I got there, he was in a lot of pain and still out of it, so I helped him to the bathroom, helped him get comfortable, and then decided to leave. As I was walking out of the door Talia was walking in. Talia was a nurse that Jon worked with, who was also a supposed friend of mine. The moment she saw me coming out, she hesitated as if she was going to walk away, but I had already locked eyes with her. I knew at that moment, something was wrong with this situation.

After the night of the surgery I began snooping around. I noticed that Jon was coming home 15 to 20 minutes later than he could have and had been for years. I just brushed it off, as several times he had said the nurses had breakfast together. As I found odd random texts from Talia on Jon's phone, as if part of the conversation had been deleted, I started noting what time he was coming in. As a foster parent I am a notorious "stalker," which is something we all like to joke about amongst ourselves. We "stalk" our children's biological families, both for clues to the life that got them to where they are, and for assurance that our children are loved and safe once they are returned home.

After installing a phone tracker, which I made Jon aware that I had done, I woke up very early one morning for no good reason and felt a pit in my stomach. I laid there and dozed until it was time for Jon to be getting off work and pulled up the tracker. I watched him get on the interstate to come home, feeling foolish for even doing so, and feeling ashamed that I would be so mistrusting. Then he turned into her apartment building. My world just collapsed around me. He blew it off, saying it was to take her medicine for her sick child. But what mother who is also a nurse does not have medicine for a sick child, or living less than half a mile from a drug store, cannot go get her own? One thing led to another, and within a couple of weeks Jon left.

It was the most traumatic thing that has ever happened in my life. I have been through an awful lot of pain, suffering, and abandonment, but Jon walking out was by far the most painful. It was not about being left with four children and an uncertain future. It was about me being in love with this person and finding out that

I was alone in that love. In his anger and hurt, which God only knows the "why" and "how" of, Jon said so many things that were even more hurtful than his betrayal and abandonment. He crumpled the beautiful picture I had in my mind of our life thus far. He told me he was only with me because of Ruben, and that he did not think he had ever really loved me and did not really know if he knew what love was. Then he told me that if we had any chance of working anything out at all it would have to be after Martin and Micah were sent back to foster care, because he could not live with them or handle our relationship with them in it. I have never felt such panic in my life.

The morning after Jon walked out, the only thing I could think to do was go to God and those who had raised me up to know that is what I needed to do. I stood up at my parent's church and could not manage to say anything other than my husband left me and I needed them to pray for us. So they did. They circled around me and prayed. By the grace of God, the prayer of a faithful church family, one amazing aunt-in-law who was on her way to beat down the door of Talia's apartment if Jon did not meet her for breakfast so she could speak some words of wisdom to him, and the blessing of a completely free marriage counseling ministry at a local church, Jon returned home the day before the bigger boys began kindergarten.

It was heartbreaking and scary, but we made it. I had to change many things about myself, as well as come to accept that even a husband I trusted wholly and would have died for could and would let me down. It was not until I lost Jon for that time that I began to see how fear drives the hurting children we care for and adopt through foster care. So many years I had counted on the security of Jon coming home, even in the worst of times. One night, he just was not there anymore. Just like that. Once it had all happened every word he said was something I had to analyze, test to see if it was truth or just more lies to keep me feeling secure. Every time he left the house I wondered if he would change his mind and not come back. Still today, when he is at work I lay in bed and cry thinking about how I have no way of knowing if he is meeting her at the smoking spot or walking her to her car or sending her inappropriate texts. When we are intimate, I want to ask him if he is closing his eyes because he is imagining her instead of me.

92

How must these children feel when they do not understand this world or the people in it, and do not have the security of knowing that no one is going to come in the morning and take them to another home? Do they lie in bed at night wondering if we are looking for better children than them to adopt? Even having a new level of understanding for my sweet boys did not help me to deal with the constant upheaval; nightly rages, defiance beyond anything I could ever imagine, constant destruction of property, skin picking, vomit chewing, violence against each other, inappropriate physical boundaries, or the seeking out of strangers to charm. It did not help me cope with the stealing of food from the garbage, stealing major amounts of food from our pantry, gorging on food, pretending they were sad and worried in front of our friends and when we went into public, but then becoming growling dictators the minute we were home.

It seems, as we have looked back at the whole picture, any behavior we tried to stop in any way became a huge deal. When we attempted to bribe, positively reinforce, or give consequence for the regurgitation Martin did, it turned into a larger monster we could not stop. He went as far as smearing vomit all over his face as well as spitting it on the ground, in his bed, or on his clothes. He did anything he could think of to make sure that we knew he was doing it and that we could not stop him. When Micah somehow realized the fear I had of caseworkers, he began describing to each caseworker how he hated being here because he got "spankings all the time," or because he "hated having to be hungry all the time." Luckily, we have such a good record with our treatment of children, and it was abundantly clear that they were not being mistreated, we just had to answer to the accusations and that was that. Once I realized that their behaviors were attempts to rile me up, get me angry, and control how I acted, I began calling them both out in public and in front of caseworkers. At a friend's house, if Micah was pouting and acting pitiful in an attempt to have someone ask him what was wrong, I would say loudly to him, "Micah, if you want someone to talk to you, just go talk to them. No one is going to respond to you pouting and moping anymore."

Every physician we had taken them to had no suggestion. We finally got Martin into an evaluating psychologist, and he did two days worth of testing. I was neither allowed to observe, nor was I given any information. We were mailed a statement a week later stating that Martin was "Borderline Intellectual Functioning," as well as "Reactive Attachment Disorder," "Possible ADHD," "Adjustment disorder - Conduct and Depression." None of those were any of the diagnoses that various others had given him. None of those diagnoses "counted" to get the agency the boys came from to help us at all. It was suggested we try a psychiatrist in a big city two hours away.

We spent six months with the university psychiatrist. She listened to us vent and helped us feel validated. She acknowledged that we are not alone and did not cause this. She also spent a lot of time brushing off everything we told her as typical, insignificant or our fault. It was because Martin was hungry. Martin was scared. Martin was stuck at the emotional level of a toddler. Martin just needed us to delight in him. Martin just needed us to play more with him. Martin needed, Martin needed, Martin needed. Martin needed a lot of things that we would never have said yes to, if we had known that was what he would need. According to what we were being told, Martin just needed to re-live his infancy stage, but we were given no good advice for what to do when he was screaming for hours or chewing puke while staring us down so we would get mad. She turned all of his behaviors back onto our own childhoods and traumas as the reason for our struggles.

It was nearly impossible to do as we were asked and always answer when he called "Mama..." when every moment he was calling "Mama" along with three other children. It was nearly impossible to stand in a time out with him while he raged when our infant was becoming a toddler and climbed up the coffee table. Later we started bringing Martin with us, and we found ourselves paying $160 per session to play puzzles for 50 minutes, and be told not to tell him no, not to correct him, not to use negative terms at all (especially not "obey"), and to allow him to decide and control where the play went. We were there to try to figure out how to take back control of our parental authority without being harmful to him, not to be told to cater to his every whim! Finally, we gave up. I refused to give out sticker after sticker to a child who is aware of his own defiance, while continuing to place other children in time out for the same thing.

As for Micah, while his behaviors were far less noticeable, they were far scarier. Micah was the one we caught choking the puppy.

94

Micah was the one who, while he was the most outwardly compliant, showed no empathy or remorse. He never apologized. He did not run up to us in times of peace, as Martin did, to hug and kiss. He told the school principal that he did not have to listen to her, and it did not matter anyway because no one could give him a consequence. He was the one who would lie about something he did while looking you in the eyes, and then do it again while looking you in the eyes. He was the one who said he would kill us. I believed him. I still do.

Neither of the boys responded to any affection, therapeutic parenting, or playing puzzles on the floor of a psychiatrist's office. They quickly created chaos, disorder, and a depressing anger to linger over our once carefree foster home. We had no idea what to do, or who to go to for help. As time passed, things went from bad to worse.

Martin's behaviors continually escalated. His tantrums got louder and more violent. Our evenings were spent listening to him scream about not wanting to take a bath or eat dinner. Micah also seemed to become more and more resentful and vindictive towards Martin. Micah appeared to have no real connection with his brother. In fact, he seemed like he hated him. He did not want Martin touching him. He did not want to play with him. He often times would even make comments about wanting to live in a house without Martin.

One night, as Martin screamed in his bedroom about not wanting to take a bath, I looked into Jon's eyes and I knew it was over. I had wanted to remain strong. I had wanted to parent these boys forever and help them to heal, but it had become obvious that things were continuing to get worse with no end in sight. I looked around the room and my eyes landed on Ruben. He was sitting on the floor playing with some Legos trying to ignore the chaos that was going on in Martin's bedroom. As toys hit the walls you could see Ruben flinch and then go back to what he was doing. That was it. I gave up.

The next day I made the phone call I had been hoping I would never have to make. I called our adoption worker and told her that we had decided we would not be able to adopt these boys. The adoption worker tried to be sympathetic while encouraging me to reconsider. I told her that Jon and I had talked and this was the only decision that we would be coming to. She said she understood and that she would contact the foster care worker that had Martin and Micah's case to let them know.

Three weeks later I found myself putting Micah and Martin's belongings into the back of my SUV again. We had been told that we were to pack their things and meet their foster care worker at the McDonalds by the DHS building. The worker would be taking the boys to their new foster home.

I pulled into the parking lot and tried to force the tears that burned in the corners of my eyes to stay put. I saw the worker's car so I pulled in and parked next to it. The worker stepped out of her car and greeted us. She then started transferring their bags out of my car into hers. I unbuckled the boys and led them over to the door of the car. I lifted them in and looked at the giddy smiles on their faces. They were not sad at all. They looked like they were about to go on a fun outing, not be moved to a stranger's home. I kissed them on top of their heads all the while silently asking them to forgive me for not having what it would take to parent them.

I shut the door and said goodbye to the worker and got into my car. I waited there silently as the worker got into her car. The boys never looked back at me. I could see the sides of their still-grinning faces. Tears rolled down my face as I watched the car pull out of the parking lot.

During the time that I cared for the boys I learned a lot about RAD (Reactive Attachment Disorder). I learned that a lot of the behaviors we saw early on with the boys were clear red flags that these boys had never attached to a caregiver and they had no idea how to be part of a family. They would always be waiting for the next best thing. The next new family that would be more fun than the last - at least that is what their brains would convince them was the case. When a child with RAD is placed in a family they immediately try to test the caregiver. They do whatever they can to drive that caregiver away because, per their life experience, caregivers always leave anyway. All the rages, all the behaviors - they were a coping mechanisms that they boys had come up with after enduring severe abuse and neglect at the hands of their biological family.

After the boys left I spent months grieving the loss of the boys I had hoped I would be able to help them become. The goal was to give them an environment where they would feel safe and loved, and I felt like I had only added to their trauma by having them moved. I am doing my best to move on. I miss them. I pray for them. I hope with every fiber of my being that they will both end up in a family that can give them what I was not able to. I did my best, and while it feels like it was not good enough, I know that God has never left me. I know HE has never left my boys. The rest of this story is up to HIM.

9

Full Circle

Waiting seems to be a common way of life in the world of foster care. After two months of waiting to be licensed by the new foster care agency to which I was transferring, I was highly tempted to make an appearance at the office and ask if they wanted me to write the home study for them. Patience is not one of my virtues, so when the cell phone sounded with that familiar ring tone that I had set up especially for foster care related calls, my initial instinct was to let it keep ringing. I was certain they were going to ask some mundane question that I had already answered a hundred times, and I was feeling feisty. "They've made me wait for months! It's their turn!" I thought to myself.

I did not make them wait long. After listening to the voicemail message from the program director at my agency, I immediately called her back. "Ms. Green, I have a few things I need to discuss with you right away. If you could please call me back as soon as possible, I would appreciate it," she had said.

It is amazing how quickly things can change. What I thought was going to be a pointless phone call had sent me reeling. The director had two pages left to finish before my home study was complete. She had just emailed questionnaires to my personal references and was hoping that I could push them to respond immediately because she needed to get my paperwork done right away. She had not one, but two babies for me if I wanted them! She had very little information other than that an eleven-month-old baby girl had been removed and placed in another foster home three days prior after some questionable findings with her newborn baby sister. The other foster home was a brand new home and had no experience with infants. The eleven-month-old was placed with them on Friday, and by Friday night they were already asking to have her moved because they were completely overwhelmed. She said that if I was willing to take both girls, she was fairly certain they would be mine. She just had to check with the caseworker and explain that I was a few days away from having my licensing number, but that I had already fostered before so I knew what I was doing.

I said, "No."

It absolutely killed me to say no because being single, it usually takes months for me to get a placement unless the children are already in care. Caseworkers tend to want couples or stay-at-home moms. If I get my placements the "normal" way, by having my home study submitted with a pile of other potential placements for a caseworker to choose from, it can take months. As much as I wanted to say yes, I had no idea how I was going to be able to take care of a newborn *and* a soon-to-be one-year-old by myself. So I told the director that I was a little concerned about being able to handle that on my own, and as much as it was killing me, I thought I needed to say no.

I immediately called my mother and somehow ended up talking myself into calling my director back and saying, "You know what... let's give this a try!"

On Tuesday, she called me and asked how soon I could take the eleven-month-old who was already at the other foster home. She said that the current foster parents were nervous wrecks and that she was no longer comfortable leaving the baby there.

I replied, "I'm ready for her tonight if you want me to take her."

I was still not officially licensed, but they moved her in as a respite placement with the understanding that she would be an official foster placement as soon as we got my licensing number. It was arranged that her foster parents would bring her over to my house themselves. That evening I opened my door to the most beautiful blond-haired, blue-eyed baby girl. Little Jessica was understandably timid and scared, but she came to me willingly and let me take over.

At that point, there was not much information on Jessica's baby sister. Madeline was born with several drugs in her system, and would be staying in the NICU (Neonatal Intensive Care Unit) indefinitely. In the caseworker's words, Madeline was "a *whole* other ballgame." With the addition of a drug-exposed newborn on the horizon, I concentrated on Jessica and started to do what I could to make her comfortable. I wanted to get her comfortable with me and into a routine before our lives became crazy with the addition of her baby sister.

The first week was a difficult one for Jessica. There had been so many huge changes for her in such a short amount of time. After the first twelve hours, I understood why her first foster parents had been so overwhelmed. Jessica was scared, confused, and exhibited many behaviors that made me suspect she had been neglected for some time. She self-soothed by banging her head repeatedly against her crib and rocking herself back and forth over and over again. She cried hysterically if she lost bodily contact with me, but refused to relax into my arms and be comforted. Perhaps the most disheartening habit that she had was when it came to taking her bottle. As soon as she saw me prepare a bottle, Jessica would run towards me, put her hands behind her back, and crane her neck like a baby bird. It was weeks before she would hold her own bottle or relax into my arms to be fed.

I often wonder what my little ones are thinking. What do they remember? What emotions and thoughts are going through their little heads? I foster babies. I foster little ones who are unable to speak for themselves, so I have to be extra observant and empathetic to the feelings they are bound to be experiencing. As a parent, I love watching my little ones as they learn and experience new things. I love the excitement on their faces as they accomplish a new task. I love their concentration when they are trying something new. I love seeing the little wheels turning in their heads when I know they are trying to get away with something or trying to figure out a way to bargain with me. I even love their little frustrated faces and the big dramatic crocodile tears that they play up when they do not get their way.

As a foster parent, I often see much bigger and more upsetting emotions and behaviors in my babies. Watching as Jessica rocked herself back and forth over and over when she was distressed because no one had ever comforted her before was heartbreaking. She was terrified of most men. It was that hysterical, nearly inconsolable, panic-stricken kind of terror. That first week with Jessica was a never-ending flood of huge emotional breakdowns, and all I could do was try my best to reassure her that she was safe and loved with me.

I remember one shopping trip when I witnessed something that I was completely unprepared to see. Jessica had been in an unusually good mood, babbling away throughout the store. When we got to the checkout, I busied myself emptying the cart and realized how quiet Jessica had suddenly become. What I saw when I looked at her face absolutely broke my heart. She was staring at an older gentleman in a wheelchair in the next lane. They say "the eyes are the windows to the soul," and her eyes were filled with tears just to the point of almost spilling over. She was not scared as she was with most men. She was sad. I am as certain of that as I have ever been of anything. The look on her face was pure sorrow.

I wiped away her tears. I kissed her forehead. I told her how much I loved her, and I told her how sorry I was that she was sad. I was used to seeing fear, excitement, even anger at times from my little ones, but complete and total sorrow in the eyes of an eleven-month-old was not something that I was prepared to see. I later learned from her caseworker that up until she came into care, Jessica had been living with her mother and grandfather. Her disabled grandfather was wheelchair dependent, and had been one of the only people who attempted to take care of her in the home. Seeing that man in the grocery store clearly reminded her of her Grandpa, and her little heart was breaking.

The waves of emotion that Jessica experienced during her first week in my home were difficult for both of us. Then suddenly on the fifth evening, everything seemed to click! We had spent the day shopping, napping, and eating – the three things that Jessica loved best. After dinner, I told her that she needed a bath, and I prepared myself for a battle. Bath time had not been very success-ful since she had arrived. I decided to use the toddler tub because it was smaller and would hopefully not overwhelm her like the regular tub seemed to. She immediately started to cry and I could see a full-blown fit approaching, so I quickly diverted her atten-tion by pouring water over her hands. She started getting inter-ested in that, and then I gave her one little bath toy that she immediately took and started playing with. After she seemed calm and almost happy, I gave her one other small toy and started to wash her off while she was playing. No tears at all! I even let her play a few minutes longer so she could start associating bath time with something fun. Success!

After bath time we went out to the living room for a little play-time. In the five days that Jessica had been in my home, the child had absolutely refused to leave my lap while we were in the house. This day, however, she decided to sit next to me on the couch. She still refused to get on the floor, but we sang songs, played Patty Cake, This Little Piggy, read books, and everything else I could think of for at least 30 minutes before we headed to her room for bedtime. It was still a few minutes early, so I thought I would attempt to put her down on the floor and see how she did. I was shocked when she started exploring her bedroom for the first time since she moved in. I decided to let her explore and started working on sorting a tub of baby clothes. I sat on the floor and started pulling items out, looking at the tags, and sorting into piles. Jessica watched me intently for a minute, then came over, and started "helping" me. She did exactly what I was doing. She pulled one article of clothing out of the bin, opened it up, looked at the tag, and then handed it to me. She stood there and "helped" me until every last piece of clothing had been sorted. Then she pointed to her crib and was ready for bed.

In the four weeks that followed, Jessica began to come out of her shell and blossomed. She was genuinely excited to see me when she woke up in the morning and when I picked her up from daycare. We had fun together! I began to see positive changes in Jessica as she began to trust me. She no longer rocked herself back and forth when she was upset, but rather came to me for hugs and cuddles. She relaxed into my arms during her bedtime bottle. I was thrilled every time I saw her have a breakthrough moment, and I loved seeing her smile.

Jessica and I had finally found what worked for us when I received a phone call telling me to go to the hospital to pick up Madeline because she was finally being released. During that same phone call, they told me that there was a hearing scheduled on the following Monday and that the girls would most likely be released into their father's care. While I was sad to be saying goodbye to Jessica so soon, I was happy that the girls would be able to go to their father sooner rather than later. It had been clear from his weekly visits with Jessica that he loved her and wanted to do what was right for his girls. I was a little surprised that they did not wait to release Madeline until Monday when she could go directly home, but I decided to make the best of it and went to the hospital to pick up Jessica's five-week-old baby sister.

Madeline was a cute little thing. That is to say, she was a cute little thing in the two hours total that she was not screaming during the time that she was with me. I knew I was in trouble when the first thing the nurses in the hospital where she had been staying for the past five weeks said to me was, "We're so sorry!"

"What does that mean?" I asked.

"Well," they hesitantly replied, "she's kind of been our little mascot for the past five weeks, so she's pretty much been held 24/7. We've been working on self-soothing today though!"

They had been working on self-soothing "today." Great.

Jessica was at daycare, so I decided to bring Madeline to my sister's house so she and my five-year-old niece and nephew could meet her. My nephew was more interested in his Wii game than the squalling infant, although he did serenade her with a lovely lullaby rendition of Beyonce's "Single Ladies" in an attempt to keep her from crying. My niece on the other hand never left her side. She held her, she talked to her, and she did her very best to appease the fussy baby. Madeline started crying again, so my niece decided to help me change her diaper. Then the baby spit up all over the floor. That did it. My niece was done. As I packed up our things and put Madeline in her car seat, she started screaming because she was no longer being held. My niece held the front door open for us and loudly exclaimed, "And she's OUTTA HERE!"

I headed over to Jessica's daycare where it quickly became apparent that I had not really thought through the logistical aspects of transporting a five-week-old and a twelve-month-old at the same time. I loaded Madeline and her infant carrier into a stroller and thought that I would just carry Jessica back out to the car. It would have been much easier had Jessica been another year older, but she was still an infant herself. Fortunately, the kind ladies at the daycare recognized that I had no clue how hard that was going to be and took care of loading Madeline for me while I loaded up her big sister.

After the first 30 minutes with both girls, I knew I was in over my head. Madeline was screaming because I could not hold her while I was making Jessica's dinner. Jessica was crying because there was a screaming thing stealing my attention. After her dinner she had ravioli in her hair, desperately needed a bath, was sobbing hysterically, and was clinging to my leg as I tried to comfort her and give Madeline her bottle. By the time Jessica should have been in bed, we were nowhere near ready. I did what any self-respecting woman would do in that situation.

I called my Mommy.

Most of my family had been on a cruise that week, and they apparently had just pulled into the garage when I sent out my "Mommy SOS." (And by "just pulled in," I mean they had not even closed the garage door or unloaded their bags from the car.) Thankfully, my mom and aunt came over and took over holding Madeline so I could get Jessica bathed, changed, bottled, cuddled, and in bed.

My one saving grace that week was that Jessica was a fantastic and predictable sleeper. Her bedtime routine consisted of us reading a book or playing for a few minutes, Jessica pointing to the kitchen indicating that she was ready for her bedtime bottle, pushing her bottle away when she was finished, giving me a quick hug, and pointing upstairs to her bedroom at precisely 7pm. We would walk into her room where she would point to her crib, grab her own blanket, roll over, and was usually sound asleep before I left the room. The best part was that she routinely slept until 7am the next morning. That was the only thing that helped get me through that night with Madeline who woke up every one and a half to two hours to drink two measly little ounces of her bottle.

Luckily the timing of the feedings that night worked out so that Madeline was fed and asleep just before Jessica woke up for the day. Everything was going well until Jessica realized that the squalling infant was still there. Then it was back to the squalling two. I somehow managed to get both girls dressed and loaded into the car in order to get Jessica off to daycare. She was hysterical with Madeline in the house. I wanted to keep things as normal as possible for her, so daycare seemed like the best option. I had Jessica in one arm with her diaper bag and my purse on that shoulder, and Madeline in her carrier in the other arm. At that point, I was firmly convinced that I was Superwoman.

I thought I could handle Madeline well enough as long as Jessica was at daycare, so I did not call my mom that morning. She ended up calling me to tell me she was coming over, and I was so glad she did. By that point, sleeplessness and the stress of an inconsolable infant had convinced me that Madeline was a nightmare in an angelic little body. The nurses were not kidding when they said that she was used to being held all the time. What they neglected to mention was that she was used to being held and walked around all the time. Madeline was not content with just being rocked. She wanted to be walked, and she let you know it in an ear piercing, nails-on-a-chalkboard, made-your-ears-bleed, continuous high-pitched screech.

My mother and I took turns walking Madeline so she would stop screaming and the other would attack the remnants of the natural disaster that seemed to have also struck my home in the 24 hours that Madeline had been there. How was it possible that something so little could wreak so much havoc on a household? In 24 hours, I had accumulated more dirty laundry than I had during the previous week having been pooped on, peed on, and spit up on multiple times. I had moved all of my bedding out to the living room and slept on the couch during the few minutes that Madeline would sleep because every little sound woke her up. My kitchen had been taken over by dirty bottles because she ate every two hours. It was as if a tornado had made its way through my home.

It was abundantly clear to me in that first day that a single, trying to work full-time, foster mom really should admit to herself that taking on a twelve-month-old and a drug-exposed newborn fresh out of the NICU by herself probably was not the best or brightest idea. I knew that the girls had a hearing on Monday and that they were probably going to be placed with their father, so I only had to make it through the weekend. At that point I did something I had never done before. I called my agency and asked if they could find someone to do respite for Madeline over the weekend.

I have always used my mom as my official respite care provider for my kids, so I had never asked to use another foster family. I have always felt that being in foster care is difficult enough for a child without having to go to yet another strange home. In Madeline's case however, she had just left the hospital and was going home on Monday. A respite family was found, and they offered to come over and pick up Madeline that night and keep her until Monday morning after I took Jessica to daycare. Based on how Jessica was reacting to her sister, and how she was already reverting back to some of the previous self-soothing behaviors that she had not done in weeks, I knew it was best for her to wait until she went home before bringing her little sister into the picture permanently.

Before my weekend respite providers came to pick up Madeline, my mother kept her occupied while I tried to give Jessica my undivided attention. I felt so bad for her. She did not understand what was happening. All she knew was that she no longer had me all to herself, and for a twelve-month-old who had never had a mother's undivided attention up until she came to live with me, losing that after five weeks was devastating for her. I was able to get her off to bed a few minutes before Madeline's respite family arrived to take her home with them.

Looking back, I realize that my mother and I probably did not display the most appropriate reaction to having Madeline leave for the weekend, but upon shutting the front door, we turned to each other, breathed deep, cleansing breaths, and exclaimed in the words of my sweet niece, "And she's OUTTA HERE!!!"

After Madeline left for the weekend and my mother and I did our little "Happy Dance of Relief," my mom left, and I stood in the middle of the hurricane disaster zone that was once my home and basked in the sweet, sweet silence. It was 7:45pm, and I had not slept more than a total of four combined hours in the previous 48 hours. I was beyond exhausted. Unfortunately at that point I was so tired that my body would not go to sleep. I had hit that point of exhaustion where I had been running on pure adrenaline for so long that my body would not shut down. Fortunately, Jessica slept her predictable 12 hours so by the time I was able to relax, I slept like a log until she woke up. That is to say, I slept like a log except for my own snoring that kept waking me up, having those full body twitches that happen when your body is so tired that you cannot see straight, and swimming in a puddle of my own drool, but I did get a full night's sleep.

The next morning, I heard Jessica's usual sweet baby babble over the monitor. I went upstairs and was greeted with her huge smile and excitement over seeing me and starting a new day. As we headed down the stairs, I saw that excitement turn into dread as she remembered that a screaming Madeline had been there when she went to bed the night before. Jessica got very quiet and hesitantly peered around the corner looking straight to the rocking chair where my mom had been rocking Madeline the night before. She looked at me questioningly, and I put her down. She proceeded to search the entire house. No room went unexplored. She finally went to the crib where Madeline had been sleeping the day before, looked inside, and realized that the baby was nowhere to be found. I honestly think that if Jessica could have talked, she would have had the exact same reaction that the rest us of had, "And she's OUTTA HERE!!!" Instead, she turned around, looked at me, smiled, giggled, and ran up to me for a huge bear hug.

Even though Madeline was away for the weekend, Jessica still was not herself. She was okay as long as I was in the room, but if she lost sight of me at all, she grew hysterical. My mom came over to help me clean the disaster zone that had become my house, but it became clear that Jessica was not ready for me to leave her sight. By my second trip upstairs to gather laundry, Jessica was hysterical, back to rocking herself, and sobbing like crazy.

No infant should ever be put in a position of feeling like they need to comfort themselves. When Jessica first came to me, she spent more time rocking herself than she would allow me to rock her. She had no way to trust that she could depend on me to comfort her. It took three weeks to get her to a point where she no longer rocked herself over and over. The fact that Jessica had completely reverted back to her old behavior after only a couple of hours with Madeline in the house broke my heart.

After my mom left, I promised Jessica that it would just be the two of us for the rest of the weekend. It took most of the day to convince her that things were back to normal for the time being, and that she could relax and be herself. By Saturday evening, she seemed to be getting back to normal. Jessica would disappear into the playroom for short stretches of time and run back out to give me hugs. I finally realized that she was going to be okay when she

108

had disappeared into her playroom for several minutes and everything grew quiet. Anyone who has ever parented a toddler knows that silence is not always a good thing. I got up to check on her when I heard hysterical baby laughter coming from the next room.

"Oh dear, what is she doing," I wondered.

Fortunately, I was greeted by the happiest, most heart-warming sight that I had seen in days. Out of all of her toys and everything that she had to play with in her playroom, Jessica had discovered a laundry basket. She had dumped out all of the dirty clothes, turned the basket on its side, and proceeded to climb in and out, in and out, in and out - for the next 24 hours! She had apparently discovered the mecca of all amazing toys. She was nothing but smiles for the remainder of the weekend, and I was so happy that what was most likely going to be her last weekend with me ended with smiles, lots of laughter, and huge hugs and cuddles from my favorite baby girl.

Monday morning came and I still had not heard from the girls' caseworker regarding court. While I was frustrated by the lack of communication, I was not surprised. I had only spoken to the caseworker one time since Jessica was placed with me, and that was five days prior when Madeline was released from the hospital. To say that I was less than impressed would be an understatement. Over the years, I had worked with caseworkers who were clearly overworked, under extreme stress, and exhausted. The very nature of their job is physically and mentally draining leading to huge turnover in the field.

The girls' caseworker made no qualms about the fact that she was burned out. She did not want to be there, and her lack of regard for the children was disheartening. I tried to "kill her with kindness," but that approach seemed to irritate her even more. I ended up avoiding contact with her unless it was absolutely necessary.

Because I had no idea when the court hearing was occurring, I decided to go about my day as usual but with the assumption that the girls would be heading home at some point. I packed up some of the girls' things, played with Jessica for a little while, and then took her to daycare as usual before going to pick up Madeline from respite.

I could not believe my ears when I walked into the respite home, and Madeline was not screaming. In fact, she seemed perfectly content. I quickly learned that the home where Madeline had been staying was actually a full house of a family of five. Madeline had been held, rocked, played with, and spoiled rotten by the couple and their three older children all weekend. We decided that if for some reason the girls did not go back to their father that day, we were going to request to have Madeline placed there permanently and do frequent sibling visits for the girls. Madeline was content, Jessica was happy with me, and we were willing to do whatever was necessary to keep it that way.

I spent the next two hours trying to reach the girls' caseworker. She finally sent me a text message saying, "Girls going to dad. Get their things. Be there in an hour." I rushed to daycare to get Jessica, and called my mom to come over and cater to Madeline while Jessica and I finished packing and played together for a few final minutes.

When their caseworker showed up at the door, it was abundantly clear that she was not happy about being there. In the ten minutes that she was in my home, she complained about the distance of the drive, how tired she was, how her legs hurt, the amount of things that I was sending home with the girls, and the fact that Madeline was crying.

Yes, the girls had a lot of stuff. They were two infants. They had complete wardrobes, diapers, formula, bottles, toys, and food. I sympathized with her. I was sorry that her legs hurt and that she was tired, but this move was not about her. Not once did she even glance at the girls whose lives were being uprooted and turned upside down yet again. My mom and I were so disgusted with her that we just sat there with the babies while we watched her load all of the girls' things.

After she loaded the car, she walked back into the apartment and grumbled, "Bring the babies." She stood outside the car with her arms crossed, rolled her eyes, and gave us dirty looks while we said goodbye to Jessica and Madeline and loaded them into the car. She never once spoke to either of the girls. I gave them each one last kiss and that woman tore out of there without ever looking back. She had a long drive ahead of her - a fact of which she made us perfectly aware. In the five weeks that the girls were in my life, I had done all that I knew how to do to bring them some kind of comfort and stability. All that I could do as they drove away was pray that they would be okay.

Life moved on, and over the next year and a half, I had the joy of fostering another baby boy. Then I got the phone call that breaks the heart of every foster parent late one night. Jessica and Madeline were being brought back into care along with their new seven-month-old sibling, and they wanted to know if I could take them. After a year and a half, those baby girls were back in foster care for the second time.

There was no way that I could take all of them. I do not think the placement worker was really thinking clearly when she called me. With all three siblings and my current placement, I would be well over the allowed ratio of children that young to one parent. I did offer to take Jessica if they were unable to find a home that could take all three siblings, but I prayed that they would be able to keep the kids together if at all possible.

I spent the next hour and a half running around and tried to get set up for a two-year-old the best I could. I started to panic because I was also moving in four weeks. What was I thinking saying yes to a placement four weeks before I was supposed to move? I could not say no though. Jessica's sad little eyes still weighed heavily on my heart even after all that time. If she could not be with her siblings, I wanted her with me. I knew that she would not remember me, but I remembered her and that was at least something that I could give her.

Fortunately, I received another call an hour later saying they were finally able to find a home for all three little ones. I was happy that the children were together, but it broke my heart that their parents could not straighten up their lives and step up for their kids. It is one of the sad realities of foster care. There are success stories, and there are parents who inevitably fail their children over and over again.

That late night call was a reminder of why I continue to foster. Because these little ones deserve someone stable in their lives. They deserve a safe place in the midst of the storm. They deserve joyful childhood memories. They deserve someone who will open their hearts and make them the center of their world. They deserve the time to heal and the time to learn to trust. They deserve to feel unconditionally loved. I believe that no matter how young they are people never forget how you made them feel. Even if my little ones do not remember me after they leave my home...*they will have known love.*

10

In My Heart, I Always Knew

My mom was visiting during a long weekend, and we both were sitting on the couch eating popcorn and giggling. "Grey's Anatomy" was on the television, and I was blissfully unaware of the evil taking place just a few miles from my house. At 8:50pm the phone rang, and I yelled for my husband to answer it. The show was almost over, and I did not want to miss the ending.

"Oh! Hi Ryan," I heard my husband say. My heart jumped into my throat. Ryan was the supervisor of our foster care agency. There was only one reason he would be calling so late at night. A child needed us. My husband mumbled to himself as he scribbled down a few notes while he listened to the voice on the other end of the phone. After he hung up, he told me that Ryan had said there was at least one child who needed a home. He had also said that there might be a sibling as well. Overwhelming feelings of excitement and anxiousness came over me immediately.

Six months prior, we had said goodbye to our second foster placement. She had been our first girl. Foster care had been rough on me. I had begun suffering from panic attacks and anxiety. Because of this, we decided to put our home on hold (foster care language for "We are not accepting new placements right now.") to figure out what our next step would be. After a lot of thought and prayer, we decided to try to adopt from the list of children whose parents had already lost their legal rights, also known as "waiting children." We already had three biological sons, so we were hoping to find and adopt a daughter. We set up a beautiful room for our princess we had yet to find. After searching through many photo listing of girls who were available for adoption, we sent out 33 letters and sets of pictures of us to agencies that held files of girls that we were interested in learning more about. We never received a single call or response to any of our attempts to be matched with a child. After getting no response we decided to give foster care another chance.

Our home had only been open for two days when we got this late night phone call. I jumped into my pre-placement panic. I was so thankful that my mother was there with me. In anticipation of her arrival, my house was already clean. I folded a few piles of laundry, made the beds, and jumped in the shower. I do not know why, but whenever I find out a placement is coming I feel a desperate urge to shower, as if I will never be able to bathe again. I dug out the baby monitor and dusted it off. We had no crib. We were planning on adopting an older girl. I found an old bassinet and sprayed it down with Febreeze. I then found a few pieces of baby clothing in a keepsake box. When I was done, I took a Xanax and tried to make myself calm down.

Later, while my mom, husband, and biological children were all asleep, I lay awake wondering about this little person who was on their way to my house. Finally, at 1:30am, headlights turned down our road. I shook my husband to wake him, and we both ran outside. The van door slid open silently in the cool night air. In the utter darkness all I heard was a tiny whimper. Then and there he had my heart, and I knew without a doubt that he was my son. I lifted him out of his car seat and held him tight. He was just over eight pounds at 35 days old. My smallest biological child had been nearly nine pounds at birth! This baby was the tiniest baby I had ever held. I pulled him to my chest and instinctively started bouncing up and down as we went inside.

114

Ryan looked pale and exhausted. He explained to us what had happened. The police had gone to the baby's house with a search warrant for stolen items. During the search, they found a locked bedroom door. Inside the locked bedroom, they discovered a child in a crib converted into a cage. The child was starving, naked, and filthy. The first responders were in shock. They called Social Services who took the older child and this baby into custody immediately. The older child had been taken to the hospital, and the baby came to our house.

Ryan was obviously shaken. He had us sign the papers quickly and then darted out into the night. I often wondered what he did after he left our home. I am sure the images he had seen that night haunted him for quite some time.

As for us, we stared in wonder at this tiny being that had just been dropped off at our doorstep. The few belongings that came from his house had the worst odor I have ever smelled. The clothes and bag literally smelled like death. I could only describe it as what you smell when passing a dead animal on the road. I quickly put it all outside. Only later would I learn the true horror of that smell.

We gave our newest boy a bath to clean away the cigarette and decay smell. He was tiny and content. I put him in the bassinet, and set the bassinet on our bed. I had never slept with any children in my room, but he was so tiny and helpless. My mommy instinct said he needed to be close to me. My mother and children slept throughout the entire process. This darling baby boy, named Charlie, slept nearly the whole night.

As the early morning sun peered in through the windows, my mom bounded into my bedroom with all the joy of a new grandmother. She snatched him up and declared that he looked like a little elf. We played in the house most of the day, only venturing out to make a trip to Walmart to stock up on diapers and bottles. A news report said that Charlie's dad was out on bail. I had no idea how he could have been released already given the circumstances, but our day went well regardless of this unsettling information.

The next day I had to hop in the shower because Charlie had spit up down my shirt. When I got out of the bathroom, my mother's demeanor had changed. She spoke words that sent chills up my spine: "They found a baby buried in the backyard of the house they took Charlie from." I will never forget the look on her face or the way my arms wanted to grab Charlie and hide.

In a panic, I called the on-call social worker. I was frightened beyond words. To this day, I do not know who returned my phone call, but she was the nicest lady. She assured me that we were safe. Charlie's father was back in jail and knew nothing about us. As I calmed down, I immediately started calling Charlie by his middle name, Michael.

Our town is small. The discovery of a hidden and neglected child, and the body of a baby being found was big news. I was scared to leave the house. They had released the name "Charlie" on the news, so I invested in a few blankets to keep over his car seat while we were out in public. I wore him, hidden, in a Moby Wrap. I was thankful we had changed his name. The details of this story were everywhere; all over the news, in foreign countries, and on my neighbors' lips. We asked our neighbor to be on the lookout for media vans. He was a huge mountain of a man, and he told me "Darling, don't you worry about them medias, you yell if you need me." Thankfully, we never did.

As the details emerged, the more I thanked God for rescuing the other child and sparing Michael. Our church family quickly figured out who "Michael" was. The news reports stated that a one-month-old "was taken into foster care," and then we appeared with a one-month-old. As quickly as people grasped who he was, they just as quickly "forgot." Everyone banded with us to conceal his identity and protect both him and the rest of my family. Donations poured in. Boxes of diapers, bags of clothes, a beautiful borrowed bassinet (better than the one we had), bottles, blankets, lots of love, and prayers flowed into our home.

Time passed quickly, yet at the same time it passed slowly. It is the paradox of foster care. We went to a few court hearings, but mostly they were kept private, and we were not allowed to remain in chambers. Michael was growing into a chubby, happy baby. He had bulked up quickly. Slowly, the horror of his previous home became a memory. Overall, it did not take too long for his parents' parental rights to be terminated, and we were thrilled to be headed towards adoption!

Michael's room had been painted purple in anticipation of the girl we were hoping to find and adopt. I told the social worker that I would not paint the room again until I knew Michael was staying with us forever. I will never forget the day she told me to "paint the room." I had known it all along. He was my son.

After a few weeks of quiet, the social worker called. "Will your husband be home tonight? I need to stop by and talk to both of you." she said. I assumed she needed to meet my husband, because she had never met him. Suddenly a surge of panic hit me. I called her back and asked, "Do you need to see him because you need to see him, or because something is wrong?" She explained that there had been a development in Michael's case that she needed to talk to us about. I snatched my boy up into my arms and looked around desperately, as if I could hide him somewhere. I changed his diaper and started to sob. In my heart I knew something was wrong.

A few hours later, my husband came home to my tear-streaked face. He looked me in the eye and told me not to worry. The giant lump in my throat insisted otherwise. The social worker pulled into our driveway. Her supervisor was with her. I knew right then that the news was not good.

The results of the DNA test Michael had previously taken had come back. The test confirmed that the man in jail was not his biological father. His biological father was a man named Aaron, and he wanted Michael. Actually, Aaron wanted his parents to take custody of Michael. They had every legal right to, but I did not care. I did not care that they had not known about him. I did not care that he was their grandson. I did not care that they thought they loved him. I did not care.

I held him tight and finished feeding him his bottle. I was distracted as I listened to the conversation going on around me. The supervisor said visitations would need to start soon. The new plan was to move Michael from our home, the only home he knew, to the home of his biological grandparents who were strangers to him. How could I have been so wrong? I knew in my heart he was mine. Why was this happening? The social worker and her supervisor left with apologies. I could not be mad at them. It was not their fault.

I sobbed. I screamed. I cried. I wailed. I fell asleep in the midst of tears. The next day, I pulled myself together. I needed to call my mom and tell her. Other than that, I had to keep it a secret. The news of this development was not public yet, and it was going to be used in the trial.

I called the social worker and asked if I could drop some pictures of Michael off for Aaron and his parents. Aaron was leaving for boot camp in a few days, and I thought he should see a picture of his son before he left. It was a hard choice, but I was praying that if I was nice, they would let me stay in his life. Our social worker met with them. She gave them the pictures, and they resoundingly said they wanted custody. It was the final blow. I was going to lose my son.

Over the next couple weeks, all the legal protocols were performed. With the initial background checks and home visits complete, it was deemed that Michael would be safe and loved with Aaron's parents. When I heard this I knew what was coming next. It was time for them to meet their grandchild. My dear friend babysat my other boys while I took Michael to meet his grandparents.

I sat in the sterile visitation room avoiding the huge mirror on wall to my right. I knew it was a two-way mirror. I tried to keep my emotions under control in case anyone was watching me on the other side of the mirror. I hugged Michael tightly in that last moment that he was all mine. My social worker, Mary, opened the door. "They're here, are you ready?" I plastered on a smile and took a deep breath. I kissed Michael on the top of his head and whispered, "I'm sorry, and I love you." Then I watched the door open.

In walked his grandparents, two very normal looking people. They seemed too young to be grandparents. Grandma gasped and started crying. I whispered, "Please don't cry." I do not know if I was talking to her or to myself. Grandpa's eyes welled up. I breathed deep and handed over my son to his grandma. Grandpa's tears spilled over as he handed Michael a small stuffed bear. It was a Dale Earnhardt bear, my mother's favorite driver. I knew they were decent people; my mother always said, "You can trust an Earnhardt fan." I felt it was a sign, though it did not make it any easier.

We talked for a few moments. They were overwhelmed, as could be expected. They had not known he even existed, let alone the type of horrors that were going on all around him in his first few weeks of life. I answered a few questions and then quietly excused myself. I took one more glimpse of Michael as I walked out of the room.

I darted across the hall into the bathroom. It was my refuge. I do not make a habit of crying in public, something I rather prided myself on. I made it to the sink where I grabbed a wad of paper towels and began to sob until my eyes hurt. I left the bathroom and remembered I did not know if Mary was bringing Michael home, or if I was supposed to pick him up. I chuckled at the thought. I was always so on top of those type of things. It humored me that I did not know.

I could not bring myself to open the door to that room again. I would not go back in that room. I stood in the hall staring blankly, wondering what to do next. Thankfully, a different social worker opened the door to the two-way mirrored room. She asked if I was okay. For the first time in my life, I answered, "No, I'm not." She went and gathered the details for me. Mary would bring Michael home. It was time for me to leave.

I had to go pick up my other children. My friend had taken them to Chick-fil-A. Thank goodness because I needed a Coke. When I arrived, she said she would be right back and went to her car. She came back with flowers and a card. As she handed them to me she explained, "They aren't from me."

I opened the card. It was from my husband. He had stopped after work the night before and bought flowers and a card for me. He had taken them to my friend's house. He had wanted to be there for me even when he physically could not. My heart swelled with love for him. I cried at the table and then bought some ice cream. It helped.

I had to run to Walmart before I went home. I laugh now, wondering how in the world I held it together. There were some clearance racks with clothes on them. I grabbed a handful of items and the ingredients to make Pizza Pasta. Pizza Pasta is my chocolate. Some husbands bring home candy when their wife is upset. Mine brings home the ingredients for pasta!

I glanced at my watch and realized I was running late. Time had flown by. I raced home. Mary's van was already in the driveway. She was holding Michael as he slept. Mary had a worried look on her face. She had heard sirens, and I did not have a cell phone. Thankfully though, she had not waited long. I took Michael from her, and we went inside to talk.

Mary told me that Michael had done well. Grandpa and Grandma had been enchanted with him. That much was obvious. You could not help but fall in love with him. I wanted to know what was next. She explained that they had to do a few more home visits at the grandparents' home. When the background checks were finished, Michael would start day visits with his biological family.

119

Aaron was gone to boot camp and had yet to meet his son. Everyone was hoping he would be able to come home at Christmastime in a couple months. My heart was too broken to worry about his feelings, or anyone else's for that matter. I was crying all the time. I was trying to accept that Michael would be leaving. That was how foster care was supposed to work. We were taught in training to help with the reunification process. This case was easy compared to the stories I had read about and been told. There was no abuse, no neglect, no damage inflicted by Aaron or the grandparents. This family was thrilled he was safe. They loved him. I could not begrudge them that. This should have been easier. I had already said goodbye to our first two foster children. This was not so different. Except that it was. He felt like he was my son. He was my son.

During the visits that were held at the DSS (Department of Social Services) office, I met some of Aaron's other family members. His fiancé, Marissa, his niece, and his younger brother all came to one visit or another. Aaron's older sister lived across the country. Her daughter also lived with Aaron's parents.

The fact that they were already raising a grandchild made the pain lessen a bit. I was glad that Michael would not be the only child in the house. Aaron's fiancé was a tiny girl who was only 18 years old. Her eyes lit up when she met Michael. Her love for him was apparent. She lived with Aaron's parents as well, and she was going to help raise Michael. I was so thrilled that I liked her. My heart began healing piece by piece.

We got the news that Aaron would, in fact, be home in time for Christmas. Michael's grandparents were given permission to have him for a week-long visit during Christmas. I had been adamant that he not be gone on Christmas day. The more I got to know his family though, the more I lessened that stance. He was going to be theirs after all. I just asked that he come home on Christmas night.

To say that I was nervous about meeting Aaron was an understatement. He was the reason that Michael even existed. Yet there was an underlying tension I could not shake. He had had an affair with a married woman. Not only was she married, but she was capable of unspeakable evil. I rarely thought of her. I still try not to. The anger in my heart would burn to the surface when she entered my thoughts.

I decided Aaron was more or less innocent. He had not been to her home. He did not know what went on there. He was barely 17 at the time, and a 23 year old woman was throwing herself at him. (It was later rumored that Michael's birth mother was asking boys to get her pregnant, and she would say it was her husband's baby.) I took the sexist stand of "boys will be boys." It hurt too much to think of anything else. The day came for me to hand over my son to his biological father.

I had all of my children with me. I saw him through the large glass doors. Instantly, he reminded me of my brother; tall, skinny, and always looking out of place. He paled when we walked in. Grandma took Michael from me with tears in her eyes. She turned to Aaron and said, "Michael, this is your daddy. Aaron, this is your son."

Aaron seemed to freeze. Marissa took him by the hand and softly said, "Come on." Michael was crying. As Grandma passed Michael to his arms, Aaron stifled a sob. That was it. I lost it. My rule of not crying in public flew out the glass doors we had just walked through. I was crying. Aaron was crying. Grandma was crying. Marissa was crying. My poor children looked confused. They sat in the ugly waiting room chairs, quiet and still for once. There were other people in the waiting room as well. I am sure we all looked a bit insane sobbing together in the lobby. I watched a family being born that day. It was a privilege to see, even if it tore at the seams of my heart. Grandma hugged me tight and thanked me for all we had done.

We went into the visitation room and put the rest of the visit's details in order. I asked to hold Michael. He had stopped crying, but was looking around with wide eyes. I gave him a long hug and handed him back to Aaron. Mary snapped a picture of that moment. I hugged Grandma, Marissa, and Aaron. I said my good-byes and told them I would see them in a week.

That week seemed like it would never end. I did not know what to do without an infant to care for. My children had grown during the last nine months. They did not seem to need me much. I took a lot of naps. I cleaned the house. I ate Pizza Pasta. My husband tried to cheer me up. I was cheerful on the outside, and I tried to enjoy my new life. It was easier, that was for sure. However, instead of reveling in the freedom, I felt useless. My boys did not seem to need my attention as much, especially since my husband was home during vacation. Regardless, I was so happy that my husband was with me during that week. It would have been dreadful without him. I knew he missed Michael too, but he is the type of person that radiates sunshine. He always sees the good side of nearly any event, even this one. After all, we had started this whole adventure in the hopes of adopting a daughter. I tried to share his view, though he may have been faking it so that I did not spiral down into a depression again.

Finally Christmas came, and I was beyond ready to see my boy. I arrived at our arranged meeting place early, but that is nothing new for me. I always carried a book in my purse, because I was always waiting for someone due to my earliness. My boys and I sat in the dark gas station parking lot waiting for Michael to arrive with his family. They were late, and I was getting anxious. The boys were anxious to get back home to play with their new toys. A few false alarms later, their car turned into the parking lot. Everyone was piled into that little car. Grandma, Grandpa, Marissa, Aaron, and Michael had all squeezed into the vehicle.

Aaron held Michael. He was not trying to hide his sadness. I felt badly for him. He was obviously upset about having to hand him back to us. The air was cold, and we all shivered in the parking lot waiting for Aaron to release the baby. He started to cry again. At last he kissed Michael, they all said goodbye, and we settled Michael into our van. My husband shook Aaron's hand and said a few words. It was an awkward first meeting. I hugged Aaron, stood on my tiptoes, and whispered, "I'll take care of him, I swear." He hugged me a bit tighter. I had an almost motherly affection towards him. It turned out that his parents were indeed young to be grandparents, only ten years older than us. In another world, I could have had a son close to Aaron's age.

We delayed the goodbye until Aaron initiated it. There would not be another overnight visit until all of the paperwork came back. Aaron was leaving the next day for tech school with the military. He did not know when he would see his child again. None of us knew then, but it would be a very long time. When we arrived home, I felt whole again. With Michael there my family was complete.

There were a few more office visitations with the grandparents and Marissa. Despite all my misgivings, I was falling in love with this family. I still hated the idea of saying goodbye to Michael, but they were so warm and loving. After two months, overnight visits were granted. The paperwork was finally finished. I called them to make plans. They agreed to meet me at another gas station. They would have Michael over for three nights in a row.

As time passed, I realized Michael needed to be with them more than with us. He would be living with them. Everything was going so well. They promised we would be part of his life after they gained custody of him, and I was so thankful for that. Marissa loved Michael as her own son. I pictured a small little family for them one day. Weeks passed, and we fell into a pattern. I would drop Michael off with them on Thursday night, and they would bring him home on Monday afternoon. This worked well until one week I hurt my back. I called Marissa and asked if I could bring Michael early, I could barely pick him up. My friend drove me to their house. This was the first time I had been there. It was nice and homey. From then on a new pattern began. I drove Michael to their house after his therapy sessions on Thursdays. It became our weekly routine. I even started to enjoy the baby-free weekends. We were preparing for our final goodbye. I was ready, but each week was another small goodbye. I did not know how many more times I could hand over my baby. How many more times could I stitch up my heart?

Michael's first birthday was closing in fast. I thought it was very symbolic that he be in his new home before starting the next year of his life. Two weeks before Michael was scheduled to leave us, we received a call for a little girl. We only said yes because Michael was not going to be living with us anymore. Four children would be enough. So we met, and said yes, to our little girl, Claire.

God has a sense of humor that is for sure. We had prayed and prayed that Michael would stay with us while also praying and praying for a daughter. Claire was a healing balm on my broken heart. I was so glad that I did not have to go home to a house with no baby anymore. There was still someone who needed my care and attention. Claire was 20 months old at the time, and full of heartbreaking delays and medical concerns. She kept me busy the last two weeks before Michael's farewell. I wanted a few pictures of all five of my kids, for the first and last time. We had a parade float wagon parked in our yard. I thought that would be the perfect place. During the photo shoot Michael took a tumble and hit his forehead. Eleven months in our care and he had never hurt himself like that. Now, the night before I had to hand him over, we had to take him to the ER.

I had a panic attack. I hated that this was how we were spending our last night together. Thankfully, he was fine. It was just a bump. The next day dawned warm for March. My husband had said his goodbyes the night before. I stared at Michael in his crib, memorizing his blonde hair and blue eyes. This would be the last morning he would wake up in this room.

Michael's physical therapist was nearly in tears when she said goodbye to him at his last session that day. He was leaving the county, outside of her work area. She had been with us for 11 months. I knew it was just the first set of tears that would be shed during what promised to be a very long day. I loaded my kids up and made the drive to Michael's new home. I pulled his belongings out of the van and carried them into the house. I then held Michael as tight as I could. My boys all kissed him goodbye. I handed him to Marissa, and then she stopped me. She handed me a small box. Inside was a Mother's Charm. It was a baby in a silver heart. I could not hold back my tears any longer. I cried, and so did Michael. I hugged Marissa and thanked her for being his mommy. She said, "It's not goodbye, just see you later." I drove home with my four remaining children. Two weeks passed, and I received a few texts and photos from Marissa. Michael seemed to be doing well.

Easter weekend was near, and Michael's grandfather called me and asked if we would babysit Michael for a couple days. We were so thrilled! They were going to keep their promise to let us be part of his life! My husband picked him up on his way home from work, and we all spent two wonderful days together. Included in his overnight bag was a letter from Marissa promising us that we would always be welcome in Michael's life. It was a strange sensation having him back in the house. He still felt like he was ours, yet he was not. We took him home Saturday afternoon and received a photo the next morning of Michael with his Easter basket.

The following Wednesday I called Mary. There was a pending court hearing about Michael's maternal grandparents petitioning for visitation. I wanted to see how the hearing went. Mary paused then asked, "Would you be willing to take Michael back?"

What? I was sure I had not heard her correctly. Fear filled my mind. I asked, "Why?!" I needed to know he was safe. She quickly assured me that he was fine. I hesitated, only because five kids would be a lot. I wanted to know how long he would need to stay. I wanted details. She said she could not give me details unless I said yes. I had to call my husband. I was out of my mind with worry, and sick to my stomach. What in the world had happened in just three short days? Kids only come back into foster care if something goes wrong. I did not want that for Michael. We had done everything right. What had gone wrong? My husband responded immediately, "Michael can come home." I called Mary, "Bring my boy home." Even though I was thrilled that Michael was coming home, I was worried that we might lose him all over again.

Mary informed us that all was not as it had seemed at his grandparents' house. There were domestic issues. A police report had been filed. Nasty accusations were flying in every direction. The worst were allegations of drug use, and that Marissa had been having an affair with Aaron's father. His grandparents lost custody. Michael was once again a ward of the state. He was once again my son. Yet, he was not.

Aaron was understandably upset. He was still away with the military when he was told the news that Michael was back with us. A plan began to brew in my mind. Aaron's family had gotten to know us and liked us. What if I asked Aaron to consider an open adoption? An open adoption is where the biological parent agrees to sign over their parental rights to the person they agree to let adopt their child. The biological parent is able to stay in contact with the family that adopts their child through phone calls, letters, and visits depending on what is agreed upon. Would he be willing to sign Michael over to us? I dreamed and prayed. Mary talked to him about it and called one night with the news that he said he was willing!

A few weeks passed with no news. On a Saturday night the phone rang. It was an unknown number, but I answered it anyway. "Hi Amelia, this is Aaron, Michael's father. Is there any way I can see him on Father's Day? I just want to see him." My heart jumped into my throat and down into my stomach. It was a Saturday night, and my husband was out with friends. I called the on-call social worker. She said that I was not allowed to let Aaron to have any unscheduled visits. I called Aaron back with the news. I told him I would talk to Mary and see if we could meet up later that week. I casually asked if he had thought more about the open adoption. He responded, "Well I was thinking, if I get a job I'm going to go for custody. If not, then I'll do the adoption." I reached for my Xanax and shakily said I would talk to him next week. My head was spinning. I could not, I would not, say goodbye again.

I met Aaron at a park the following week. Mary approved the visit, and I wanted to get an answer out of Aaron. His car pulled into the parking lot. A girl got out of the car with him. It was not Marissa. Her name was Sarah, and it turned out that she was the mother of Aaron's other son, Joshua, who was only four months younger than Michael. Apparently there were a lot of things I had been kept in the dark about. Sarah ran out of the car. I heard Aaron's sister say, "Don't Sarah, you'll scare him." Sarah came running up to the stroller and attempted to take Michael out. I stood dumbfounded for a moment and then picked him up. Reluctantly, I handed him off to Aaron.

Sarah said, "Look, he's dressed like mother like son." She was not referring to me. Both Michael and Sarah were wearing blue and orange. I cringed and bit my tongue. I had an instant dislike for her. I could not get over the insensitivity of that statement. After all, this was the first time she had met him. I had been raising him for 15 months, and she had just claimed to be his mother.

We sat and talked. She mentioned she was about to graduate a year early. Sarah was barely 17 years old. Her tone was nearly bragging, "I was only 15 when I got pregnant." I smiled. I am sure it came across as a grimace. It was the very cliché of "starting off on the wrong foot." There was something I just could not stand about her, but I could not put my finger on it. She talked as if Michael was hers. "I told Aaron, I'd support him whatever he chose, but I love that little boy like my own." Implying she had some say in not only Michael's future, but also the future of my family. I needed to get away from her, quickly, so I gave Aaron time alone with Michael near the swings, and Sarah followed like a lovesick puppy.

I struck up a conversation with Aaron's sister, Caroline. She was only 20 years old and had just given birth to her third child. I could see maturity in her where I could only see selfishness in Sarah. We talked about the adoption options. "I couldn't give up my kids," she stated. The more I talked to her, the more I could see that she did not approve of Sarah. She said Sarah was claiming to

126

have two sons, claiming Michael as her own. She was begging Aaron to keep him and raise the two boys together. Aaron's sister mentioned that Sarah had kept their son away from Aaron and his family when she and Aaron had been fighting. I was not sure what Caroline thought of me until we put Michael in the van. She could see my willingness to have an open adoption and keep her involved in her nephew's life. The nephew she had only met that day. She turned to me and whispered, "I'll see what I can do."

I called Mary and updated her on what had happened and my opinion of it all. I loved Mary. She took what I said to heart. She then arranged for visits to be held at the office, but I was confused. If we were moving forward with adoption, why were we still doing visits? Regardless, the visits continued and Aaron brought Sarah and their young son with him to the next visit. That day Michael and Joshua met for the first time. Aaron and Sarah came to the scheduled visits for the next few weeks.

Then Aaron missed a few visits. The third week was the final strike. If he did not show up the visits would stop. He showed up, but with Marissa! I was shocked! What had happened to Sarah? After everything that I had heard, I was shocked to see Aaron with Marissa. They said they were working things out. I just walked to my car and shook my head. Unfortunately, the next week Sarah was back and she made certain that Aaron told me to not have any contact with Marissa. I never saw Marissa again.

Aaron texted me one day asking if we could talk about the adoption plans. "Yes!" I screamed at my cell phone. I asked what he had in mind. He answered, "One week a month and share holidays, if that's okay with you." I was stumped. That sounded like joint custody to me, not adoption. I did not want to hurt his feelings or sound like I was trying to be controlling, but I had to find a way to tell him that was not going to happen. I thought about trying to explain it via text message, but then wrote that we needed to talk in person instead. My husband had the next week off from work. He came to Michael's weekly visit with me. Surprisingly Aaron announced, "I'm going to sign the papers today." I instantly held my breathe.

Mary wanted us to offer one visit every three months. I was afraid of scaring him off, so I said, "We'll do once a month." With that, Aaron signed the papers. I hugged him. I knew it was hard for him. I knew he wanted more time with Michael than that. I knew he loved Michael. I knew he was afraid of upsetting Sarah, but he signed anyway. I was so proud of him.

After he signed, we walked back to the waiting room where Mary nearly jumped up and down. She was so happy for us. She had felt terrible back when she had to be the one to tell us that Michael would be going to live with his biological grandparents. I think we both felt a weight lift off our chests, but the adoption was not final yet. There were two more court dates. I went to one, and my husband went to the other. The judge approved the plan of an open adoption. After the plan for an open adoption was approved, Aaron stopped attending visits. He missed three in a row, and the visits were cancelled. Aaron and I kept in contact via text and email.

On Halloween we signed our "Intent to Adopt" form. I had my husband sign the form the moment he came home from work. I raced the papers back to Mary before closing hours. "Be patient while I get the paperwork together," she said. I was. I was. I was. And then I was not. Christmastime was upon us once again. The year before, we had been in the middle of saying goodbye to Michael. This year he was with us, still not ours, but with us.

Aaron asked to see Michael around Christmas. He and his father both came. Michael's grandfather had not seen him since he had been placed in foster care the second time. He blamed himself for losing custody. I had been left to believe that the accusations about he and Marissa were true. After seeing him, I am not certain that was the case. Tears ran down his cheeks as he thanked me for bringing Michael to see him. Michael's grandpa promised it would not be so long before the next visit.

The New Year dawned and my phone calls to the lawyer became frequent and habitual. She was waiting on the paperwork from Mary. To this day, I do not understand what took so long, other than Mary was very, very busy. Mary had become Claire's social worker as well. While everything was going on with Michael's case, we were also dealing with Claire's issues, medical needs, and court dates.

During one particular court hearing for Claire, her biological parents did not show up. I was beyond disgruntled. However, I was thrilled when Mary told me, "I sent the papers to the lawyer for Michael's adoption." I dashed home and called the lawyer. She said all was in order. All we had to do was sign. She sent the papers over.

It was an intense weekend of waiting. On Monday morning, I drove the papers to the lawyer's office personally. Michael slid the signed documents into the mailbox himself as I snapped a picture. The lawyer called soon after and announced, "It's all done. It's going to the judge's office. I'll call you when he's signed. It can be a few days or a few weeks." I jumped every single time the phone rang for the next two days.

On February 7th, nearly two years after Michael had come to our home as a tiny, helpless baby, the phone rang. Once again, a phone call would change our world. The lawyer proclaimed, "I'm speaking to Michael's mother!"

I admit I screamed in her ear. My kids came running. I shrieked, "Michael is ours! Michael is ours!" We jumped around for a few moments full of joy. I scrambled to call my husband. He did not answer. I tried my mother, and she did not answer. I called my best friend. She did not answer. They were the only three phone calls I needed to make, and no one answered. I started the process over. Finally, I got them all on the line. The news was spread to the most important people in my life, the ones that had been there each and every step of the way. Then I posted the news on Facebook. Michael was legally ours! I finally showed his face to the world. The online album that held over 600 pictures of our beautiful Michael was finally able to be shared with everyone. The congratulations poured in, and my tears began anew. I finally let out a breath I had been holding for two years. He was ours.

Michael has been our legal son for six months now. Michael's grandparents reunited and were on their way to happily ever after together. Sadly, we did not know that when Michael's Grandpa saw him last Christmas, that would be the last time we ever saw him. He passed away just three weeks after the adoption was finalized at the young age of 41 years old.

Aaron is engaged to Sarah, and they are raising Joshua together. Caroline officially moved home from California. She regained custody of her daughter and has had two more children. She is newly pregnant with her fourth. She and her husband are living with Aaron's mother. Aaron's brother is doing well in the military. Michael is his spitting image. Our open adoption is working out wonderfully. As for Sarah, I am trying to move past my initial dislike, but it is an ongoing battle.

Our family has been sewn together beautifully. It has been

crafted by God's own hand. We prayed for a daughter, and we prayed that Michael would be able to stay. I never dreamed that we would be blessed with both. Our family has grown to include five children. We do not know where we will go from here. All I know is that we have an empty bedroom and open hearts.

11

The End of Our Foster Journey

The end of our foster journey – just typing those words seems so odd. For the past three years our lives have been entrenched in foster care and adoption. We started out simply enough with just one biological child in our home. Our sweet baby boy was only months old when we started taking our foster care training classes. I remember our licensing worker commenting to me at a training class that it might be better for us to wait. I suppose she was suggesting that fostering was not the best thing for us at the time. Honestly, it infuriated me. Did she think we were not prepared? Did she know something I did not know? Looking back the answers are probably yes and yes. Is anyone really prepared for it all though? Any true knowledge about foster care has to be learned on the front lines. You can sit in a classroom and discuss different scenarios for days, weeks, or even months, and I promise you, it will do you no good. Every case is different. Every child is different. The foster parents out there getting their hands dirty are the ones making a difference. I am grateful that we did not back off and that we pushed ahead and fostered at that time in our lives. In our journey we have received countless phone calls about children needing a safe place to go. Sometimes they came to us. Many times they did not. I have never said no. Looking back that is not advice I would give. It is okay to say no. It is okay to take care of you and your first family. It is okay to ask questions. For me, I let blind faith lead me and I am not disappointed in my journey. Every bit of it shaped me into the woman, wife, and mother that I am today.

Just two weeks after our license was officially approved, we received our first phone call. I was at home making strawberry jam while my little baby boy, who had not yet turned one, slept. I can barely remember the quiet of those days. It was that very same licensing worker who had initially tried to discourage us from fostering that ended up calling us about this newborn baby girl. I instantly broke down in tears. It was starting. It was overwhelming. I was filled with love for this child, and at the same time was heartbroken over the reality of her life. She was born exposed to methamphetamines. The details are all a blur, but I remember dropping my son Andrew off with a friend while I went to the hospital to pick up our new daughter. I met our CPS (Child Protective Services) caseworker outside the hospital. We talked for a few minutes about nothing and everything. She was surprised and taken aback that this was our very first foster placement. Regardless, she was kind and encouraging. We ventured up to the Labor and Delivery floor, and after a quick stop at the nurses' desk, I was ushered into the nursery. That was the first time I saw Ashlynn. She was so big! When I heard that she was born drug exposed I had imagined a child born preterm or with growth restrictions. Ashlynn weighed in at nine pounds! She had a head full of thick black hair and gorgeous dimples already visible even without her infectious smile that would take a few months to appear.

Ashlynn was her mother's eighth child. The first four had been removed four or five years previously for neglect. Her mom, Rebecca, had never completed the services she had been offered in order to regain custody of those children. Because of her lack of effort, her rights to her four oldest children were terminated and the children had since been adopted. The next three children she gave birth to were all removed from Rebecca at birth one by one over the following years because they all tested positive for drug exposure at birth. All of them had been adopted also. Termination for her seventh child had occurred less than a year prior to Ashlynn's birth. In our state, even if a baby had not been born drug exposed, the prior terminations alone were grounds for immediate termination of parental rights. Somehow, Ashlynn's case slipped through the cracks and the court had decided to let Rebecca work a case plan in hope she would turn her life around and be able to parent this new baby.

In fact, at the initial meeting to discuss the removal of the child and case plan, I was told to bring all of Ashlynn's belongings, because chances were that they would release the baby to Rebecca's aunt with whom she was staying. They were hoping to fast track her case to get the baby returned. It turned out that this aunt was a relative by marriage and there was something about her background check that did not sit well with the CPS supervisor. Months later, after a failed home study, I was told the aunt was no longer an option for placement. In the meantime, I fell into the routine of caring for two very young children. We celebrated our biological son's first birthday and hoped that someday we would celebrate our little girl's as well.

That daydream faded quickly. As a new foster parent, I was naïve and did not understand all the laws and rules that come with foster care and adoption. More specifically, the Indian Child Welfare Act, or better known as, ICWA was what blindsided me when it was brought to my attention that it applied to our new baby's case. Our sweet Ashlynn was born to a Native American mother so ICWA applied in her case. My husband and I are not of considerable Native American ancestry so we were ruled out as an ICWA compliant placement. Rebecca had not ever registered with her tribe. She had not wanted any of her children to grow up on the Reservation. She told me that herself. However, after Ashlynn's birth she wanted access to the health care and financial support that tribal membership could offer her. She decided to register, and with that the tribe could officially stand in and block termination of parental rights when the case plan with CPS officially changed.

I held tight to my tiny hope that there would be an exception made. I was hoping that, if they saw that she was bonded and attached to us, we would have a fighting chance. After all, she had not had a visit with her biological mother since she was three months old. Rebecca had skipped out on her inpatient rehab facility along with all the services and counseling that CPS had requested her to do.

I remember the day in August that we went to court for the final hearing in Ashlynn's case. Our family and friends were praying for a miracle. My stomach was in knots as we sat in the back of the courtroom. As expected, the tribe intervened and the judge ordered the child to be transferred into an ICWA compliant home as soon as one could be found. Just outside the courtroom doors, in what seemed to be the tiniest room they could find, my husband and I sat down with the CPS caseworker and the Tribal Representative. I was a mess. I could not help but cry hysterically. I tried to calm down, but it was all too much. The representative gave her sincere apologies and even shared that she too had been a foster parent. She had loved a baby girl from birth until she was nearly two years old and then, unexpectedly, a relative came forward and her baby girl was gone forever. I could see that she was holding back tears as she told her story. I am confident that her sharing that story with me is what helped me to know she had empathy for us and that she was not making this decision lightly. She was doing what she had to do. A family who had recently moved from our city back on to the tribal lands was their choice for placement. I took her up on the offer to slowly transition Ashlynn into her new home and the opportunity to meet Ashlynn's new parents.

I cried my eyes out for days and weeks. It is a strange thing to mourn for a child who is still in your arms. I did my best to love on her every minute I could. I would find myself getting her out of her crib as she slept just to rock her in my arms as I sat in a chair in her room. Over the next six weeks, we met with her new family twice. Melody, the new adoptive mother, Ashlynn, and I all met for lunch just once. Melody was tall and beautiful. She was kind and I liked her. Meeting with her was strange in so many ways. What do you say over lunch to someone who will be raising your baby? That is how it felt. Maybe this is the conflict that birth mothers who are placing their child for adoption feel. It broke my heart to know that I would not be the one raising Ashlynn, but if I was not going to be allowed to raise her, I felt comfortable with Melody being the one that was chosen to do so. She and her husband, David, struggled with infertility and it seemed that no children would be coming to their family biologically. They had chosen adoption as their path and they already had a three-year-old adopted daughter. Our next visit was at the same restaurant, but this time we each brought our whole families. It was great to get together and laugh. We talked about getting together for barbeques in the future. None of these things would happen though, and I blame myself as much as them.

The next week, the tribal worker came to my house at the set time. I had all of Ashlynn's things packed. I had even bought a bright pink plastic tote to load up her overwhelming supply of clothes. I cut out custom vinyl letters for her name and cute flower designs to place on the tote. I finished her scrapbook and filled it with pictures. I wanted to show that she was loved while she was with us. No baby of mine would be loaded up in plastic bags and shuttled off to another home. I hugged her and held her tight. I tried to hold back my tears. Finally, I had to load her into the car seat in the back of the tribal worker's car and watch them drive away. I remember walking back into my house and realizing I would probably never see my daughter again.

The day after the final hearing for Ashlynn, I had received another phone call from our agency. They were hoping to place another newborn infant. They knew that Ashlynn was scheduled to leave soon. We had initially thought Ashlynn would be moved two weeks after the hearing, but it ended up being six weeks after. In the mean time, a little boy named Jackson had been born, and they wanted to know if we would take him.

I told them, "Yes."

I excitedly called my husband to tell him the news. I think he thought I was crazy. We had just found out we were going to lose a child we had fallen in love with. Were we really ready to do it all over again so soon? Looking at it from the outside, I am sure we did look crazy. I already had Andrew who was fourteen months old, Ashlynn who was five months old and had not moved quite yet, and I was taking on another newborn. Despite the logistics of our situation, I could not say no to this new baby. I felt that somehow in the midst of the sorrow of Ashlynn's lingering goodbye, Jackson would be our miracle.

When the worker arrived at my home the next day holding sweet baby Jackson, he was wrapped in a hospital blanket wearing a simple white long-sleeved, cuffed bodysuit. He was tiny. The next day, when I took him to the pediatrician, he weighed in at five pounds. He had lost a significant amount of his birth weight and we had to work hard to get him caught up. He was born at 37 weeks, so not premature, but due to his mother's drug abuse and poor nutrition his growth was restricted. He was not born positive for drugs, but his mother did admit to hospital staff and CPS that she had used drugs within a week of his birth. She also admitted to using off and on throughout her pregnancy. She was doing her best to prepare for him when he was born. She had served some jail time to pay off fines from domestic violence charges. She had lined up housing and even had a few of the necessities she would need for him. I had instant love and compassion for her. She was making an effort. Her improvements were slow coming, and she slipped and relapsed several times, but she kept at it. She found a great deal of support with a local church. To this day I know that their connection with her is what brought her though.

The first time I met her, we were sitting in a CPS conference room. This meeting was held about a week after Jackson had been taken into foster care. Jackson's mom was there along with a friend from her church who also served as a mentor in a crisis pregnancy center. I was still new to fostering and those meetings intimidated me. I could not even begin to imagine how she must have felt. She had no prior history with foster care. This was her first child and she was grasping for options for recovery and wanted to be re-united with her baby boy. Unfortunately, she was not sure who the father was. She named two or three men that could possibly be the father. She had thought it was her incarcerated fiancé's child. She had listed him on the birth certificate, but when Jackson was born he did not look anything like this "father." It was obvious that it was likely not him, and she had to share more names. One of the men named was married. She was terrified of what this news would do to his relationship and what it would mean in the case. After all the information had been laid out (reasons for coming into care, supports that the birth family needed, safety issues, etc.) it was determined that Jackson would stay in our home as a foster child. They gave his mom, Amber, and I a few minutes to talk and catch up on how he was doing. As we sat down in the lunchroom of the CPS office she asked boldly, "So why are you a foster parent? Do you want to adopt? Are you trying to adopt my baby?" I had no idea how to answer her. Of course I wanted to say 'yes,' but this was hardly the time to have that conversation. She wanted her child back. She wanted to hear for herself that I was not trying to steal her baby from her. I calmly told her that Jackson was adorable. I loved taking care of him, but my goal was for her to be his mom. I told her I was willing to support her in that.

Weeks ticked by and she consistently came to all her scheduled visits with Jackson. We, on the other hand, started to get comfortable in caring for Jackson and hoped he would stay. At a month old, Jackson weighed nine pounds. He had some reflux issues, but once we added in some special medication all of the issues disappeared and he thrived. When Jackson was four months old they finally had all the paternity testing scheduled. I took him to the county office to have his blood drawn. I never saw any of the possible fathers myself, but the technician who drew Jackson's blood had also just taken blood from one of them. She pretty much declared that the man she had seen right before us must be the father, and said that he seemed like a nice enough guy. Months later, after meeting him, I realized how she had known. Jackson looks very much like his biological father. That technician did not need a blood test to know. And yes, it was the married guy.

I was not given the official news for several weeks. In fact, it was during one of my regular home visits from CPS that the news came pouring out. I remember it vividly. I was sitting on the floor with Jackson; he was five months old at the time, when the worker said matter-of-factly that the biological father had been identified. The worker said that all they needed to do was ensure he had a crib and Jackson would be moved to his father's home. The father in this case was non-offending, which simply meant he was not the cause of the child coming into care, so he could be deemed as safe. My heart shattered and I literally sobbed right there in front of the worker. I was caught so unbelievably off guard. Just the week before, Amber and I had talked about adoption again. She was entering a long-term treatment center. She was not sure what would happen with the case. She said that adoption might be the best choice for him and I promised to be as open as possible with her if we adopted Jackson. All of my hope suddenly went down the drain with this news.

Then, the case took an even stranger turn. The biological dad and his wife were also expecting a baby any day. It turned out that they had some prior CPS history concerning their previous children. In fact, Dad and his wife had two daughters who were not returned to them just the summer before. Instead, a grandparent had legal guardianship of them now. Because of this a deal was made. They would wait and see if the new baby ended up coming into care. If that did not happen, Jackson would be moved to their home. Our heads were spinning and our hearts were breaking while we waited for the decision to be made. We had our first visit with the father and his family after the New Year. They had indeed brought home their new baby and were preparing to add Jackson to their family. I just could not understand it. He had a baby. Why did he want to take this one too? What did his wife think of all of this? Did she really want to be raising the baby he had as a result of an affair?

As nice as they all seemed it just did not feel right. I felt like CPS was rushing. They wanted Jackson out of foster care. Why could they not consider letting him live with his birth mom? The facility she was in allowed mothers to have their children stay with them. I knew that questioning CPS was not my place, at least to do so openly, but if I was not going to fight for Jackson's safety and well being who was? That was when I heard CPS tell me something so true, but so ugly about the foster care system. They explained to me that the standard to which a biological parent is held is far different than what we, as foster parents, must meet. What we see as appropriate parenting, income, living conditions, and so on are not the standards that the birth families are held to. Their only income may be government assistance, they may not have enough bedrooms, they may have made really poor decisions in the past, but it does not matter. They do not have to be ideal at all. "They just have to meet the bare minimum." Minimum. Minimum! It seemed that was all Jackson deserved according to them - the absolute least available. I was infuriated, but it made no difference. The transition date was set, and that was the end of the story. At least that is how CPS saw it.

As Jackson's case swirled around us, we had also said yes to another foster child. After this new little one had been in our home for a few weeks, an assistant for their Guardian Ad Litem (GAL) came over for a visit. The news had already come that Jackson was going to leave, and here sat this assistant to talk all about our new foster child. I was completely hung up on transitioning Jackson out of our home. I could not help but talked about Jackson's case and shared how odd the whole situation was. Before I had even finished the story she already knew the identity of the birth father. I had not told her the child's name or birth parents' names. Ironically, her office had represented the biological dad and his wife's children in the previous CPS case, and they were not happy to hear about what was going on in Jackson's case. She looked it up and they were, in fact, Jackson's new representation as well. The GAL had happened to be in the courtroom the previous month when biological dad had been introduced, and she had interjected and requested to represent the child. The judge allowed it, and this was a pivotal change in the case.

The GAL had not been notified by CPS about the intent to move Jackson to his biological father's home. The assistant was furious and knew the GAL would be too. She said that she could not guarantee anything, but she said they would intervene and demand a hearing in front of the judge to discuss placement before he was moved anywhere. When she walked out my door I was literally shaking. I remember thinking about how grateful I was that I opened my mouth. I knew the situation did not seem right, and I now felt validated that my concerns were real. So rarely had I felt like I actually got the opportunity to advocate for a child in my care. Sure, I took care of their day-to-day needs, but I always did as I was told. However, in this case, I felt as if I had just saved my son. I saved him from what could have been. On transfer day, I packed up a few things because I had not actually heard from CPS that it was not going to happen, but I had strict instructions from the attorney to call them if they tried to set up a time to move Jackson. Late in the afternoon the call finally came, and the move was being postponed.

The next week a special hearing was called, and it was determined that Jackson would remain in our care until the next permanency meeting which was months away. I was torn. I knew that it was only a matter of time before he would have to leave, but I knew that I needed to keep him safe. Over the next several months, Jackson's birth mom continued to do well in her program. By the time the permanency hearing rolled around, she had been in her inpatient treatment program for six months. She had completed all of her parenting classes, domestic violence classes, and counseling. Jackson's biological dad and his wife had also been court ordered to complete some services as well. I was so grateful for this. They both had to attend parenting classes, and they had to have in home meetings and counseling, as well as random drug testing. My concerns were not completely eased, but I felt that the situation was better than it would have been. The system was doing a better job of setting him up for success.

We did, at one time, become brave enough to speak to Jackson's biological dad about adoption. He was nice about it on the surface and said he would think about it. As expected, nothing came of it. A week before the permanency hearing, I sat in a small room in the CPS office surrounded by case managers, supervisors, Jackson's birth mom, the biological dad and his wife. I had also invited our licensing worker with our agency to be there with me. This was going to be the hardest meeting of my life. The plan for transition was discussed and each of the birth parents expressed their gratitude to my family. CPS thanked me, and in an effort, I think, to mend my broken heart, they offered me the transition on my terms. It was decided that if the judge went along with CPS recommendation to move Jackson to his father's home, it would happen on Friday instead of at the hearing on Wednesday. This did not go over well with the birth family, but CPS drew the line and said that it was the normal transition for the child, since he had already begun spending weekends at their home.

The hearing came and went. Jackson officially was to go live with his father. His father and the birth mother would have to file custody paperwork on their own once the case was dropped from CPS in three months. I packed up my son's things: toys, clothing for the next size or two, shoes, personal care, and diapers. I wanted him to have everything that was his even if it broke my heart to give it to them. I loaded it all into my car and I drove to our meeting place. This was the same spot that I had driven to every weekend for the past several months in order to drop Jackson off for weekend visits, only this time I would not be picking him back up. That reality sunk in so deeply that I had tears in my eyes before I pulled into my parking space. Jackson's father was already there waiting. We loaded up all of Jackson's belongings into the back of his car. Then I got my precious nine-month-old baby boy out of his car seat and handed him to his father. I tried, but I could not hold my tears back. I had hoped to hold it together, because I could not imagine what he thought of me. To him I was just a babysitter. I was part of the system that was separating him from his child, and from a life free of interference. To me, though, Jackson was my son. I had loved him every day since he was born, and it was hard for me to let him go. We talked only for a few moments. He thanked me for caring for his son. I asked him to please invite us to Jackson's upcoming birthday party even though I knew it would never happen. He nodded and loaded Jackson into his car and drove away. I sat there for a few minutes motionless, and then proceeded to cry my eyes out. I knew I could not drive while I was so overcome with grief. When I finally calmed down, I made the trip home.

I have not spoken to Jackson's father since that last goodbye. I was fortunate enough to become friends with his birth mom. She is kind and generous and has allowed us to see Jackson a few times over the past several years. I am sure we could see him more if we asked, but I want to allow her the time she needs with him since she shares custody. I still remember the day that I saw pictures from the first birthday party she had for him. She had posted them on Facebook. Immediately, my eyes filled with tears, but these were grateful tears. She had planned the exact kind of party I would have and gave him gifts that I would have wanted him to have. In my heart I still have a special place for Jackson. I do not think I will ever stop feeling that connection to him. You cannot love, nurture, and care for someone for as long as we did without developing a bond with them.

Since Jackson left, we have been blessed with more biological children, and have been able to adopt two of our foster children. Finally being able to adopt has helped to heal the hurt that was caused by saying goodbye to several children that we love, but some of those scars will never go away.

I am confident that I was stretched, molded, and refined into the wife and mother I am today because of those experiences. The Lord sees immense potential in each of us. It is hard for us to see ourselves the way He does. However, my time as a foster parent expanded my world, and made it easier for me to freely give love those who need it.

141

12

One Week at a Time

My husband and I were still what most would call "new" foster parents. We had only had one case so far, and that had ended in the two children we were caring for being returned to their biological family. After a few months of no potential placements, our social worker called to see if we would be interested in possibly taking a baby girl. It was not a sure thing, but two days later, she called back and said it was official. The next morning we picked up a beautiful baby girl named Daisy.

Daisy's biological mom, Jane, was a minor with severe Bipolar Disorder and did not have much family support. The goal of foster care is always reunification first, but we were told to expect that Daisy's case would likely drag out due to Jane's age and the fact that Jane was also a ward of the State. The social workers also warned us not to get too close to Jane because she was known to be dangerous and violent.

When you take a foster placement, your life becomes defined by the weekly scheduled visits that the child is supposed to have

143

with their biological family, as well as by the court hearings that are typically scheduled every three to six months. These visits and court dates usually determine the course and eventual outcome of the case. Often, you will find yourself living week to week, not knowing what each new visit or court date might bring.

Throughout our entire journey with this precious baby girl I always prayed, *"Lord, help us love her like she is ours forever, and hold us up if she is gone tomorrow."* During the next year, that prayer would be tested many times.

Week 1

As Daisy's first scheduled visit with Jane approached, I could not help but worry that Jane might take off with Daisy. I had only been Daisy's foster mom for a few days, but I could not help but feel protective of her. I had been told Jane was unpredictable. Jane was living in a group home for teenagers in foster care, and I had no idea if the visit would even be supervised by anyone.

After I dropped Daisy off, I anxiously waited for the time to pass so I could have her in my arms again. When I returned, everything seemed as if it had gone well. I was immediately relieved to see Jane carrying Daisy out of the building to me. After she strapped Daisy into her car seat, Jane hopped in a car that was waiting for her and left the group home. I knew that was against the rules of the group home, but I had no idea what I was supposed to do about it.

Later I received a call from the baby's caseworker letting me know that Daisy's mom never returned to the group home after I saw her leave. I was told to call next week before our next scheduled visit to see if she came back. I was heartbroken when I heard Jane had run away. Regardless of our desire to adopt, we hoped to see Jane learn how to be a good mom to Daisy and raise her herself.

Week 2

Jane returned to the group home the day before her scheduled visit with Daisy. It appeared that she knew how the system worked and how to manipulate it. She was able to have her visit with Daisy despite the fact that she had broken the rules.

Week 4

The day before our next scheduled visit, I received a voicemail from Daisy's caseworker letting me know Jane wanted to cancel. She gave no explanation, which left me curious as to why she would cancel. I also wondered how it would affect the court date that was approaching.

Early the next morning, I got another call telling me that Jane had changed her mind and she wanted to have the visit that day. They asked if I could still bring the baby, or if we had made plans. I told them that I had already made other plans. The staff understood, but Jane did not. I could hear Jane in the background yelling, "She's not her baby! Wednesday is too long not to see my baby! She needs to bring her. It's not fair." The staff at the group home told her that it was her own fault because she had asked to call and cancel the visit. The next day she went missing from the group home again.

Week 5

We attended Daisy's court hearing. Jane was there as well. The judge did not go easy on her. Daisy also had her regularly scheduled visit with Jane. After the visit Jane gave me some clothes to take home for Daisy. Fortunately, most of them were the right size for her as opposed to the previous time she had sent clothing for her. At the end of the visit, as I buckled Daisy into her car seat, Jane covered her ears and told me to "take her away" because she did not want to listen to Daisy cry.

Jane was supposed to be moving to a new group home, but she had run away again. No one knew where she was or where she would be placed when she returned. That was the fifth time in four weeks that Jane had run away.

Week 6

I received a call asking me if we could change the visit location from the group home to the CPS (Child Protective Services) office. I was thrilled. I preferred the visits be at the office anyway. It would forced Jane to actually spend time with Daisy, instead of passing her around and showing her off to the group home girls like she always had in the past.

Week 7

I did not care for the new group home where Jane was placed. At the last group home, they took precautions and understood that we needed to remain as detached from Jane as possible for safety reasons. The last group home even told us that we should not get too personal with her, but Jane had a way of being so friendly when you saw her. She made it hard to keep your guard up. We had to be careful, but we also had to be friendly when we did see her each week.

The new group home handed Jane the phone when I called the first time. I was a bit taken aback and did not know how to handle that. Thankfully, Jane was polite and understanding as I explained we were going to need to change the visit schedule, but not once did she ask about Daisy. I could not imagine what it would be like to have to give Daisy back to someone who did not seem to care about her.

Week 8

The weekly visits were starting to take their toll on me. My stress level was at a new high. *"Lord, hold us, please!"* I was constantly worried about Daisy's safety during her visits. No one seemed to be supervising them the way I thought they should be.

I called the group home to confirm Daisy's visit for that Wednesday. The group home "Dad" asked if I have been told about their request to increase the visitation times. He said that one-hour was not enough time for Jane to bond with Daisy. He then went on to list a bunch of degrees he had earned and told me that he had been doing this for a long time and that he knew what he was talking about. I felt like he was talking down to me, and that he thought I was trying to keep Daisy from seeing her mom. That could not have been further from the truth. It made me wonder what Jane was telling them about us. She had a way of making people feel sorry for her even when she was the one not doing what she was supposed to.

The group home "Dad" went on to say that he was going to talk to the supervisor about the visits. He wanted them to be increased to twice a week and to be two hours each. He said, "I hope it's not an inconvenience to you since I know you live pretty far away."

It would have been a huge inconvenience to us, but we were "just" the foster parents. We had all of the responsibility on our shoulders, but none of the rights. That was what we had signed up for and we knew it, but it did not seem fair.

I was glad that someone was taking the time to care about Jane, but it was going to take more than a couple of weeks or months in that home to make her responsible enough to parent Daisy.

The next day, I got a call from the same group home that had just been talking about requesting more visitation time. They had put a "psych hold" on Jane. Needless to say, the next visit was cancelled, and Jane would be moved yet again when she got out. It broke my heart that she was being bounced around so much. She continued to be kicked out of group homes due to her violent, unstable behavior and inability to obey authority. She needed stability, and chances were she was never going to have it.

Week 9

We had a monthly visit with the baby's caseworker at our home. She said that Jane's visitation schedule would have to be made around Daisy's needs from that point on. So far we had been at everyone's beckoned call just to make the visits happen, even when Jane went missing and the visits had to be made up after she came back. I started tearing up. It had been a tough two months. It was then that she told me she was there to check up on us as well. I tried not to laugh because, until that moment, it had not felt like anyone had been looking out for us. We talked about our right to respectfully say no if we were asked to do a last minute visit. It was nice to feel supported, if only for a moment. One specific verse came to mind:

> Psalm 34:4 "I sought the Lord, and he heard me,
> and delivered me from all my fears."

Week 10

I heard from Jane that she had gotten a job. She was very happy to tell me that fact after the visit that week, and I congratulated her.

The new group home she was living in was very nice. It was technically a facility for troubled youth. They wanted her to stay as a permanent placement, but it would ultimately be up to her to prove she could follow the rules. It appeared she was actually doing some things to work her case plan to get Daisy back. I was happy that she seemed to be doing better, but I was worried that it would not last. More than anything, I would have loved to see her succeed. Just the week before, I had prayed that someone would come into her life and care about her enough to help her. This new home seemed like a good fit and the staff truly seemed to care.

If reunification did happen, I felt like I might be able to be okay with it. It would hurt, but I knew that God was in control. He alone would choose who Daisy was going to be raised by.

• •

It did end up being too good to be true. Shortly after Jane looked like she was starting to head in the right direction she ran away from the group home, again. She had managed to last nine days at the new home before running.

Jane's life and this foster care case were both a mess. No one was doing her any favors by continuing to give her chance after chance after chance. I could not believe that she was allowed to continue visiting with Daisy as long as she wandered back to the group home the night before a scheduled visit. No one knew what she had been doing or who she had been with. It did not seem safe to me, but no one else seemed to have too much of a problem with it.

I really had thought this new place was going to be good for her. I was so disappointed in Jane, but I needed to stop expecting her to change for Daisy. If she had not already changed there was very little chance that she ever would.

Week 11

On Thursday afternoon, my husband, Brandon, called the new group home. This was the fourth home that Jane had been in since we met her. He told the group home staff that we had made plans for Friday, since Jane had gone missing again, so we were not available to transport Daisy to a visit the next day. He requested they reschedule the visit for Saturday. Brandon could hear Jane in the background. She could only hear half of the conversation, but she started yelling immediately. The group home "Mom" handed Jane the phone. Jane accused Brandon of trying to keep Daisy from her. She said that she was going to call CPS on us because we were trying to keep her from her baby. She said that we were the reason she kept changing group homes, because we kept changing the visits on her. She said that Daisy was not our baby. It was not the first time that she tried to throw that in our faces. We were well aware that Daisy was not legally our child. Her accusations were

148

ridiculous. We had only changed one visit in the last 11 weeks, and she was claiming that she had moved from group home to group home because of us? She was just saying anything she could to try to get her way.

Regardless, the visit was rescheduled for Saturday. I ended up taking Daisy to the visit myself. I was a nervous wreck. Jane's new group home was in the middle of an area we frequented. It was also very close to where Brandon worked. When I got there she was cold and distant. I complemented her on looking nice and pretended like nothing had happened.

Week 12

Brandon arrived at Daisy's scheduled visit only to find out that Jane had ran away yet again! No one bothered to call us. It was the first time Jane had actually missed a scheduled visit without calling to reschedule.

The stress of Daisy's case was weighing heavily on me. I was not sure how much longer I could do this. Watching Daisy play on my living room floor throughout the week helped remind me that I would do anything for her. Even put up with this nightmare of a case.

That next morning I received two voicemails from the group home because Jane had returned. They wanted to set up a visit for her because she was pitching a fit. Of course she wanted to see Daisy immediately! According to her, our world needed to come to a screeching halt because she decided to come back and wanted to see Daisy. I decided that she would just have to wait for a bit like we had to do so many times. We agreed to bring Daisy for a visit the next morning as opposed to that day.

Week 13

When I dropped Daisy off at the visit with her mom, Jane acted like nothing had ever happened. You never would have guessed that she had just disappeared for a week and missed three visits.

As she was saying goodbye to Daisy, she said that it was "just so hard to let her go." She kept kissing Daisy and said, "But I can't afford to go to jail for you, because that's what'd happen if I ran off with you. I'd go to jail." Oddly, I was comforted by her words.

Jane still thought that she could make us do whatever she wanted, and the group home that she was currently in was catering to her. You could tell that she loved to feel like she was in charge.

Week 14

Daisy had another visit with Jane. Thirty minutes after I dropped her off, I got a call from the group home. Jane had asked them to call me. She could not get Daisy to stop crying, and she did not know how to make her stop. I told her that Daisy was teething and her teeth were probably bothering her. I explained to her that Daisy liked it if you stuck your knuckle in her mouth. Daisy had been chewing on anything she could find that week, but her favorite thing to chew on was our hands. I told Jane to bounce Daisy on her lap while Daisy was standing, or to try the bouncy seat that she had for her. She thanked me and said she might call me back to pick her up early because she was having such a hard time with her. I told her that would not be a problem. Ten minutes later she called and asked me to come get Daisy.

I walked in to get Daisy, and as soon as she was in my arms, she calmed down. She was calm, but was doing that sucking-in-of-air sound that is so pathetic after a long cry. She had been crying for 50 minutes by the time I came back. Jane squeezed her cheeks and gave her a bunch of big kisses and Daisy started crying again. This had started to be a trend. Daisy had been crying at the last few visits when I came to pick her up as well.

Week 15

Jane was depressed, hollow, and just not present at the weekly visit. It was very odd. She seemed to be going through the motions, but was not engaging with Daisy at all. She had a far off look in her eyes. She loved Daisy, but seemed unwilling to change.

After that visit Jane went missing again.

Week 16

Daisy's caseworker called me to let me know that an aunt of Jane's had called her and was requesting custody of Daisy. Daisy's caseworker spoke with her, and said she seemed like a decent person. They decided to send someone out to do a relative assessment. I remained shockingly calm about the news. My husband was definitely not as calm as I was. I told him that if Daisy did end up having to move we would deal with it when it happened.

Week 17

We had our monthly visit with Daisy's caseworker. I told her the details of the visits that had gone on for the last three months. There had been 17 visits scheduled and Jane had missed nine of them.

Daisy's caseworker said that she told Jane if she did not stop running away they were going to terminate her services. Daisy's caseworker went on to tell Jane that, if they did that, the plan would change from reunification to adoption. Jane told her that she would "just fight for Daisy after she turned 18." Daisy's caseworker made sure she explained everything to Jane very clearly. That way if she did come back to fight for Daisy, it would be clear that Jane knew her actions were going to result in her parental rights being terminated. I asked if she thought Jane was going to give up fighting for Daisy altogether. The worker said that she was not sure, but she was not convinced that Jane understood what was going to happen.

Monday morning we received a call letting us know that Jane had returned to the group home over the weekend. I was told that she had a visit scheduled for Wednesday afternoon. I was thankful that they did not demand that we change our schedule to bring Daisy that afternoon for a visit because she had "missed her baby."

It had been 17 days since we last saw Jane, and 17 days since Jane had seen her daughter. As usual, I was a bit nervous about seeing her.

Week 19

It all hit me at once. Suddenly I felt helpless and I wanted to give up. I could not fathom having to give Daisy back to Jane or to Jane's aunt who had popped up out of nowhere. Though I tried to ignore it, I could not help but hope we would be able to adopt Daisy. With every visit, it got harder and harder to accept that she most likely would be returned to her biological mom or moved to the aunt's house eventually. I did not want to hand her over for her visit that day or any other day. I did not want to let her go be with someone who was practically a stranger and had more important things to do during the end of her visit than properly say goodbye to her daughter.

Week 21

The group home called. They said there was an emergency placement meeting the night before, and that Jane was being moved to another new group home immediately after it.

Week 22

Jane wanted to show Daisy off at a Christmas party, so she was allowed to have an extended visit. They counted that as her Christmas visit. Jane would be spending Christmas with her biological family. We would have Daisy all to ourselves the entire week of Christmas and would not have another visit until after the New Year. It was a very welcome break.

Week 23

Our adoption worker called to see if I knew anything about the aunt that had inquired about gaining custody of Daisy. I, personally, had not heard anything since the last time I asked Daisy's caseworker about her. Our adoption worker told me that they had not heard anything either. Eventually we heard that the aunt, Renee, had her fingerprints done and her home had been certified. She said that she was willing to foster, adopt, or be a legal guardian to Daisy.

I had faith that God would do what was right for Daisy.

Week 24

Jane returned to the group home after being gone for the holidays. She called to check in on Daisy. She had never done that before. We had talked numerous times on the phone, but this was the first time she had ever specifically called to check on Daisy.

Week 25

Brandon took Daisy to the visit that week. Jane was normally not very nice to Brandon, but that week was different. At pick up she said to Daisy, "Don't worry, you're coming home with me next month." I was so glad that I was not there to have to bite my tongue.

To our surprise, we found out that Aunt Renee had been approved. This meant that Daisy would be leaving us to go live with her. Daisy's caseworker said they were planning a long transition period, but I was not sure if that would happen. We had always known that Daisy might end up leaving us, but we honestly had not expected it - not like this. We knew that we would survive somehow. *"God hold us, we need You now."*

I was a blubbering mess when I first found out and I still was to an extent, but I had a feeling everything would be okay. I knew I had to trust God to get me through this and to keep Daisy safe.

It was not easy and I had to do my best to keep anger from taking hold in me. I knew that the prayers I had prayed since day one were being answered. *"Lord, hold us up if she is gone tomorrow."* I would be lying if I did not admit that I kept asking, *"Why God? Why have you called us to this only to have our hearts broken?"* I did not want to have to buy another little suitcase, or pack up another child to leave us. We knew that God had called us to this and He had not left us. Eventually, my husband and I found ourselves oddly at peace with the fact that Daisy would be leaving. I think we were probably more numb than at peace, really.

I tried to keep the thoughts that led to anger out of my mind. I tried to remember that I must show Christ's love even when I did not want to. I also needed to pack everything that belonged to Daisy including the things I did not want to. There was no reason to hold on to them. The pain they would cause us by seeing them would be too much anyway.

Brandon was not thrilled that we would be supervising the visits with the aunt that would be leading up to Daisy being moved into her home. I had no idea how we were even going to manage another visit because of our already very busy schedule.

One day I found myself in the children's luggage aisle picking out a suitcase for Daisy. It hurt to even look at them. We had always said that no child who left our home would ever leave in boxes and garbage bags. I bought a cute pink bag with purple flowers on it. When I got home I packed up all her clothes that were still a bit too big for her and made a log of them. I made a mental "to do" list, but not knowing exactly when Daisy would be moved made things difficult. The date for Daisy's move had yet to be set. I was a planner. I knew my baby would be leaving, but not knowing when she would be leaving made things even harder.

All too quickly the day came for Daisy to meet Aunt Renee and have her first transition visit with her. Aunt Renee was nice and seemed like she wanted to help make this easy on us as well. I was grateful for that. It was hard to sit across from her and watch her play with Daisy. I could tell that Daisy was a bit uncomfortable with this lady she did not know and would have rather have had me hold her. I stopped myself from giving in to Daisy's stares that I knew were saying, "I want you to hold me, Mom." I knew that Daisy needed to get comfortable with Aunt Renee if she was going to be living with her.

We had a visit with Jane after meeting Aunt Renee, and Jane told me that she wanted to make sure we still got to see Daisy after she left us. She said it with so much compassion. Jane was very excited about the new arrangement. Aunt Renee would have to prove that she would not allow Jane to be around Daisy all the time after Daisy was moved.

After our meeting with Aunt Renee and the visit with Jane, I called our adoption worker. She listened to me talk about Daisy being moved and the visits we had just had. She was still surprised that Aunt Renee had been approved and that the plan was to move Daisy in with her. She had always thought that this case would end in Daisy being adopted by us.

She could tell I was struggling. I am sure my voice gave it away even though I had tried to hide it. Our adoption worker told me that grieving is like standing in the ocean being hit by waves. If you fight the waves when they come they will exhaust you and when a huge crashing wave comes it will crush you. However, if you rode the waves as they came, you would be able to cry and grieve in whatever way you needed to and then keep going. That helped me a lot over the next few weeks.

Week 26

Having to say goodbye to a child you love is a normal part of foster care. You have to let them go and trust that God will protect them. We needed to let go and pray without worrying. I had no idea how to do that, but I continued to try.

I put together a picture book to send with Daisy. I put it together quickly, and have to admit, I held back a lot because it hurt to share some of it. I planned on giving Aunt Renee a CD with all the pictures we had taken so she would have them as well. I was not even sure if she would keep it for Daisy since I had included a couple of pictures with us in them.

Daisy had been with us since she was one month old. During this transition time she turned seven months old. It felt like we were losing our daughter. We *were* losing our daughter. She had come to us as a very young baby, and now she knew us and preferred us to anyone else. As I packed up her things, I prayed that the sparkle in her eye and her amazing smile would not leave her as she transitioned to Aunt Renee's home.

154

Wednesday was our regularly scheduled visit with Jane. After that, we had a visit scheduled for Friday with Jane, Aunt Renee, and Daisy's caseworker. I was impressed that Jane had helped co-ordinate a group visit. The visit went well and an unsupervised extended visit was scheduled for the next Monday morning at Aunt Renee's home.

I was mentally exhausted. I kept myself awake until I knew I would be asleep within minutes of going to bed. I just did not want to think about having to say goodbye to Daisy. Just the thought of not seeing her every day made my chest feel heavy and tight. I knew that we had done what we were supposed to do. We fully support family reunification when it is safe and appropriate. We were doing our best to accept this outcome, but it still hurt like crazy.

Brandon compared it to watching your child go through terminal cancer, but our child would not be in Heaven, safe and well. She would be an hour away in someone else's care. While Aunt Renee was nice enough, her personal lifestyle choices were still questionable. We also worried that she would let Jane be around Daisy when she was not allowed to be after Daisy was moved. We were worried for Daisy's safety.

Brandon took Daisy for her extended visit with Aunt Renee. Once the visit was over, he returned home with Daisy. There was no sparkle in her eye when she saw me. She did not reach for me like she normally would have. It was obvious that the visit had been rough on her. This was so hard. It was so much harder than I thought it would be, and we were not even to the hardest part. We had not even had to say goodbye for good yet.

Week 27

After the extended visit a date was set for Daisy to move in with Aunt Renee. We would have to say goodbye the following Friday. Upon learning of the official date, my husband and I made plans to go away for the weekend after Daisy was moved to hide from reality.

Before the final move, another joint visit was scheduled for Aunt Renee, Jane, and Daisy. Aunt Renee cancelled at the last minute claiming she had car trouble and could not make it. Jane, on the other hand, was doing everything that she was supposed to do at that time. She was attending all of her classes and had shown good progress over the past three months. The plan for the next hearing was still to terminate Jane's reunification services. I had no idea if her recent progress would change that or not.

If all went as planned, Daisy's case would continue to move towards adoption. Aunt Renee had said she would be willing to adopt Daisy, but we were not sure that she really meant that. Daisy's caseworker told me that we could contest it if we wanted to. From the very beginning, we knew that was not something we would do unless we really thought God was telling us to do it. We felt like we needed to let Aunt Renee try to parent Daisy if she claimed she wanted to.

We had one last scheduled visit at the group home on Wednesday with Jane before the big move. As hard as it all was, I tried to think about anything positive that would come from Daisy moving. That was all that got me through the dark times. First of all, we would not have to deal with all of the drama revolving around her case anymore. Secondly, Daisy would be with family. Family always comes first. We knew that and agreed with that, no matter how hard it was to accept.

We arrived at Aunt Renee's house for the final visit before the official move. Aunt Renee acted surprised as she opened the door to greet us. I had confirmed with her the day before, so I did not know why she was acting like that. I had Daisy in my arms and three bags of Daisy's belongings. I told her that I also had a bin of clothes in the car. She asked if I needed help, and I told her, "No, I will just go back for it." She looked inside and then said, "Um, well, oh, uh, let's just go back to my room." She then directed us down a dark hallway into her bedroom. Before we got all the way down the hallway I noticed an older lady standing in her robe staring off into space. I had no idea how many people were in the house or who any of them were. When we got to Aunt Renee's bedroom I did not see a crib. All I saw was a bouncer. I knew her home study stated that she would buy a crib if she got custody. I was a little bit panicked as I tried to tell Aunt Renee everything she needed to know about Daisy. I do not think she expected me to come inside, so I was trying to rush through everything so I could leave.

When I got home from the visit I just sat in the car for a bit. I physically could not move. I was paralyzed with pain. I had to hide for a few minutes and cry the ugly cry. I felt like life was

156

crashing in around me. The days were passing quickly and all too soon it would be time to say goodbye. I was losing my girl. I had no idea how to prepare for that.

I returned four hours later to pick up Daisy one last time. Aunt Renee met me at the door, and then Jane came to the door with Daisy. I do not know when Jane got there, but I was glad that Daisy had someone she knew with her. When I took Daisy from Jane, she kept looking back at Jane and Aunt Renee, and not at me. She was full of smiles and laughter. I was amazed because, usually, when I came to pick her up you could tell she had been crying and was desperate to get into my arms. It did my heart good to know that she had enjoyed her time with them. Aunt Renee did say that Daisy cried every time she held her, but there are certain people Daisy just did not care for at first. I was hopeful that she would get over that quickly.

Week 28

The caseworker ended up taking Daisy to Aunt Renee's house to officially move her in with them. Seeing Daisy drive off in the back seat of that car broke our hearts. Brandon could not move. He could not function. He was an emotional mess. The sight of our baby girl in the backseat driving away haunted me. It was such a horrible feeling watching her drive away from us.

We went away for the weekend like we had planned to grieve and reconnect. We wanted to avoid going home and dealing with reality right away. We did the same when our previous placements had been returned to their biological family as well.

Five days after saying goodbye to Daisy, I got a picture of her via text message. She looked like she had grown up so much already. The text was from Jane, and she offered to arrange a visit for us. I nervously replied that I would like that. We planned a visit for that Saturday morning at Aunt Renee's house. We had no idea if this was a good idea or not. We wanted to see her so badly, but we did not want to make her sad. We did not want her to want to come home with us when she could not. Regardless, it was just one visit. After that we would decide how we needed to proceed.

I was curious to see how attached Daisy would be to Aunt Renee. I was scared that the usual sparkle in her eye would not be there. I was scared that she would cling to me, yet I desperately wanted her cling to me. I was a mess.

Brandon continued to break down practically every day. A friend who had gone through the same thing said that it is hardest on daddies to lose their little girls.

I was doing okay. Like our adoption worker had told me, the pain came in waves, but I was holding my own – for the time being. Any strength I had was coming for God, not from me. I missed her terribly, but I was not a wreck. God, truly, was answering my continual prayers of, *"Hold us up if she is gone tomorrow."*

Week 29

We finally got to see Daisy. It was an interesting visit. Brandon and I both got the impression that Aunt Renee did not want to adopt Daisy. She had assumed that Jane would get her act together and parent Daisy eventually. Unfortunately, Jane had run away again after doing so well for three months.

Aunt Renee told us to feel free to call and come see Daisy anytime. She had also asked the social worker if it would be okay for us to take Daisy for an overnight visit. The social worker said that would be fine. She ended up almost begging us to take Daisy overnight. She wanted to go on vacation the next month and needed us to watch her. Of course, we jumped at the chance. The more we talked, the more obvious it became that she did not want to adopt Daisy. She was slowly starting to realize that Jane would not be in the position to parent Daisy any time soon.

As for Daisy, she lit up when she saw me and started crying until she was in my arms. It was so wonderful seeing her again. She was laughing and smiling during our entire visit.

We talked with Daisy's caseworker after the visit to make sure she knew what was going on. She had also gotten a similar impression from Aunt Renee that she did not want to adopt Daisy. She told us to stay in contact with Aunt Renee as much as we could or were willing to. It was hard on us emotionally, but we wanted to be there for Daisy no matter what.

Even so, I was not sure that I was ready to have my heart broken again if we did this with Daisy and Aunt Renee. If we did overnight visits and we stayed connected, I was not sure I could handle walking away and saying goodbye again when the time came. Part of me wanted to walk away and let the healing begin now, but I knew in my heart that Daisy was worth the possible heartache.

Week 32

Daisy had been living with Aunt Renee for four weeks. We had seen her for one hour three weeks ago. We had our first overnight visit with her planned for Saturday through Sunday.

When I went to pick her up, she practically fell out of Aunt Renee's arms to get to me. Once she was in my arms she had me in a death grip. She wrapped her arms so tightly around me that she started to pinch me. She was smiling and giggling and almost hopping up and down.

I was worried she might not remember us, but apparently I had not needed to. Aunt Renee was very amused seeing Daisy respond the way that she did.

Week 34

Out of nowhere we received a call from Daisy's caseworker. She asked us if we would be willing to foster Daisy again. I was in shock. The worker was not offering up any details, but that did not matter. Our girl was coming home! We may never know the full story of what happened in the six weeks she was living with her great aunt, but all we needed to know was that Daisy was home safe with us.

After Daisy was brought back to us I ended up experiencing a new level of exhaustion. Daisy would not let me put her down. She would wrap me in a death grip if I tried to put her down in her crib. Aside from that issue, things went well.

Shortly after Daisy's return, Brandon called Aunt Renee. She asked how Daisy was, and if she could see her. Brandon said yes, but explained that he had to talk to Daisy's caseworker about it first. She thanked Brandon over and over again for calling and letting her know how Daisy was doing. She said she understood how we must have felt when she left.

Before Daisy left us, I never felt like she was going be my daughter forever. I had hoped she would be, but I never had a peace that she would be. After she returned home though, everything felt right. I immediately felt like she was going to be my daughter forever. Of course, I knew nothing was set in stone, but my girl was back in my arms and I was content to just be happy about that.

Week 36

For quite a while after Daisy was moved from Aunt Renee's house back into our house we did not hear from her caseworker. For once, I was just fine with that. I struggled daily with my emotions surrounding this case. The fact that we had not heard from her meant that Jane had not returned to a group home. I hate that I was happy that we did not have to deal with visits, because it also made me sad for Jane.

I sent a text to Aunt Renee telling her that we would be happy to meet up with her so that she could see Daisy. She replied that she would call back with a time, and that she would love to see Daisy.

Week 37

We were supposed to have a visit with Aunt Renee, but she cancelled because of car trouble. Four weeks had gone by, and Daisy had not had any visits with Aunt Renee or Jane.

Week 38

Because we had not had any visits it was getting easy to forget that Daisy was not mine. She felt like a part of our family - a permanent part of our family.

Week 42

A visit was scheduled with Jane to be held at the CPS office on a Friday morning. Jane was still not back in a group home, but the supervisor approved a visit anyway. I was put in charge of supervising the visit. I was fine with that because I knew that Daisy would need me, but I was a nervous to see Jane. We had not seen or heard from Jane in nearly four months. I had no idea if she would show up at all.

Jane did come for the visit and it ended up being torture for Daisy. When she got there I handed Daisy right over to her. As soon as Jane started to take Daisy into the visitation room she started crying. Her little face turned red, she had tears streaming down her cheeks, and she was trying desperately to see me. I kept waving at her so she would know I was there. I had to bite my tongue to keep from saying, "Mommy's here. Mommy is not going anywhere." I am sure Jane would have gone crazy if she heard me call myself "Mommy" to Daisy.

160

I spent the next 30 minutes trying not to have a panic attack. As soon as Daisy turned six month old she was no longer interested in being held. She always wanted to be down on the floor where she could play with toys. Jane did not know this because she had not seen her in weeks. Daisy did not want to be held on a anyone's lap anymore. For 30 minutes Jane and her sister passed her back and forth as Daisy cried. Jane's sister said she was always like that with her, and that she was just a cranky baby. She said that Daisy was cranky all the time at Aunt Renee's house.

Anyone who meets Daisy asks me if she is always "that content." My answer is always yes, unless she is hungry. I made sure I told Daisy's caseworker about that. She was the only one who had actually seen her in both homes. She did not act surprised when I told her.

Daisy ended up screaming and crying during the entire visit. I had to sit in the next room and listen to her scream all the while wondering what kind of mental and emotional damage this was doing to her. We had been busy rebuilding her trust in us. What was this one short hour going to do to all of our hard work? That night it took over an hour longer than normal to get Daisy to go to sleep. My baby was scared and confused.

Week 45

We had a home visit with Daisy's caseworker. We talked about Daisy's upcoming birthday, and we both assumed that Jane would probably want to see her. The next hearing had been scheduled and the recommendation was going to be to terminate all of Jane's services. If that happened, Jane's visitation schedule would be reduced to once a month, if the visits even happened at all.

Week 47

We had managed to schedule a visit around Daisy's birthday so that Jane could see her. Planning the visit had been very stressful. A lot had changed in Jane's life since we had last seen her. None of which was good. I was anxious about the visit, but I knew it was an important visit for everyone. Leading up to visit day, I had been battling my own fear. For almost a year I had prayed, *"Lord, help us love her like she is ours forever, and hold us up if she is gone tomorrow."* Never did I have a prayer more clearly answered then this one. The uncertainty of this case was very real. We did not know if Daisy would someday be returned to Jane or if we would be able to adopt her. One night, as I was looking for a Bible verse on fear, I came across this one and I audibly gasped as I read my prayer hidden in it.

Isaiah 41:10 " Fear thou not; for I am with thee; be not dismayed; for I am thy God: I will strengthen thee; yea. I will help thee; yea, I will uphold thee with the right hand of my righteousness."

Jane ended up calling and cancelled the visit 15 minutes before it was scheduled to begin. I was sad for Daisy. I was angry with Jane. In eight weeks there would be a hearing at which it was assumed that Jane's services would be terminated. After that, Daisy's case would be headed for adoption. Jane certainly was not doing anything to make herself look like a capable parent to the court.

Week 55

The next few weeks seemed to run together. We tried our hardest to make it to the next court hearing, but obstacles kept coming up and we were not able to go. I was overwhelmed with stress, and the anxiety that I experienced leading up to that court date often left me in tears. We found out that Jane did not attend the court hearing either, and that her attorney asked for it to be rescheduled. The judge rescheduled the hearing by 30 days and also ordered a visit. Daisy's caseworker did not have any way of contacting Jane, so we had to wait and see what would happen.

Week 59

The week of the rescheduled court hearing came around quickly. I was at peace and ready for whatever might happen. As the date drew closer, we received a call letting us know that a visit had been scheduled with Jane.

I was actually excited about this visit, but the night before I ran into one of the ladies who worked at a group home that Jane had lived in. She and I talked for nearly 20 minutes. It brought back all of the memories of Jane bouncing from one group home to the next, and us having to deal with all the drama that surrounded Jane.

By the time I reached the CPS office the next morning I had worked myself into a nice little panic attack. I got there early, so Daisy and I played in the visitation room while we waited for Jane to arrive. Out the window I saw Jane get off a bus and run across the street. She was ten minutes late, but she had made the effort to get on the bus and come. That showed me that she really did want to see Daisy. From the moment she walked in the room things were pleasant and friendly. She referred to me as Daisy's mom, and we made small talk. We also talked about Daisy's biological dad whom she will likely never meet. I was able to find out more details about Daisy's biological family and tucked them away in my brain for Daisy when she is older. We talked about what Jane's plan was now that she was 18 years old and out of foster care. She shared with me that the court hearing we thought we were waiting for had happened two days before. She told me that she had informed the court that she would no longer fight for Daisy. It was obvious she was beginning to realize that adoption would be best for Daisy. I made sure to take some nice pictures of Daisy with Jane before it was time to go. Jane gave me a phone number where I could contact her.

After the visit, I called our social worker right away to find out what happened at court. She said that reunification services were terminated as planned and the case was being referred to the adoptions department. Though we still needed to wait for Jane's parental rights to be terminated, we were finally on the road to adoption. Daisy would be our daughter, forever.

I truly believe that my prayer, *"Lord, help us love her like she is ours forever, and hold us up if she is gone tomorrow,"* was answered as God carried us through the greatest storm of our lives. He allowed us to love this little girl who will soon be ours forever with a "forever" kind of love right from the start. This journey has indeed been a roller coaster of a ride - one that I am glad that we climbed on and had the faith to see through without giving up.

13

Mine for Five Months

"Can I have two little girls for Christmas?" I said playfully into the phone. My husband, who was on the other end, knew I was serious. He also knew there was no use in telling me "no."

After our agency initially called me to ask if I would take two sisters that were part of a sibling group of four, I did not hear back from them for three days. I had said yes before asking my husband what he thought about it. He knew I was still heartbroken from our first foster daughter leaving, so he would have said yes to anything. After three days of not hearing anything from the home finder, I decided to call them to see if they had heard anything. After a short conversation, it looked like the girls would not be coming to our home. Something about that did not feel right to me, and I continued to hope that they would end up being placed with us.

Later that day I received another call. Despite what they initially thought, our agency would need a home for the girls, and they were calling to ask us if we could pick them up the next day at 2pm. Excitement welled up inside me. I had known that they were going to end up with us as soon as I got that first phone call.

The next day I drove to the agency to meet and pick up my two new foster daughters. I had my current foster daughter, Lizzy, in the car with me. She was my second placement, and had been with us for around six months. As I mourned my first foster daughter being returned to her biological mother, Lizzy was a much-needed distraction. She was a very busy child, and she had a very complicated case. Her visits with her biological mom and legal dad were very hard on her, and in return, very hard on me. We were doing the best we could under the circumstances, and I welcomed the two new girls as a change in pace to the long days through which Lizzy and I had been wading.

I walked into the agency and was quickly led into one of the social worker's offices. As I sat there, I watched Lizzy go from one thing to the next. The child truly could not hold still. After a bit of small talk between the social worker and me, the door opened. In walked two people. Each had a child in their arms. I had been told that the girls were two years old and one year old. The 27-month-old looked like a typical two-year-old, but had very short curly hair. However, the 15-month-old looked more like a six-month-old drowning in her clothes that were obviously not her size. She looked oddly small to me. She almost looked like she had dwarfism.

I immediately felt overwhelmed. This baby looked much younger than I had thought she was, and the two-year-old was acting very out of control as soon as she entered the room. As I watched these two girls play on the floor in front of me, more people came through the door with the girls' brothers. The boys were older than the girls, and the oldest immediately started taking things out of his book bag for all the children to play with. He constantly told all the younger children what to do and what not to touch. He talked very quickly, and understandably appeared nervous. As I stared at all the children, the social worker began to talk. He said that the kids' mom had been staying in a shelter with all four children. She appeared to have some drug issues, and someone reported that to CPS (Child Protective Services). The kids had come into care with nothing, so each of them had been given a duffle bag with clothes and a few other items. The 15-month-old was swimming in her clothes because they were not hers.

I signed the placement paperwork, and then it was time to go. I had three little girls now, and only two hands. No one offered to help me get them out to my car, but I figured that I might as well get used to it. This is what my new normal would be like. I picked up Tyra, the 15-month-old, and grabbed two year old Tamara's hand. I said a silent prayer as I started to head out the door with them while Lizzy trailed after us. As I reached the car, I was very thankful Lizzy had decided to behave in the parking lot. I strapped all the little girls into their car seats, and we headed home. The car ride home was quiet. Tamara and Tyra were wide-eyed as they studied the situation. They looked as if they were trying to find something familiar that they were not going to find in my car.

We arrived home and I somehow managed to get them all in the house. I decided that a snack was in order. I put Tamara and Lizzy in booster seats at the kitchen table and I put Tyra in the highchair. Tyra was still quiet. I searched her little face that had small, delicate features for a clue as to what was going on inside her head. Tamara had begun to say a few words here and there. She seemed convinced that she needed to feed Tyra a little bit of everything I put on her plate. She also appeared to be slightly obsessed with Tyra's bottle. She kept taking it and drinking from it. I noticed that Tamara still held her tongue as if she was an infant when she was sucking on Tyra's bottle. It occurred to me that, although the emergency foster mom had told me Tamara used a sippy cup, she had probably used to a bottle when she was with her biological mom. I decided to let her have her own bottle against my better judgment.

The girls had on the most hideous clothes. Not only were they ugly, but they also fit poorly. No wonder Tyra looked like she was swimming in her clothes. Her duffle bag had a tag on it that read, "infant girl, 18 mo. old." They had been given bags labeled for their age, but Tyra was so small that nothing in the bag fit her.

As the girls snacked on some cereal, I snapped a few pictures of them. I immediately captured Tamara's gorgeous smile, but Tyra was still wide-eyed. She did not crack a smile. She studied me very intently.

My husband, Ryan, came home from work, and was greeted by Lizzy and her two new "sisters." He walked over and greeted them both, but they did not pay much attention. Ryan also commented on Tyra's size. He thought both of them were beautiful.

167

We were all still strangers though, and did not know what to think about each other quite yet.

The girls finished up their snack, and when I got them down from the table they immediately began to search the house. They came across Lizzy's toys and sat down to play with them while glancing up at the TV every once in a while. Tamara babbled mostly nonsense and Tyra was very quiet. I sat close to them and would talk to them about the toys they picked up. Eventually it was time to change their diapers. I had picked up some clothes for the girls, but I had been expecting a one-year-old that fit in twelve-month-old size clothes. All of the clothes I had bought for her would be too big. I went down to our basement where I store my many bins of children's clothing, and pulled out the tub that held some six-month-old size clothes. I pulled out an outfit that looked comfortable and took it upstairs. Sure enough, it fit Tyra perfectly. Our new 15-month-old was the size of a six-month-old. She could walk and eat just fine, but was just very tiny.

Nighttime came and it was time to put all my little girls in bed. I was hoping to avoid the girls waking each other up at night. I moved Lizzy into an empty bedroom where I had set up a pack-and-play. I set up a second pack-and-play in the dining room where I planned on having Tyra sleep. I had a crib in Lizzy's room, and I decided to put Tamara in that. Tamara was the oldest of the three girls by a few months, but she seemed to be more capable of mischief.

Sure enough, after putting the girls to bed, I heard some noise. I followed the noise into the room Tamara was in and found her out of the crib playing with a few toys on the floor. I immediately groaned inside. I was worried it was going to be a long night. I picked up Tamara to put her back in the crib and she started to cry and do her best to wiggle out of my arms. She was not going to go to sleep without a fight. I decided to "swaddle" her in her blanket in hopes it would calm her down. I laid the blanket out on the floor. I calmed Tamara down and then laid her on the floor on the blanket. I rolled her up in it, much like a burrito, and tucked in each end of the blanket. She was as snug as a bug in a rug. Actually, she was far "snugger" than a bug in a rug, but I knew if she was not wrapped up tightly she would be out of the crib again as soon as I left the room.

I laid Tamara down in her crib and left the room. I stood by the door and listened to her whine and cry for a bit. Thankfully, the whining quickly stopped and she fell asleep. I had lived through day one with my three unconventional triplets. I was relieved they were in bed for the night.

The next few weeks passed in a blur. It was Christmastime and we had lots of Christmas things to do! I did not let being a mom to three girls under the age of three years old stop me from getting out of the house and doing my normal Christmas shopping. They went with me everywhere.

Lizzy was often the one who caused the most problems in public. She was always throwing a fit because of something. I had gotten used to it though, and just kept moving even if it meant scooping her up and holding her under one arm while pushing Tamara and Tyra in the shopping cart with the other.

Tamara was no angel herself. She gave me her fair share of problems as well. She spent her first few weeks at our home taking every single toy out of Lizzy's hands that she could. She was a fighter! Not only would she try to take the toy, but if Lizzy tried to keep it from her, Tamara would attack her! She would wrestle Lizzy to the ground and do whatever she needed to do to get the toy she wanted. It was as if she could not see a single toy besides the ones Lizzy wanted to play with.

I spent most of my time playing referee to Lizzy and Tamara. I quickly found myself becoming mentally exhausted from breaking up fights, chasing three toddler girls around the house, dealing with tantrums, and wrestling Tamara into bed each night. Some days I would quarantine the girls in the playroom with me and I would lie on the couch and zone out. I would suddenly find myself half asleep. I could hear every word they said and I would break up little fights, but I still tried to get some much needed rest.

Christmas morning came and I had three little girls to spoil. Before coming to my house, Tyra and Tamara had been living in a homeless shelter with their brothers and mom. I had been absolutely thrilled to go to the store and buy lots of presents for them. The girls did not seem like they knew what to do with a wrapped present, so we helped them open each one. Tyra toddled around in a pair of warm jammies that were too big for her. The sight had me giggling all morning.

Tyra had turned out to be such a sweet little girl. She loved being held and cared for. She loved her bottle that she was too old for, and I loved giving it to her because I had not had a baby that young before. She loved my husband and would do a happy dance when he came home from work. He would come in and scoop her up into his arms. They were quite a sight. He has always been a big guy and seeing him holding a little tiny girl made my heart just melt.

As the weeks turned into months, I started to try to get Tamara and Tyra healthier. From the very beginning you could tell they had not had a lot of food available to them. They only seemed to recognize pretzels and were obsessed with them. Both girls still loved bottles, and I let them have them even though they were too old for them. Tyra appeared to have some type of digestion problem. Her bowel movements were very hard and sometimes were partly white. I had never seen anything like that before. I decided to take her off of cow's milk and gave her baby formula. After a couple days she started to have regular bowel movements.

Tamara had the opposite problem. She was blowing out every single diaper. Her bowel movements were very loose and very messy. It was as if her body could not handle the normal food that it was not used to getting. It took a couple months, but eventually she started to have normal bowl movements as well.

Both girls were thin and had very little hair. When I took them to the doctor Tamara was in the normal range for weight and height, but Tyra was labeled as "Failure to Thrive." Fortunately, they both put on a healthy bit of weight quickly. Their skin began to look nicer and healthier. Their hair started to grow. They also seemed to get a little bit happier and behave more normally with each passing day. Every once in a while though, Tamara would act very oddly.

One day I had put Tamara in her crib for a nap. She was not very happy with me. She started to throw a fit, and I decided to leave the room. When I came back in she had not calmed down at all. She looked a bit like a caged animal. She was grunting and groaning. She was glaring at me, but it was as if she was looking right through me and not at me. I stared in disbelief because I had never seen her like that. I stood back and listened to the noises she was making. They did not sound like her normal cries. They sounded so angry. Eventually, I picked her up out of the crib and took her into the playroom. In a few short minutes she was playing like her old self and the emptiness in her eyes was gone. She never acted like that again. I do not know what brought it on. I

170

wondered if she had just been mad. I wondered if she missed her mom or dad. She was only two years old and had no way to communicate what was going on in her head or how she felt about being taken away from her mom. My heart broke for Tamara as I sat close to her, and she played with toys on the floor. Life is not fair when you are in foster care.

Tamara and Tyra's brothers had been placed with a foster home that was licensed through my agency as well. Their older brother, Luke, had a birthday coming up, and his foster mom called me to invite the girls. I was happy that the girls would get to see their brothers. They had not seen them since being placed in foster care. Their biological mom had moved back to the state that she lived in before the kids were taken away. Our agency was working on getting a visit set up, but their mom was so far way that it had not worked out yet.

The day of the birthday party arrived, and I was running late as usual. I pulled up to the foster mom's house and unloaded Lizzy, Tamara, and Tyra. As we walked up to the house I noticed that it was a little shabby. We knocked on the door and it swung open. A group of five children almost tumbled out on top of us. The foster mom had three biological daughters who were older and also had Tamara and Tyra's brothers who were six years old and four years old.

Luke was the four-year-old. He was a tiny little thing just like Tyra. He was similar in build and had similar facial features. I later found out that Liam, the six-year-old, had a different biological dad than the younger three children. He did not have the same facial features as the other children, but had the same coloring.

I walked into the house and could not help but notice the dirty carpet. The foster mom immediately started apologizing for everything. She apologized for how dirty the house was. She apologized that the kids had started eating without us. She apologized for how simple the party was. It did not matter though. The birthday boy looked as happy as could be. He ran around with a dinosaur hat on his little head and a big smile on his face. He was just happy to be celebrated. We went into the kitchen to cut the cake. The kitchen was so dirty. There was a thin layer of food smeared on just about every surface. I cringed, but acted as if I did not notice.

My girls and their brothers were all over each other. You could see that they loved each other. They rolled around on the floor and kept touching each other for no reason. They tumbled into the kitchen and squished into seats with each other. Liam made sure to try to feed Tyra everything he had. You could tell that he was used to taking care of her. I watched and wondered to myself what it would be like to be a six-year-old that was in charge of making sure a 15-month-old had food. My mind then wondered what it would be like to have that 15-month-old ripped away from you and you were left with no answers as to "Why?" or "Will we ever be together again?"

The party winded down, and it was time to go. The girls said their goodbyes and we got in the car to leave. I could not help but feel guilty that I could not take the boys home with me too. These children belonged together.

A court date was set and with it came a visit for Tamara and Tyra with their biological mom and dad. I was asked to bring the girls to the agency after court. The parents had finally come back to the state to attend the hearing, and the agency wanted to make sure they arranged a visit for the same day. I did not attend court because I did not have a babysitter for the girls. From what I was told, the hearing was a big mess. The judge was not quite sure how to deal with the biological mother living in another state now. He told our agency to work out a plan with the DHS (Department of Human Services) in the state she was currently living in, and to have all the kids moved to a foster home in that state. That would take time, and my agency was not sure how to go about that. We were left hanging with no clear plan of what was going to happen to our girls.

As I got the girls out of my car in the agency's parking lot, I heard a male voice yell, "Tamara!" Tamara whipped around. I grabbed her coat sleeve and turned to see who had just yelled her name. It appeared to be her dad. I assumed that she knew him from the huge smile on her face. I checked to make sure there were no cars coming and I let go of her coat so that she could run across the parking lot to him.

He picked her up in his arms, and she immediately started giggling. It was obvious she was excited to see him. I had Tyra in my arms, and he said hi to her. She had a bit of a scowl on her face. I walked into the building with them. I walked through the doors and I immediately knew who their mom was. I knew it was their mom because she looked just like Tyra. I dutifully handed Tyra

172

over to her as she held her hands out and started to call her odd pet names like "Moo Moo." I took a couple steps away to give them some privacy. I locked eyes with little Tyra. She was not happy and her eyes seemed to say, "Please, do not leave me with them!" My heart broke, but it did not matter. I had to do what was expected of me. I was expected to hand these children, even if only for a few hours, to people who were strangers to me, and pretend like it did not bother me at all.

I went to a shopping center to waste away the time the girls were to spend with their parents. I returned to pick them up, and Tyra was thrilled. She almost leapt out of her dad's arms to get to me. I could tell that Tamara would have rather stayed with her family. I felt horrible for her. Thankfully, she did not throw a fit. She came with me, but it was a quiet ride home.

Another court hearing was scheduled for about six weeks later. The judged wanted to make sure progress was made on moving the girls to the state in which their mom was living. Our agency told the judge that they had contacted the DHS in the other state, but they did not want the case. Our agency did not know what to do. The judge then said, "Fine, give them back to their parents." Everyone was dumbfounded. The District Attorney was not happy. He decided to try to get CPS (Child Protective Services) to fight the ruling. He told our agency, "Do not give those children to anyone. You keep them right where they are until I get this under control."

I was horrified. Give them back to their parents?!? They had not done anything they were supposed to do to regain custody! The biological mom had lost them because she was doing drugs. No one had drug tested her since the children were taken from her! No one knew if she had a place to live. She had no job. She had no income. No one knew if she had any way of feeding the children. No one knew if she was even capable of taking care of them!

After the court hearing, a visit was supposed to take place. I took the girls to the agency only to find out that their mom and dad had hightailed it back to their state instead of coming to see their kids! The judge wanted the kids to go back to these people? I felt so bad for the older boys, the girls' brothers. They were old enough to know why they were at the agency. They had been told that they were going to see their mom and dad. Liam was obviously upset. The boys' foster family was upset as well. They had made plans to take their older girls out for some family time during the boys' visit - the visit that now was not happening.

I could not handle the sadness on Liam's face. I told his foster mom that the kids were due for a sibling visit anyway, and asked if I could take them for a few hours. They happily agreed. I loaded all the kids into my car. I had never taken care of this many kids before. I went through the McDonalds drive thru. I ordered them each a happy meal and an ice cream sundae. I brought them back to my house and we had an outdoor picnic.

I took pictures of the kids together. The oldest boy asked me, "Why are you taking so many pictures of us?" I chuckled. I needed to capture as many memories as I could. I knew in my heart my girls would not be staying with me. I had been battling it for the entire length of their stay with us. Every time their mom did not come for a visit that my agency had tried to set up my heart would whisper, *"Maybe, maybe they will stay. Maybe you will be able to adopt them."* I had to push those thoughts out of my mind as fast as they came. In my head I knew that this case was far too complicated, and that the judge was uninterested in what was best for my girls. He wanted their case off his docket, regardless of the safety of my girls.

That night I returned the boys to their foster home. During the whole ride, Liam made suggestive comments about how he would like to live with me rather than his current foster mom. It broke my heart to not be able to offer that to him. I simply did not have enough bedrooms for my agency to even allow it.

Winter had turned to spring, and spring was quickly making way to summer. On Memorial Day weekend my husband and I always have a family cookout. This year I had planned it all around the kids who would attend, and most of all around my girls. They started out the day in their swimsuits and played in the water until they were hungry. They sat on a blanket on a beautiful day in May eating hot dogs and all the other things I had put on their plates. After they were done eating, they played some more until they were exhausted. I put three happy girls down for bed that night.

The next morning I got up and I got the girls out of bed. Everything about that morning was normal. The girls were crabby from all the playing and lack of naps the day before. I had been breaking up fights all morning and was annoyed with them for acting so badly. My phone range around 10am, and I answered it. It was one of the supervisors from my agency.

"The girls had court this morning. The judge was irate that they had not been returned to their mom and dad yet. He ordered them home immediately. I need you to bring them to the agency at 2pm today. We will have a transporter take them to meet their parents," the supervisor said.

I felt sick to my stomached instantly. My girls were leaving. I called my husband, and he came home immediately. I began to pack up everything the girls owned as fast as I could. I had been doing laundry for the past few days so all their clothes, thankfully, were clean. I could not imagine having to pack up dirty clothes to send home with them.

I was able to pack them up fairly quickly. Then I got them all dressed up one last time. I put beautiful sundresses on all three of my girls. I had come to enjoy dressing Lizzy, Tamara, and Tyra all up like three little triplets. I wanted to do it one last time. I did their hair and put matching bows in their curls. I took a picture of my three angels in front of our front door. It was time to get going, but we had a few stops to make first.

First, my husband and I took the girls to get some lunch. Then we went to a park that is very close to my agency to spend our last two hours with our girls. We played. We snapped pictures. We hugged and kissed them. When I woke up that I morning I never would have thought I would be spending the day saying goodbye to two little girls that had come to feel like my daughters.

The clock ticked the minutes away. It was time to take them to the agency. The girls were so young, we had not told them what was going on. It would not have meant anything to them anyway. They were all smiles and giggles. They had no idea that they were about to be ripped away from the people who had cared for them for the last five and a half months.

We carried our girls into the building and were met by their social worker. She was carrying a couple of out-of-date car seats. She made some small talk with us, and in an apologetic way, told us about how court had gone. We had not even been informed that there was a court hearing scheduled for that day. That really upset me. How dare they not tell me! Had they informed me, I would have at least known there was a chance this could happen today. I could have gotten their things in order, or had them say goodbye to people they knew.

But I had not known, and in the tiniest way, I was happy about that. The day before had been perfect. We had a wonderful day with all of our family. I had no idea that it would be the last time any of those people would see my girls, but they got to see them. I could be thankful for that. It is because of those moments that I know God was taking care of us, even though we were facing a very hard and very sad goodbye.

The social worker loaded the girls' brothers into her car first. After she was done, I buckled my sweet girls into the dirty car seats. Tamara was thrilled to see her brothers and did not have a care in the world. That made me happy for her. Despite my worry about their safety, I knew she would be happy to be back with her family.

As I buckled Tyra in, she looked at me with worry in her eyes. She did not like the strange car. She knew something was wrong. She was young, but she knew. I kissed her and told her I loved her. I kissed Tamara and told her the same. The last thing I remember seeing as I closed the door was Tyra in the backseat reaching for me. She was getting ready to cry. I closed the door and walked away. It was awful. I had no choice. There was no other option for me but to walk away from a child who thought I was her mother. It broke my heart into a million pieces.

To this day, I have never seen or heard from Tamara and Tyra again. They were too young to remember us, and we had no relationship with their biological parents, so that was it. I was their mom one day, and the next I was not. I still think about them often. I still have pictures of them on my walls. I think about how they are older now and wonder what they look like. I try to picture them with longer hair, but I just cannot imagine it. They will always be the age they were when they left in my mind.

My husband and I went on and were able to adopt Lizzy. Her case was crazy from start to finish, but in the end, she ended up being ours. There are still moments when I wonder what it would be like to still have my "triplet" girls all here with me. In those moments, I hug Lizzy a little tighter than normal and say a prayer for Tamara, Tyra, and their family.

14

Fighting for Our Kids

It was a Valentine's Day I would never forget, but for all the wrong reasons. Our three foster children, Luis, Marisol, and Carmen, had been living with us for just over a year, and we were only days away from their permanency hearing. Our plan to adopt them was supposed to be moving forward, but my husband and I had no idea that we were about to be blindsided in a way we had never expected.

Rebecca, the children's caseworker, called the week before the hearing. The kids' biological father had resurfaced in Mexico. The Mexican Consulate's office had sent over a home study and reports stating that he wanted the kids. The papers claimed that the children needed to be sent to Mexico immediately. To say that we panicked would be an understatement!

Rebecca had been involved in another case, a few years prior, where a different set of siblings that had been in foster care were sent to Mexico to live with their biological parents despite documented physical and sexual abuse. It had appeared that the judge on that case did not want to deal with it anymore. Rebecca was worried that history might repeat itself, even though it was a different judge.

She also informed us that the paperwork stated, because the biological father was a Mexican national, our children were also considered Mexican nationals. Their biological mother was a U.S. citizen herself, and all the children had been born in the United States, but that did not seem to matter to them. The Consulate also claimed that because the kids were Mexican nationals the Consulate had the right to overrule the local juvenile court regarding their placement. They insinuated that they had the same power as the ICWA (Indian Child Welfare Act) in which a child's tribe can choose to place children in native homes only.

At the time, we lived in an area where most of the cases involving children of Latin decent never made it to the termination phase. Either the children were reunified with their biological parents, or the kids went to other family members. We were in a rather unique situation. Andrea, their biological mother, had never really been involved in the case. She attended the first court hearing, begged the judge for a visit with them that she did not even show up for, completed half of a parenting assessment, and then disappeared. By the time we received the phone call about the biological father wanting custody it had been ten months since the caseworker had seen or heard from Andrea. The kids had not seen her in 13 months, and we had never met her.

The kids' biological father, Antonio, had been in a state prison for domestic violence charges when the children were taken from their biological mother. The initial goal was reunification with a biological parent, as it always is in foster care. Because Andrea was nowhere to be found, Antonio was the next option. He had been sentenced to two years in prison, but it was assumed he would only actually serve one year. Surprisingly, instead of being released after serving his time, Antonio ended up being deported to Mexico. Early on in the case, at a placement review hearing, Antonio's public defender announced that he did not even know the location of his client. Rebecca, the caseworker, also did not know. She had sent a notice to the Mexican Consulate's office, and they reported back that they had not had any contact with him. It had been months since that placement review hearing, and we had not heard anything from either of the kids' biological parents. The fact that both parents had basically disappeared led us to believe that this case would end in a quick and easy adoption. Nothing could have been further from the truth.

After being in our home for a few months, all three kids had been referred to an in-home counseling agency. They had witnessed a lot of domestic violence and had suffered neglect at very young ages. We were working through some minor behavioral issues. Our therapist at the time was a former adoption specialist from California, and she was well versed in working with the Mexican Consulate. It ended up being a huge blessing that she was scheduled to come out to the house the day after we received that devastating phone call.

After informing the therapist of what I had been told, she told me that the Consulate was not able to make the demands that they had. The Consulate could intervene on behalf of a biological parent, but not in the manner of taking over the case or overruling the local courts. They could hire a lawyer to represent the parent. They could get copies of court paperwork. They could make recommendations. However, they could not just take the kids because they wanted to! She gave me the name of two lawyers she knew in California who she thought could help us. We called Rebecca and informed her of the therapist's recommendation. Rebecca talked to her supervisor, and then called us back to confirm that we should try to find a lawyer and intervene in the case.

Immediately, I got out the phone book and started calling family lawyers. I left messages with many, but never received a return call from any of them. I spoke with a few others who said that such a situation was something they were not familiar with and did not feel they could help me. I talked to a few who insisted that this type of case was an immigration issue and advised that I consult an immigration lawyer. I contacted three immigration lawyers who insisted this was not an immigration issue, and that it was a family law issue! With court only four days away I was getting frantic.

I finally spoke to one of the biggest adoption law firms in our state. They recommended that I call a smaller firm in the area that specialized in both immigration cases and family law cases. My husband and I met with two lawyers from that firm the very next day. After hearing our case, they felt we had a strong enough case to file for adoption on our own, without needing parental consent.

We also found out that we needed to pay them $2000 the very next day as a retainer fee so they could begin filing the proper paperwork. $2000! We did not have that kind of money lying around! I went to my grandparents who happily agreed to give us the money. They had come to love their great-grandkids, and wanted to help us fight for them. I was so thankful for their help and finally felt like I was on the right track.

One of our newly hired lawyers came to court with us that Friday. It was the craziest court hearing we had been to up until that point. Normally, court was closed to all but the involved parties. That day my husband, myself, our lawyer, the kids' caseworker, the DCFS's (Department of Children and Family Services) lawyer, the Guardian Ad Litem (GAL), biological dad's public defender, three representatives from the Mexican Consulate, the judge presiding over the case, and the "head judge" who presides over all of the juvenile courts were all present at the hearing. Very quickly it became quite clear that no one knew the correct/legal protocol of how to proceed in a case like this. My biggest fear was that because no one knew what to do, they would all agree to just send the kids to Mexico in order to not have to "do" anything. Just the thought of that made me weak in the knees. At the end of the hearing, the goal was changed to concurrent planning. Our motion to intervene was taken under advisement, and everything was tabled until the next scheduled placement review hearing.

Our lawyer advised that we file for adoption of Luis, Marisol, and Carmen. They suggested that we file with a court other than where the kids' foster care case was heard. The basis of our adoption petition was that we did not need parental consent for the adoption because the parents had legally abandoned their children and were unfit to parent them. To legally file this, the children could not have had any significant contact with either biological parent six months prior to filing. It was easy to prove that in their biological mother's case. The kids had been in care for 14 months. She had not seen them even once during this time. No one knew where she was or how to reach her. She had disappeared after that first hearing. Antonio had been in jail even before the kids came into care. He did not receive, nor ask for, any visits while he was in jail. However, we did have some contact with him while he was in jail.

I had known when the kids came to us as foster children that the possibility of them being placed with Antonio once he was released from prison was very real. I had wanted to develop a relationship with him in case that happened. I asked Rebecca for permission to send him a letter and some pictures while he was in jail, to which she agreed. During the next four months, I helped the kids write him four letters and he had sent them a few letters in return. His letters were short in length and not very personal. One letter from him was nothing more than a picture he drew for each child. He did mention in one letter that he feared he would be deported, and that he did not know how that would affect the kids. He also discussed his total shock and disbelief at the behavior of their mother. We received a picture of him from a local relative of his, but the kids did not even recognize Antonio. Would these few letters ruin our chances of being able to file for adoption?

The children had a CASA (Court Appointed Special Advocate) who was assigned by the courts. He had met the kids about three times during their first year in foster care. It was painfully obvious that he was only going through the motions because his job required a community service involvement. He was very uncomfortable around the kids and had no real interest in their case. He said that he would leave every decision up to the GAL. Unfortunately, the GAL had never met the kids in person. Regardless, she felt the kids should be sent to Mexico. She also did not have any concerns about the domestic violence arrests related to Antonio and Andrea's tumultuous relationship. In fact, she said that given Andrea's erratic behavior toward the case, she probably deserved it. We could not believe what we were hearing! She said flat out that the kids were too young to say what they wanted, so their opinion did not matter. It was devastating to listen to the person that was supposed to protect our kids speak so lightly of these issues. It was obvious that we were the only ones who would be fighting for our children's safety.

After finding out we had filed an adoption petition, DCFS (the Department of Human Services) and the "team" decided the best option was to bundle the two cases together. The higher court would now preside over both the adoption case as well as the foster care case. If the judge ruled in our favor for adoption, with the grounds that the children had been legally abandoned, the parents' rights would be automatically terminated in the foster care case. The Mexican Consulate assigned a new lawyer to represent Antonio, in addition to the public defender that had been representing Antonio in the foster care case. Notices were sent to both Antonio and Andrea (at her last known address) to notify them of our intent to adopt. They legally had the right to contest the adoption and in turn, would need to prove that they had not abandoned the children and were indeed fit to parent them. Antonio decided to contest the adoption, which did not surprise us.

At the next permanency hearing everything went crazy. No one agreed on anything. A court date should have been scheduled, however everything was continued until further notice because of the chaos that had erupted in the courtroom. All the lawyers and agencies spent the next few months battling each other outside of court. Eventually, it was agreed upon that DCFS would work with the equivalent agency in Mexico and offer Antonio another chance to work a service plan. He had not completed any services while in jail, even though they had been offered. DIF (Departamento De Infantales y Familias), the agency in Mexico, was required to send paperwork showing what services Antonio completed, as well as the curriculum for their classes, trainings, and testing. There were many arguments over whether Antonio and the Consulate were required to translate those documents into English, or if it was our job as the petitioners to get them translated. We had to have all of our documents translated into Spanish on our dime, so our lawyer thought Antonio's side should be responsible for theirs. That was never done. Our lawyers made several requests for Antonio to provide DNA proof that he was the biological father of all three children. Antonio flat out refused.

Two months before the next scheduled hearing, I received another phone call from Rebecca that floored me. Andrea had been arrested, and her newborn son had been taken into foster care. When she asked if we would take him I had to pick my jaw up off the floor just to answer her. We had heard that Andrea had given birth to a child a year prior, but no one had any idea where she or that baby was. We were completely shocked that she had *another* baby after that one! Nicholas, the newest baby, came into our home at two and a half months old. We later found out that the first baby she had given birth to since losing her older children was living in Mexico with his paternal grandparents. Now Nicholas, the second baby she had given birth to since losing her older children, was with us as well as her older children. We immediately fell in love with him. When Rebecca first called me about him, he was in another foster home. Andrea and her new boyfriend were in jail at the time. By the time Nicholas came to live with us, two weeks later, she was out of jail and had already had a few visits. Andrea had complained to the caseworker about the care that Nicholas was receiving in his first foster home and requested that he be moved. She had no idea that he would be moved to us. Since Nicholas was having visits with Andrea, I was concerned how that would affect Luis, Marisol, and Carmen. I called Rebecca, and she assured me that the older children would not have to attend visits with their biological mom. Andrea had failed to respond to any of the legal notifications regarding the older children's case, so DCFS was not going to offer her any type of case plan for their case.

I had never met Andrea. I had never even seen a picture of her. Now I had Nicholas, and I knew I would probably be meeting her very soon. At the visitation center there was one entrance for the biological parents and a separate entrance for the foster parents. I asked if I could wait in the adjoining cafeteria to avoid having to meet with Andrea in the lobby. As soon as I walked in the door and laid eyes on her, I knew who she was. It was such an odd sensation! There she was, the woman I had been so curious about for nearly two years. The woman whose children I had been raising for the past 20 months. Now I had her newest baby. Would she abandon him as well?

Two weeks after that visit a court hearing was held for Nicholas' case. My husband and I always attend court, so we were there when the judge asked for the names of all in attendance. When we announced our names Andrea whipped her head around and stared at us. She knew our names from Antonio. She was beyond shocked that we were now involved with Nicholas' case. She was very unhappy to see that Rebecca had been assigned to his case as well. Andrea had initially lied to the police and CPS about her name, and it took about a week for anyone to put the two cases together. The judge presiding over Nicholas' case recognized us and realized the cases were related. Andrea had to backtrack with her lawyer, because she had told him that her other four children were living in California with her mother. He had no idea until right then that three of her children were already in foster care. It was not until after that hearing that Andrea even asked Rebecca how Luis, Marisol, and Carmen were doing. After seeing us at this hearing she decided that she wanted to contest the adoption as well.

Legally, Andrea should have never been allowed to intervene on the case. Our case against her was solid. She had missed every deadline. She had never responded to any of the court's notices. Legally, she had missed the boat. Sadly, the judge never even questioned her involvement, and allowed her to intervene.

I had thought the last hearing had been a disaster, but that did nothing to prepare us for the disaster that happened next. The judge presiding over the contested adoption was not overseeing this hearing because the case was up for a review only. The commissioner judge, who was hearing the case on this particular day, had no idea what the case was even about until we started. Antonio was supposed to be calling in from Mexico. There was a woman who had been asked by the court to interpret the call, but she was not a court appointed translator. She was under the impression she was just translating a few statements from Antonio, but the court was trying to get her to translate the entire court proceedings. It was a jumbled mess from start to finish. I was called to the witness stand to testify, which I had not expected. The last question asked of me was how did the kids feel about possibly having a visit with Andrea. I had to tell the court right in front of her that the kids had told me that they did not want to see Andrea. Seeing the sad expression on her face as I spoke was heartbreaking. Despite the fact that her past actions made her look like she did not care about the kids, I knew that my words had cut her deeply. It was then that the translator interrupted and said she could not continue. This was not part of her job description. She did not have the authority to translate court proceedings and asked the court to find someone else. After all of that, the commissioner judge made no changes to the case plan. The next court date was set, and, yet again, we left the courthouse without seeing any progress made in our children's case.

Finally, the next court date arrived. There had been two consecutive days set aside for court, but it became very obvious after the first day that two days would not be enough. As usual, no one could agree on anything. Court was continued, but it was only scheduled for one day. It was around this time that Andrea decided she could no longer afford this case. Her focus shifted to getting Nicholas back. She decided to sign adoption consents for us to adopt the kids. Finally! We were half way to becoming the legal parents of our children that had felt like ours for the past two years!

Despite the craziness of the adoption case we were dealing with, we had agreed to take in two more foster children. Their cases had been moving forward as well while we were fighting this uphill battle. Though Addison and Lily were siblings, they each had their own separate case. Due to a legal technicality, seven-month-old Lily was being reunified with her biological mother while Addison was not. At the same time, ironically, Nicholas was being reunified with Andrea. It was a very emotional time as both of our babies were leaving. Nicholas spent his first birthday with us. We were able to have a great celebration for his birthday and a goodbye party for him and Lily. It was bitter sweet.

Nothing about our oldest children's case was easy. As if everything had not been crazy enough, the judge presiding over the case passed away unexpectedly which added to the chaos. A new judge had to be assigned to the case, but she was not scheduled to do so until January. She tried to oversee a few of the cases that the commissioners could not handle until her term started, but we were unable to get a court date for any time during the remainder of that year. Our next hearing was not scheduled until March. It had been two years since we had initially filed for adoption. We knew we were going to need at least two more days of court hearings. These were all day hearings – from court opening at 8am and lasting until 5pm. The expenses continued to mount, and we were always looking for ways to raise money to pay for them. Many people asked us how we were able to keep going without any end in sight. In our hearts these were our kids, and we loved them just as much as if we had given birth to them. They were completely attached to us as their parents, and we were, literally, willing to do anything for them. After the New Year our court date arrived. We did not know if we could win this case, but for their sake, we were willing to try. The thought of sending them to Mexico with strangers was heart breaking. The kids would have been devastated! How could we *not* keep going?

Two more days of court were scheduled. One was a full day, and the other was scheduled to end at 3pm. My husband and I were both called to testify. At one point the Consulate lawyer that was representing Antonio asked me to translate one of the letters that Antonio had sent the children while in jail. I know some Spanish, but not enough to accurately translate a letter under oath. Our lawyer put a stop to that. Antonio's lawyer questioned me about Mexican holidays and Catholic celebrations, none of which I was very familiar with. I testified that we were open to having a relationship with Antonio, just as we were willing to have a relationship with Andrea. Whatever holidays and religious celebrations they wanted the kids to be aware of, we would try to share with them. We are not Mexican, so we cannot fully bring them up in the heritage and culture their biological family could. The judge called a halt to the lawyer's line of questioning, which she felt was pushing too many lines. That did not stop him from trying the same things on my husband. At the end of the second day, after all the witnesses had been called, we were told that we would be notified of the court's decision within 30 days.

Finally the call came. On a Friday afternoon in June our lawyer called. The judge had made her ruling. She agreed that, while Antonio had made token efforts to communicate with the kids, he had failed to do so in a significant manor. He had not sent money, or gifts, or any type of support during his time in jail or after he was deported, even though he had the means to do so. This judgment left no room for an appeal. It was well documented, and Antonio even admitted in his own testimony that he did not send more than those few letters after we had initiated communication with him. The ruling was worded as such that the parental rights were terminated, and the adoption granted all in one motion. They were ours!

There are no words to describe the relief that washed over me. It was finally over! After living as a family for three and a half years, we were all finally a family legally. The kids asked to change their names, which we supported. They kept part of their original names, but added a name that they chose. This took some getting used to, but for them it was therapeutic. Luis had just turned five years old when he came to us, and he was nine years old when he was adopted. Marisol was three years old when she came to us and was eight years old when she was adopted. Carmen was two years old when she came to us, and almost seven years old when she was adopted. Our everyday life had not changed, but everything *had* changed. We no longer had to worry about losing our kids. They no longer had to worry about where they would grow up or with whom. The peace, happiness, and joy of having their adoption finalized lifted a huge weight off of our shoulders. Parenting our children is a complete joy that we do not take for granted.

It was not easy. It was not quick. It was not without many heartbreaking moments. Yet, God never failed us! Our marriage and our faith were strengthened while we walked that scary road. It was so hard not knowing what the outcome would be, but God knew. The love in our home has grown and overflowed. Later, we were thrilled to be able to adopt Addison and Lily (who came back after being reunified with her biological mom for three months), which only added to our happiness. Someday, we would like to adopt again. God has made it clear that He has big plans for our children and our family.

15

The Undiagnosed Child

After seven and a half years of infertility, pregnancy losses, and failed infant adoptions, my husband and I ventured down the path to foster-adopt. Once we were approved, we began to submit our home study for children we would find on online databases. There are many online databases containing the 125,000 children in foster care that need adoptive homes. One day, there he was – our son. We knew it. He had my red hair and blue eyes, and my husband's mischievous twinkle in his eye. We submitted our home study hoping and praying that we would be chosen as his forever family. After many phone interviews, because the agency handling his case was across the country from us, we finally got the call. We had been chosen! He was ours! After five more months of paperwork, we flew across the country childless, and flew home with a four-year-old. His caseworker told us many times that they suspected he had ADHD (Attention Deficit Hyperactivity Disorder). "Pfft! No big deal! ADHD? No problem!" we thought. We finally had a child! Who cares about ADHD, right?

189

In foster care there is what is known as "the honeymoon period." Usually, when a child first comes to live with you, they are a bit timid and behave themselves for the most part. We definitely did not get a honeymoon period. From the minute Zach entered our life he turned it upside down and inside out. He had long rage sessions where he displayed freakish strength that even a grown man does not possess. I had no idea what was going on with my child. He would spend three to four hours a day screaming, crying, hitting, kicking, and destroying the house. Nothing, and I mean NOTHING, snapped him out of his rage sessions until he exhausted himself so much that he fell asleep. Anyone and anything in his path during his rages was destroyed. He was so full of anger and hate. I never knew what would set him off each day. Some days it was something as simple as me saying, "Okay, time to brush your teeth."

When he got mad he would spiral into a downward tailspin and was unable to recover. I tried talking to family and friends, but no one understood. They said things like, "Oh, all kids throw temper tantrums!" and "You wanted kids! Hahaha!" But this was not a normal temper tantrum. This was something much, much more severe.

I had been in the childcare/teaching field my whole adult life. It was my career. I had even taught emotionally disturbed high schoolers at one point. None of that had prepared me for this. The hardest part of it was that he only behaved this way while he was alone with me. When anyone else (including my husband) was present, he acted like the most angelic child on the face of the earth. This split personality, or Dr. Jekyll and Mr. Hyde phenomena, made it impossible for anyone to understand what was really going on. He had a charismatic charm about him that drew people in and wrapped them around his little finger. They would say to me, "How dare you make up such nasty things about Zach! He's an angel!" Out in public he would shower me with hugs and kisses, but behind closed doors if I hugged him he would stiffen up like a statue and scream "Ouch!" This was all part of his act. He wanted people to think he was perfect. He wanted to hide the deeply hurting and troubled child that only I knew. The lack of support and belief from my loved ones just threw me deeper into my isolated hole of confusion and depression.

What I did not know then was that I was suffering from Post Adoption Depression. Motherhood was not what I had expected it to be. My child was not the child I had dreamed he would be after looking at his picture all those months beforehand. Adopting had also stirred up the memories of the pregnancies I had lost, and made me wonder how different life would be if those babies were here with me instead.

I talked to Zach's caseworker about his outbursts. She said that once we finalized the adoption he would stop because he would feel secure with his spot in our family. However, once we finalized the adoption his behaviors escalated even further. I tried talking to his counselor, but she kept blaming me. I was not "nice enough." Ha! If you knew me you would know that I am one of the nicest, most-patient-with-children-people on the planet! I tried talking to my husband, but Zach's triangulation had succeeded in pitting us against each other. I had no one to turn to. No one understood. I knew there was something wrong with my child far beyond the ADHD diagnosis. I knew he was not happy, he was not healthy, and he needed help. I was not going to stop until I found answers, and got him the help he needed to live a happy and healthy life.

The lowest of lows was the night I called the police on my five-year-old. I had been surprised and thrilled to find out I was pregnant after we finalized our adoption of Zach. I had no idea how this news would send him spiraling totally out of control. One night he attacked me with a baseball bat, putting holes in the doors, and he even tried to strangle the dog. I had hidden all the knives, but did not think to hide the baseball bat. I later ended up in the hospital for 24-hour monitoring for the pregnancy I was carrying. It was then that my doctor told me if Zach was still living in the house when the baby was born he did not know if he could let me take the baby home.

The worst part of that night was when the police showed up. Zach charmed them with his innocent act, and they laughed at me and told me next time to "just spank him." I realized that they had no clue about the amount of strength that Zach was capable of during a rage session. This was when I realized that unless you are living with a child with these kinds of rage issues, you could not comprehend the power behind their anger. The police left laughing, leaving me with a very volatile and unpredictable child.

I felt hopeless. I knew something had to change. My unborn baby's life was now at risk.

A friend recommended I read the book "The Trouble With Alex" by Melanie Allen. The book is about a foster-adopt child with RAD (Reactive Attachment Disorder). I had never even heard of RAD before. I sat down one evening to start the book and I read it clear through the night until 2am when I finished it. I set the book down and knew then and there that Zach was battling RAD, a severe disorder that needs extreme therapy and intervention in order to heal. Even then, the statistics of those who actually heal are very low. I was on a mission, but first I needed my loved ones to believe me. I could not seek and implement the help that Zach needed without support.

I began videotaping Zach's outbursts and showing them to my loved ones. That is when they finally believed me. I made them watch a video called "Child of Rage" on YouTube so they could grasp the level of mental instability we were dealing with. None of them were able to make it to the end of the video because it was too disturbing. The disturbing thing is that this was what I was living with. They could just turn the video off. I could not. The average person would have thrown in the towel, and just given up on a child like this. He would end up aging out of foster care and perpetuating his birth family's history. Another family had attempted to adopt him before us and gave up. This only added to the list of those who had rejected and abandoned him. He assumed that if he could push me over the edge I would give up too. I was not willing to quit. Oh, I thought about giving up many times, but after all the years I longed to be a mother, I was not going to turn away from it now.

I searched and searched for a therapist who understood Reactive Attachment Disorder. This was easier said than done. Unfortunately, many therapists have no clue about attachment issues and blame the adoptive parents' parenting skills for the child's extreme behaviors. Zach had it down to a science. He was a pro at going into the therapist's office, charming them, and telling them how mean his parent was. So far, this had resulted in the therapist always blaming the parent! This tactic was not helping him get healthy. It was only pushing his level of pain deeper and deeper and preventing him from embarking on the path to healing.

I finally found someone who had studied RAD and knew how to help us. His fee was $100/hour out of pocket. It did not matter. I had to help my child, even if it meant going into debt. The first visit with the specialist was a Godsend. He got it! He was not charmed into Zach's manipulation and triangulation like the last several therapists had been. We could actually, finally, make progress!

At our first appointment the therapist did a full evaluation of Zach. He determined that Zach had Fetal Alcohol Spectrum Disorder (FASD), was exposed to drug use in utero, Reactive Attachment Disorder (RAD), Severe ADHD, Oppositional Defiant Disorder (ODD), Obsessive-Compulsive Disorder (OCD), and Anxiety. Bipolar Disorder was not completely ruled out because Zach's birth mom suffers from severe Bipolar Disorder and that may end up coming out when he is older. We had no clue that Zach had FASD.

A FASD diagnosis means Zach will forever be about half his chronological age socially and emotionally. He will always have severe issues retaining information. That is why we must re-teach him basic living skills every single day of his life. His brain lacks the ability to remember. It means we have to have visual reminders all over our house, and he still cannot remember to wash his hands after he uses the bathroom. It means peers do not understand his immature play, and that his younger siblings will one day surpass him socially and emotionally. It means he will most likely be dependent on us for the rest of his life. It means all the hopes and dreams we had for his future have to be modified.

We had assumed that his wide-set eyes, large ears, flat top lip, and curved pinky were just genetics from his biological family. These are all the signs of alcohol use in utero. On top of the things he was exposed to in utero, Zach was subjected to every kind of abuse and neglect you can think of in his first two years of life before he entered foster care. We found a picture of him with his birth father on his birth father's public social media page. Zach looked like one of those starving children from a third world country. His arms were like toothpicks. He was so malnourished it nearly made me throw up just seeing the picture. I cried myself to sleep that night. In his packet of information we got from the agency it said he would eat scraps from the garbage in his home, but if he got caught his father would beat him. Due to the lack of food and neglect, he developed an eating disorder. He would gorge on food, if allowed, until he purged. If he felt out of control, he would take control of one of the only things he could - food, by not eating at all.

Because he will always crave the sugars in breast milk/formula that were withheld from him, he literally developed an addiction to carbohydrates, and the natural sugars they contain. This abuse and extreme neglect in his first two years of life made it so he trusts no one. When he was young, he was supposed to be able to trust his mother to do things like feed him, bathe him, change him, love him, care for him, but he was left with nothing. As a very young child, to get food he learned to charm strangers. For Zach trusting someone else to care for him meant being left to die in his mind. That was too scary to risk doing again. He was living his life in a constant state of fight or flight. Zach was angry. He was confused. He was wounded. All he knew was he had to be in control. As a result, he controlled everything that he could control. Every aspect of every day had to be on his terms.

If you gave him a warning like, "Okay, we are going to clean up for dinner in five minutes," he would say, "No I will do it now." It seems harmless, but that is an example of how he had to manipulate every single minute of every single day so that he felt in control. Trying to manipulate everything and everyone around him was exhausting. He continued his known behaviors of pushing away his caregivers and charming strangers in order to feel in control of meeting his own basic needs. His fear of abandonment ruled his life, and he was never going to let another caregiver disappointment him again. He was not able to differentiate his birth mom and myself. To him "Mom" meant someone you cannot trust because they cannot care for you and keep you safe. His years of anger toward his birth mom were being taken out on me.

It was recommended by several specialists that Zach enter a Residential Treatment Center at the age of five because his brain needed a complete rewiring. We thought long and hard about this and decided we would do everything possible to keep him in our home. We would explore residential treatment only if we completely ran out of options. Even though he had turned my life into a living hell on earth, the thought of him sleeping somewhere else and feeling scared hurt my heart too much. That is when the hard work began.

My dear friend, to whom I am forever indebted, came over and without saying anything got on the phone. She called any and every agency and service she could think of and said, "Can you help this family?" She found classes and lectures for us to attend. We got frustrated and undermined as we went against a school district that had also been charmed by Zach. They did not agree that he needed any additional support. We had to get all these services outside of school on our time. Each evening was spent at some appointment or service. It was all consuming. We went to the specialist every week. We are currently still in debt because of all of all the services and therapies that we had to pay out of our own pocket because they did not accept state insurance. We started working with a local Crisis Intervention Team. They sent therapists into our home to work with Zach and our family through play therapy and skill building. We got Zach into horseback riding therapy. We also got him into a day program. Being at home with me was just too hard for him. I got a parent mentor who came to the house just to listen to me. It felt nice to be listened to! We got Zach on a mood stabilizer and started him on a gluten-free diet. We started him on supplements. I got into online support groups. I read and researched more than I had ever done during my entire four years of undergrad. I needed to know everything there was to know about FASD and RAD. We implemented Nancy Thomas' theories from "When Love Is Not Enough." We did not understand all her theories, but we just went with it. That meant only having caregivers in his life who will follow this approach religiously. That left us with very few people we could actually leave him with.

We also did regression therapy. We took Zach back to his infancy, where he was mentally stuck due to trauma. We nurtured his inner infant that never got nurtured. We rocked him to sleep at night with a bottle. We ran in his room in the morning when he woke with a bottle. We gave him pacifiers to soothe him. We rocked him and read books to him. He had never got the consistent rhythmic nurturing of rocking and feedings as an infant. As a giant five-year-old he was silently craving that. He could not move forward with his childhood until his inner infant could heal. The only way to heal it was to revisit his infancy. This lasted a few months until his need for it seemed to fade away. He asked for bottles less and less. He put the pacifiers away after awhile. He also was in need of major self-esteem repair.

195

It has been 15 months since we implemented all of these changes, and it has been 15 months since Zach has had a rage session. I cannot say everything is "sunshine and rainbows," because that would be a lie. I can say that Zach has nearly done a complete turnaround from the child he was when we first brought him home with us. We still have to be completely hyper vigilant in our parenting, especially since our daughter was born.

Zach was sexually abused by his older sibling before coming to live with us. Because of this, his brain still thinks that it is okay to sexually abuse your siblings. His brain is still haunted by the constant watching of porn to which his birth mom's boyfriend subjected him. This is something we are still working on in therapy as part of rewiring his brain and replacing the bad with the good. He has never hurt our daughter, but he has talked about it. Imagine holding your precious newborn baby girl you struggled to have for nine years, and having your son nonchalantly ask when she will be big enough for him to have sex with. Imagine having to remain emotionless so that he is not scared to share his thoughts like this in the future, because that would only delay his healing.

He has already inappropriately masturbated during a play date. We do not have play dates anymore. This forces us to use a whole new level of parenting supervision that most could not fathom. We cannot do simple things like run to the bathroom, or go put a dish in the sink in the other room. We cannot ever leave him unattended with his sibling. His therapist recommends that even if/when we get to the point where we fully trust him we must never give him the opportunity to lose that trust. It is exhausting. We constantly supervise his every move, always worrying about our daughter's safety. Our friends and family say, "Oh Zach would never do that!" Maybe not, but why risk it?

We have a door chime on his bedroom door so that when he gets up in the night we can get up with him. We have been advised not to leave him and any other children with one babysitter, because we cannot trust that they will be able to handle Zach's level of hyper-vigilant supervision that is needed when caring for the other kids as well. This means if we want to go on a date we have to find separate sitters at separate locations to care for our kids. The cost of multiple sitters on top of what dinner costs is not worth it, so we have stopped going on dates.

196

At age seven he still uses his bodily functions as a weapon by urinating or having bowel movements in his pants or his bed on purpose, to try to get attention or to make us angry. He sometimes will deliberately throw up his dinner all over the dinner table to try to get a rise out of us. He still chooses to use his affection in a fake way to try to get what he wants. We do not allow fake affection. This can look extremely strange to people in public when we do not allow our child to hug us as part of his "show." We tell him he is welcome to hug us for real when we get home, but he never does.

He subconsciously craves that life of chaos and turmoil that he was born into. It is what he knows. It is his "normal." It takes everything in our power to remain calm and in control of ourselves. Every single night I pray for the patience, strength, energy, understanding, focus, wisdom, insight, and the desire to parent Zach. What I wish is that we would have known about Zach's diagnoses prior to adopting him. I wish we could have started him on the path to healing the minute he entered our home. Unfortunately we wasted a year and half in turmoil because we did not know how to help him. I wish that they taught us about attachment disorders in our adoption classes. I wish that these children did not sit in foster care for years falling through the cracks. I wish they got the proper medical care they truly need to heal from their early childhood trauma. I wish they were not subjected to therapists with a monthly turnover rate so high that they are never able to develop a bond. I wish caseworkers knew about Reactive Attachment Disorder. I wish caseworkers were not overworked and underpaid so they could actually give these children on their caseload the time they need. I wish that caseworkers did not withhold information about children.

So often it seems that these important details only come out after the child is already placed in your home. It would be so helpful to know these from the get-go. They say, "That which does not kill you will only make you stronger." I guess I am one of the strongest people around. At the end of the day, my marriage is stronger, my faith is stronger, and my will and ambition are stronger. I know now that I can and will do whatever it takes to help my children be happy and healthy. That is my ultimate goal for them. Along the way I have lost friends and family members who just do not get it. Frankly, at the end of the day I am so burnt out the last thing I want to do is pick up the phone and call a friend. My friends who have endured know that if they want to communicate with me they better text me. I cannot talk on the phone in front of a child with RAD anyway, because it triggers their loss of control. I remember being on the phone once and Zach was hurling objects at my head, screaming, and spitting in my face. He had to get my attention because when he feels out of control he feels like he is going to die.

I have lost that thing called, "me time," but I have gained the profound privilege of turning a child's life around. I grew up with this saying by Ralph Waldo Emerson on the wall of my bedroom and I guess it has always stuck with me.

"To laugh often and much; To win the respect of intelligent people and the affection of children; To earn the appreciation of honest critics and endure the betrayal of false friends; To appreciate beauty, to find the best in others; To leave the world a bit better, whether by a healthy child, a garden patch, or a redeemed social condition; To know even one life has breathed easier because you have lived. This is to have succeeded."

People ask me all the time, "Is it worth it? Would you do it again?" These questions are hard to answer. Of course, I would like my life to be easier, but then I would not be who I am today. I am really proud of this person I have become. I love the unlovable. I give unconditionally to someone who literally lacks the ability to love me back. In fact, he hates me for loving him. I hug a child throughout the day, every day, who does not hug me back. Now that is living a Godly way of life. Some days it drains me to the core. I do not want to wake up and do it all over again the next day. Other days I catch a glimpse of hope: A real smile, or a real hug, and I know I am doing something right. It is definitely not a "normal" life, but it is our "new normal."

I have people say all the time, "I would love to foster, but I do not think I could handle it." They are probably right. Not everyone can handle it. I do not tell my story so people feel sorry for me, or for them to view my child as a monster. I write this to raise awareness, and to share the very real, and very raw, life that I live. What I wish the most is that three years ago someone would have said to me, "It is HARD. It is really, really hard. But it will be worth it."

16

A Story of Grace

As a mother of three young children, I felt overwhelmed at times, but so incredibly blessed. Our life was busy and full, but happy and content. Then I felt God pulling our family towards orphan care. I looked into overseas adoption, domestic adoption—any option besides foster care. I thought, "I could never be a foster parent. There is too much risk, too much hurt involved."

However, God firmly told me, "It is NOT about you." So we submitted to His will and began the process of becoming certified as foster parents. I understood that God wanted us to sacrifice our comfortable lifestyle for the sake of a child who had no other options. What I did not realize was how our decision to foster would impact the other side of the arrangement, the biological parents, and how I would be affected by that relationship.

The process that we thought would take 90 days took nine months. My husband lost his job and we could barely provide for our current family, but God said, "Keep going." We trusted in God's plan, and eagerly prepared for the time when we would welcome a disadvantaged child into our home. We never considered that we might also invite the child's parent to be a part of our family as well. The whole point of foster care is to rescue the child from the unfit parent, right?

After a long nine months, we were finally certified and could not wait to get "the call." "The call" came quite a few times for different children - five in all. We said yes to every single one, and each time the child was placed somewhere else before we could pick them up. Extremely frustrated, we called our caseworker. She listed about 20 children that we could choose to foster, and shared with us why they were in care. It came down to a newborn boy, which was what I had desired all along, or a ten-month-old little girl. We prayed about it, and God said, "Take the ten-month-old." It is amazing to think how such a seemingly small decision could change our lives so much.

Grace was nine months old when she sustained a severe burn on her leg that prompted an investigation by CPS (Child Protective Services). Her mom was ironing on the floor, and being the curious little girl that she was, she crawled over to the hot iron while mom was not paying attention. Grace's mom, Angela, was terrified that her baby girl was going to be taken away. She had aged out of foster care herself, and knew how traumatic and scary it was to grow up in the system.

Angela was on track to break the cycle of foster kids producing another generation of foster kids. She had attended college and joined the Army, where she served our country for nine years. She left the Army after suffering from severe depression and post-traumatic stress disorder. After being discharged from the Army, she continued to suffer from even more mental disabilities such as bipolar disorder and schizophrenia. She was homeless many times. She met a man 20 years older than her and began a relationship with him that led to her pregnancy with Grace at the age of 34.

Angela had always wanted children and thought that waiting until she was older was a wise choice. Now she was not so sure. Because of all the medications she was on, Angela could not sleep at night. She averaged an hour of sleep on a good night, and was often suicidal. She checked herself into the psychiatric ward at the veteran's hospital about once a month.

When Angela received notice of a complaint being filed with CPS and that she would be visited by a caseworker, she had a breakdown. For the safety of her daughter and herself, she needed to check herself into the hospital immediately. She was frantic and had no one to help her. Her family was in another state and was struggling with difficult circumstances themselves. She took the bus to the veteran's hospital, which just happened to be next door to a children's hospital. Outside, she saw a woman she had met a couple of weeks before. She told her friend how desperate she was and that she was having suicidal thoughts and needed to check herself into the hospital immediately. She asked her friend to please look after Grace until she got out, and the friend agreed. Angela signed a note of written permission for her friend to watch Grace and left for the hospital.

The next day, CPS went to Angela's home to begin the investigation concerning the burn on Grace's leg. When they arrived, no one was home and the landlord had not seen Angela or Grace, which was unusual. They tracked down Angela in the hospital and asked her where Grace was, to which she responded, "I don't know." Grace was now a missing child.

Five days later, the friend who was caring for Grace saw a news story about the little girl who was considered missing. She immediately called 911 and CPS came to pick up Grace. She was now a ward of the state. Grace was placed in an emergency foster home, where she stayed with an amazing family until our family was chosen to be her long-term placement.

My heart was pounding as my husband and I sat outside the CPS building waiting for Angela's visit to be over so we could bring Grace home. I could barely breathe knowing that we were about to meet our second daughter. We watched as Angela walked out of the building and got into someone's car. Knowing nothing about Angela at this time, we slunk down in our seats, worried that she might see our car and follow us after we left. How silly and judgmental that seems now.

After Angela was out of sight, we got out of our car and walked inside. We nervously followed the caseworker upstairs and down the hall to where Grace was waiting. As we walked into a bright yellow room, we were met with the biggest grin and happy shrieks from Grace. I will never forget the moment my eyes met hers. It was as if I was seeing one of my biological children for the first time. I truly feel that God had shown her our faces because we were instantly a family. In our paperwork, the caseworker even wrote that Grace was playing and laughing with her foster parents immediately. We had no adjustment issues with her and our biological children were immediately in love with their new sister.

It was the end of October when Grace came to live with us, and when I heard her story, it was so familiar to me. After searching the Internet, I realized that I had read the news story about how she had come into state custody a week before we were certified as foster parents. After reading the story, I instantly had compassion for her mother, Angela. I had no idea how God was going to use that compassion to show His love through me.

The first time I met Angela was during a visit at the CPS office. She came in looking very professional, with her hair done and a beautiful shawl around her shoulders. She brought shoes and clothes for Grace and two books about Jesus. I was anxious to reach out to her, and brought as many pictures of Grace as I could get developed. She was so gracious. After this visit, we communicated every day for a month by email. I later found out that Angela walked to the library every day to check her email for the pictures that I would send of Grace.

As Christmas approached, I hoped we could get together with Angela to celebrate. I had not heard from her in about a week, which was very unusual, so I checked with our caseworker to see if she had talked with her. She had not, but made some calls and discovered that Angela was back in the psychiatric ward at the hospital. Angela would be spending Christmas there. My heart was broken for her. Without a second thought, I told her that I would be there to visit her on Christmas Day.

At this point in our foster care journey, we had a total of six children. Three of them were biological, one was Grace, and the other two were a sibling set that we had unexpectedly taken in two weeks before. I was a very busy mama. Going to the psychiatric ward on Christmas Day was not something that I would have ever imagined myself doing. I asked my mom to go with me. We wrapped presents and took pictures of Grace for Angela. I had no idea what I was going to do or say.

When we got up to the psych ward, it was so quiet. We could not find anyone who worked there and we had no idea how to get past the two sets of locked doors that led to the patient area. We considered leaving, but I knew that the Lord did not bring me there on Christmas Day to leave without seeing Angela. Finally, a nurse came out and went through all of our presents to make sure they were safe to bring in. A picture frame was not allowed because of the glass in it and a thick ribbon tied around a throw blanket had to be thrown away. I had never even considered that some of these items could be potential weapons or a means to end her life. We were finally cleared to enter the ward, and I nervously prayed for the Holy Spirit to take over.

We walked into the common area and I looked around for Angela. When I saw her, I barely recognized her. She had on hospital garments and her hair was pulled back in a do-rag. Her eyes were filled with sadness as I embraced her and wished her a merry Christmas. We sat down at a table and gave her the gifts and pictures of Grace we had brought. After she went through them, I updated her on how Grace was doing. I told Angela how much we loved Grace and that she was such a happy little girl. Angela was trying so hard to hold back her tears, and she was so grateful that we had come to visit her. She had never had visitors before.

The nurses and some of the other patients approached us and shared how sad Angela always was and how happy they were that we came to visit and "love on her." After we had been there only 30 minutes, it was announced that visiting hours would be over shortly and we needed to wrap things up. I asked Angela if I could pray with her and she graciously accepted. I cannot remember what I prayed, but the words that came out of my mouth were not from me. They were from the Holy Spirit, loving and comforting this deeply hurting woman through me while I held her hands and bowed my head with her. Just as the Bible says in Psalm 34:18, *"The Lord is nigh unto (close to) them that are of a broken heart..."*

After Angela was released, we met at the zoo and celebrated Christmas and Grace's birthday. I was able to get some great pictures of them together. She began attending church with me once a month and would wear her t-shirt with our church logo on it every time I saw her. After getting to know Angela better, our family began inviting her over twice a month for breakfast at our house and to see Grace. It was a little awkward at first, but the kids always made her feel at home, calling her "Mama Angela" and giving her hugs.

Angela was off and on in her relationship with Grace's father. He had shown up to court only one time. His rights were terminated early on in the case because of this. That was a blessing, since he had been abusive towards Angela many times in the past. Despite the fact that Angela could barely take care of herself, CPS was hopeful that if she got her medications straightened out, she could get Grace back. Over the next six months, though, it became evident that this would not be an option. She moved from her apartment to an assisted living facility. Her medications had made it so hard to function that she had begun having hallucinations again and was often suicidal.

The assisted living facility was close to our home, so we would go visit her and pick her up for church or for a visit at our house. My husband and I picked her up for one of our court hearings in July. At this point, Grace had been in state custody for about nine months. Before we got out of the car, we said a prayer out loud, and asked God that whatever decision was made would be in the best interest of Grace. As we walked in, Angela was very somber. Our caseworker handed us each a copy of the court report and we read through it. I could barely hold back the tears when I reached the point in the report where it stated that, "Angela reports that Grace's foster mom is her only friend." Shortly thereafter, our case was called. Our two minutes in front of the judge went something like this:

Judge: *"Ms. Smith, I have in front of me a piece of paper that states that you are relinquishing your parental rights to Grace. Is that correct?"*

Angela: *"Yes, sir."*

Judge: *"Ms. Smith, do you understand that by giving up your parental rights you have no say in medical decisions, where she goes to school, or anything else in the future?"*

Angela: *"Yes, sir."*

Judge: *"Ms. Smith, did anyone threaten, coerce, or bribe you into sign this document?"*

Angela: *"No, sir."*

Judge: *"Ms. Smith, do you believe that this decision is in the best interest of Grace?"*

Angela: *"Yes, sir."*

Judge: *"By order of the court on July 11, 2011, parental rights of Grace Smith are terminated. We are off record now. Ms. Smith, I can tell that this decision did not come easy to you. I wish you the best of luck in life."*

There was no doubt that was the hardest moment of Angela's life and one I will never forget. Saying goodbye that day was so hard and uncomfortable. How do you react when the mother of your foster daughter just relinquished her rights so that you could adopt her? I hugged her and told her that I respected her so much for her decision and that she was now a part of our family too. I told Angela that I wanted her over for holidays and as many visits as we were capable of making. We invited her over for breakfast that following Sunday to reassure her that we were serious about keeping her involved in Grace's life.

When I picked Angela up for breakfast that Sunday, she came with toys that she had bought at the thrift store for all six of our children. It was such a generous and thoughtful thing to do with her very limited income. The kids were so excited and showered her with kisses of gratitude. We had a huge breakfast of biscuits and gravy and lots of bacon, Angela's favorite.

Before she left, I had her record her voice on one of those Hallmark books for Grace, so that Grace could hear her birth mother's voice whenever she wanted to. Angela was very touched by that. We were moving that next week, so I let her know that it might be a few weeks before we saw her again, but we would bring her out to the new house soon.

When I dropped her off at the nursing home, the passenger door would not open for some reason, so I had to get out and let her out. I am so glad that happened, because it allowed me to give Angela the last hug I would ever give her. I looked into her tear-filled eyes for what would be the last time and said, "I love you."

Three days after we moved into our new house, I got the phone call I had been dreading. My husband called and said, "Is your mom there? Go somewhere by yourself. I need to tell you something." I went outside and stood on the porch. I could hear the pain in his voice as he said, "Angela shot herself." "What?!" I shrieked, over and over again. "What?! No! No! Why would she do that?!" Sobbing, I screamed, "She's supposed to come over next week. We had it planned, she was supposed to come over! Why would she do that?" Logically, I knew why, and I had known that this was likely to happen. But you are never, ever prepared for a phone call like that.

I wept all day long. I wept for the way Angela's life ended. I wept for Grace and that she would never have a memory of her birth mom. I instantly regretted not calling or visiting her more often. I just kept saying over and over again, "I'm so sorry, Angela. I'm so sorry."

The funeral was the next day at the nursing home. Other than residents, it was my husband and I, two of my dear friends, and our caseworker. My husband shared a little bit about our family involvement with Angela, what a good woman she was, and that she would be terribly missed. At the end of the service, we fittingly sang "Amazing Grace."

The woman who ran the nursing home brought us letters that Angela had left for us. I never thought I would be a recipient of a suicide note. This is a portion of the one she left for Grace:

"To my daughter,
I will always love you. Mommy had to go. Your new mother will take good care of you. She will feed you when you need to eat, change your diapers, and tuck you in at night. When you remember her, please remember me. I'm sorry I had to go. I couldn't deal with the pain anymore. Whenever you're alone, I'm there with you.
Love, Mommy"

The next few months were filled with lots of paperwork, and right before Christmas, we were blessed to finalize Grace's adoption and give her our last name. It is still hard to believe that this part of our journey is over. The Lord used it to teach me so much.

When we became foster parents, I had no intention of getting close to the birth parents. They were the "enemy" in my mind. This experience has changed the way I view all of them. They are hurting people who need love just as much as these children do. Many of them were victims of the foster care system themselves. Angela was a beautiful person who loved her daughter very much. You may never know what a person has been through or is going through, so extend to them the same grace that the Lord Jesus has given us, and love them with everything you can while they are with you. You just might be their only friend.

"And the King shall answer and say unto them, Verily I say unto you, Inasmuch as ye have done it unto one of the least of these my brethren, ye have done it unto me." Matthew 25:40

206

17

The Reason

They say that everything happens for a reason, and I have always believed that to be true. That is, I believed it to be true up until the day that I sat in stunned disbelief in the back of a courtroom as my whole world came crashing down around me. The judge had just ruled that the little boy who I had loved as my own for the past year be turned over to the joint custody of his teen parents effective immediately. No warning. No transition. No goodbye. My baby just never came home.

For as long as I can remember, I wanted to be a mom. I dreamed of long road trips in an RV with my husband and gaggle of kids (five to be exact) while I traveled the country with my family. I looked forward to creating our own traditions like wearing ugly Christmas sweaters on Christmas Eve and decorating gingerbread houses. I wanted to load up my brood in my soccer mom minivan every fall to visit the local pumpkin patch, eat kettle corn, and get lost in the corn maze. I longed to be a room mother at my children's school, do all of those Pinterest crafts that drive some mothers crazy because no *normal* person has time for that mess, and chaperone every field trip over a 15 year span. I dreamed of being *"that* mom" - the one who thoroughly embarrasses her child by shouting, "That's my *baby!* Mama loves you, Sugar Dumplin'!" during his high school graduation. Yes, I had big plans when it came to what my family life would look like.

It turned out God had a different plan for me. At the age of 30 I had a hysterectomy due to complications from severe endometriosis. Still single, with no biological children, I spent the next few years praying and desperately trying to figure out what God had in mind for me. I knew I was meant to be a mother. I just had no idea how that was going to happen.

In the fall of 2008, I decided to take a leap of faith and become a foster parent. I had always shied away from foster care because of the usual fears related to having to say goodbye to children who I loved as my own, but as time went on I finally began to trust that God would not have planted this seed in my heart only to leave me hurting and devastated. I began to trust that He would heal me through the hurt as I loved my children and let them go. I decided to take a leap of faith and dove headfirst into the crazy, unpredictable world of foster care, allowing myself to love my kids with my whole heart despite the inevitable hurt.

When I opened the front door on a spring afternoon in 2009, I had no idea just how much the seven-month-old on the other side would change my life. Josh flashed a slobbery, two-toothed grin in my direction and I was a goner. For a baby who had been in numerous homes in a short amount of time, Josh was a surprisingly well-adjusted little charmer. I was shocked at how easy everything was with him. He slept through the night, he took great naps, he flirted with the ladies, and he was always happy and smiling. Our life together was quiet and easy amidst the general chaos of foster care.

As is usually the case, we knew very little about Josh's situation early on. He had previously been with a relative who told CPS (Child Protective Services) that they could no longer keep him, so he officially became a ward of the state. CPS had initially been unable to locate Josh's mother, but they managed to find her at school about a week after he had been moved into my home. Josh's mom, Beth, had just turned 16. Over the next couple of weeks I learned that she was essentially homeless. "Couch surfing," she later called it. The bits and pieces that I learned about her life through Josh's caseworker pulled at my heartstrings in a way that almost had me more concerned about her well-being than Josh's. I knew that Josh was safe and loved with me, but his mom was just a child herself and she was struggling.

Three weeks into Josh's placement, I made a decision that would change everything. I asked to meet Beth. I never had any intention of taking in a teenager, but there was just something about this girl that made me want to at least *consider* the possibility. I am not really sure what I was expecting that afternoon as I sat in a CPS lobby with Josh while we waited for his mom to arrive. I had already been running through different scenarios in my head. If she walks in at 5'10" and outweighs me by 50 pounds, all bets are off! I may be a little crazy (all foster parents are), but I am not stupid. When the door opened, and a little girl all of 5' tall and 90 pounds soaking wet ran in to scoop up Josh, I immediately thought, "We just might be able to make this work."

Looking back, I do not think that Beth had any idea that I was seriously considering taking her into my home as a foster child. As we sat around a conference table with Josh's caseworker, my agency case manager, Beth's father, and a family friend, we talked about Beth and her decision to put herself in foster care. Due to her age, the county wanted it to be her decision. Ultimately, she wanted to be in a home with Josh, but she was under the impression that she would be living somewhere else for a while. She was definitely scared of what coming into care would mean as far as her lifestyle was concerned, but she put up a brave front and seemed willing to try.

Over the next two hours, we talked about every topic imaginable; her school, her pregnancy with Josh, her drug use, her home life, her love of cooking, and even her fear of thunderstorms. As the visit came to an end, Josh's caseworker pulled me aside and asked, "So what do you think?" I looked across the room at Beth as she and her family said their goodbyes to Josh and said, "I'm willing to try if *she* is."

I still remember the look on Beth's face when I asked her, "Would you *want* to come live with me?" Her eyes grew huge and her jaw dropped to the floor. I could see the wheels turning in her head as she realized that I was serious and that she had a huge decision to make. "It's definitely going to be a big change from what you're used to. You'll have a curfew and rules, and I'll expect certain things from you. But I have a lot to offer you too if you're willing to take it," I added. Beth looked down at a smiling Josh for a second before looking back up at me and nodding "okay," and in that moment I knew that our lives were about to get interesting.

Beth did not move in right away, so Josh and I had a few extra days of "normal" before the chaos of being a single mother to a teenager and an infant in foster care really began. It took a few days for CPS to get the paperwork together and for me to re-arrange the house to accommodate a teenager as well as an infant and myself. I moved Josh into my room, and let Beth have the extra bedroom for herself. The fact that Josh was in care after having been removed from Beth prompted that decision. Beth had not been parenting Josh up to that point, and I wanted to make sure she was willing and able to do so before depending on her to take care of his needs at night.

The first night was not at all what I had expected. The case-worker dropped her off after dinner, and because it was nearing Josh's bedtime, I thought I would let Beth give him his bedtime bottle. Josh had been with me for several weeks, so I hoped she would take the opportunity to reconnect with him. When I asked her if she wanted to feed him, Beth looked at me as if I had asked her to eat a slug. She did it, but it was very obvious that the task of feeding her son could not end fast enough. I tried not to read too much into it. I tried to tell myself that she was simply over-whelmed by the huge changes that were happening in her life. Unfortunately, Beth's reaction was a foreshadowing of what was to come over the next seven months.

We spent the first several weeks after Beth moved in attempting to develop some kind of routine and to find ways for Beth to work her service plan that CPS had required in order for her to re-gain custody of Josh. Beth's lack of relationship or any feeling of connection with her son became extremely apparent when it came to taking care of his needs. It was a constant battle to get Beth to interact with Josh on any level. Feeding him, bathing him, or even playing with him all seemed to be chores that she was required to do in order to get her allowance. She was very sporadic when it came to giving her attention to her son. Once every few days she would decide she wanted to play with him, only to push him away five minutes later.

Beth told me once that she only had Josh because she thought it would bring her some attention. She said that plan backfired on her because once he was born everyone only paid attention to *him*. Her resentment was apparent when we were in our home. In public, things were completely different. Beth was extremely possessive when it came to Josh, and was always very quick to point out that he was her son when anyone complimented him. She reveled in the attention that being a teen mom brought her, and Josh was the prop that she used to make her role complete.

On top of Beth's treatment of Josh, we constantly battled other behaviors that many foster parents experience like lying, sneaking around, and stealing. The constant lying drove me crazy! I honestly do not think that Beth knew *how* to be honest. She would lie about the most random, unnecessary things. She would tell elaborate stories of being a drug runner and driving a getaway car for her brother when she was three years old. She made up deaths of friends and told everyone who would listen that she had been an international model who flew around in private jets. The stories were completely outrageous, but the lying about everyday things made me want to pull my hair out. I would ask her an innocent question like, "Did you ask Nana if she could pick you up?" and her immediate response was almost always a lie.

I think I could have dealt better with Beth's behaviors if Josh had not been a factor. It was clear that Beth was a hurting teenager with a tough past who desperately needed someone to love her, but Josh was directly affected by Beth's jealousy and resentment. As time went on, I began to notice a huge change in his behavior. That smiling, easy-going baby boy was becoming confused, sad, frustrated, and clingy. He began hitting Beth in order to get attention from her. It took two hours to get him to go to bed at night as he would cling to my neck and sob if I even attempted to leave him. Josh would wake up several times throughout the night, crying out for me to hug him before falling back to sleep. Beth's treatment of Josh and the stress it was causing was taking its toll, and I told CPS that I would no longer force Beth to care for him. I had been doing the majority of the parenting anyway, and what little she did do was hurting Josh.

After I took over all of Josh's care, Beth seemed relieved that she no longer had to deal with it. Unfortunately, a new problem developed as a result. Beth became resentful of the relationship that Josh and I had developed. She became angry and defiant. She would pick fights and throw temper tantrums that would rival those of any two-year-old. Then she made the huge mistake of becoming belligerent with her CPS caseworker and her therapist. Her behavior forced my agency to put a safety plan in place when it came to her contact with Josh.

Being a single, full-time working foster mom to an angry teen and her infant son was hard enough without having to follow an official safety plan. When my agency had Beth and I sign the papers that said that Beth was not allowed to have unsupervised access to Josh, Beth scribbled her name seemingly without a care in the world. I, on the other hand, panicked. Not only was my agency requiring that Beth have 24/7 supervision, but Beth was not allowed access to Josh while they were both living in the same home! I knew that these demands were going to be impossible for me to meet as a single, working mom. As much as I did not want to be yet another person who let her down, I felt like I did not have a choice. I asked to have Beth moved to another foster home.

I felt like I had failed her. As difficult as things had been, parenting Beth had not been a *completely* negative experience. There were good times too. I loved being able to witness so many of Beth's "firsts," as her life up to that point had not been easy or "normal" by any means. I loved watching her excitement as we celebrated holidays, went on family outings, and decorated her bedroom together. I loved hearing positive feedback from her teachers and seeing her happiness at having someone actually care enough about her education to ask. We had private jokes and mother/daughter time that we both looked forward to.

Beth was a smart girl, and she had so much potential. Unfortunately, her lack of ambition and sense of entitlement were traits that she simply had no intention of changing. She grew up watching as her parents lived off of the government and received assistance from charities and other people, so in her mind, she was entitled to the same. Being in foster care did not help matters either. As a foster child aging out of care, Beth knew exactly what assistance she would be receiving. Her response to every question regarding her future with Josh included some sort of assistance from Medicaid to WIC to subsidized housing and free college tuition and childcare. As much as I tried to show her a different way of life, she simply did not want to change.

212

The morning after Beth left in early January, I was busily rushing about getting Josh ready for daycare and me ready for a long-awaited doctor appointment. I had been battling recurring pneumonia since coming down with the flu in September, and was so excited to finally have a fresh pair of eyes look at the problem and try something new to see if it would help. Josh and I were on our way out the door on that cold winter morning, and I was distracted by my rambling thoughts. "Things are finally going to be normal again! I can breathe better just knowing I do not have to worry about Beth's drama 24/7! I can start to make this house a stress-free zone for Josh!"

Those thoughts and more were running through my head as I stepped onto a metal grate and felt my foot slide out from under me on a sheet of invisible ice. My hands were full with Josh on one side, and his diaper bag and my purse on the other. My only thought was *"DON'T LET JOSH GET HURT!"* I did the only thing I could think to do and twisted so Josh would fall on top of me, rather than on the ground or underneath me. That is when I heard it - the cracking sound of a stick breaking in half. The searing pain in the lower half of my leg and ankle made me think that it more than likely was not a stick that had snapped in two. I knew something was broken, but as I sat there on the ground, I kept wishing it away. "It will be fine. I will just sit here for a few seconds, and the pain will go away."

I immediately checked on Josh, and thankfully, he was completely unscathed. Thank goodness he did not try to run away! He was more concerned about why Mommy suddenly decided to fall to the ground and not get up. I looked around hoping that someone was within calling distance to help me, but it was pretty clear that I was on my own. I have no idea how I did it, but I somehow managed to stand up and stagger back into my apartment with Josh in tow. I dropped everything inside the front door and crawled to the couch only to realize that I could not stand up to sit on it. I propped myself up on the floor and wondered what to do next.

Just then, Josh came toddling over with my cell phone in his hand. "Nana?" he asked questioningly, as he held the phone out to me. My boy was smart! He knew that Nana was the best person for the job. If anyone could fix Mommy, Nana could. Josh was so good. He could have gotten into all sorts of trouble while we were waiting for help to arrive, but instead, he got some books from his bookshelf and shared them with me until my mom got there.

I ended up calling my doctor's office because I was going there anyway and told them to add a broken leg and/or ankle to the mix. It made no sense to pay for an ER visit when my doctor's office had radiology onsite. By the time we made it to the doctor's office, I was not sure what all I had injured. I was fairly certain my leg was broken, but my ankle hurt as well. I could not completely pinpoint the pain. The doctor's office actually did the exam for my breathing problems first. Later, they sent me for x-rays where I heard the tech exclaim, "Oh! *That's* not good!" I ended up doing a breathing treatment while they called the orthopedic office to set up an appointment for me and put a huge splint on my leg. I am certain I was quite a sight.

At the orthopedist the next morning, we found out what I actually did. Apparently, when I twisted I pulled the ligaments holding my ankle together which also happen to be connected to the smaller bone in my leg. The pressure from the twisting snapped the bone. The doctor said that the break was "inconsequential" and that it should heal itself in a few weeks. It did not *feel* that "inconsequential," but at least he did not seem too concerned about the fracture. The ankle, on the other hand, was a different matter. Leave it to me to injure myself in a way that stumped a man who had been practicing for 20 years. His plan of attack, when it came to healing, was for me to remain completely non-weight-bearing for eight to ten weeks. That plan was much easier said than done for a single foster mother of a 15-month-old.

While being wheelchair-bound for weeks was not exactly practical, it did give me the opportunity to spend much more quality time with Josh. My mother moved in to help us out, and I had a few months to focus on making life as peaceful and normal as possible for my little boy. Beth never called or asked about her son, and CPS was not going to arrange visits unless she requested them. Josh and I got back into a great routine without all of the stress and drama surrounding Beth. We spent our time reading books, singing songs, cuddling, and watching his favorite episode of Barney.

That time with Josh taught me just how deep a mother's love can run. I quickly learned that the best sounds in the world are your baby's laughter and the little "I love yous." I learned that baby hugs and kisses and "cuddle time" with your little boy can make a bad day turn around in an instant. I learned what it means to be a mom. While I certainly never planned to be housebound for weeks with an injury, I will forever cherish that extra time with my little boy. I was able to bond with him in a way that I had not been able to while Beth was still living with us. It also gave me the opportunity to get to know Josh's father.

Two months after Josh came to live with me, CPS was able to determine paternity. Kyle had just turned 19, and he found out the day before the first major hearing in Josh's case that he was his father. My first impression of Kyle at the courthouse was that he was extremely angry and bitter. It was understandable to an extent. Finding out that you are a father is life changing. Finding out that your son is also in foster care and that you will now be required to work hard to get custody of him when you never did anything wrong in the first place had to be frustrating to say the least. Kyle walked into court and immediately asked for sole custody of Josh. While his intent looked good on paper, it seemed pretty clear that Kyle only wanted custody so Beth could not have him.

Over the summer Beth and Kyle made a few attempts at reconciling. One moment they were getting along really well, and we would meet Kyle for dinner so he could see Josh and spend some time together. A week later, Beth would insist that Josh belonged to her and that Kyle needed to back off. Kyle would get angry and call CPS trying to get Beth in trouble. The next week, they would be back to being best friends and wanting to build a long, happy life together as a family. It was exhausting. Neither one of them saw Josh as a person. He was a possession, a weapon to be used to hurt each other, or a lovely little prop to make their make-believe family complete. They were a couple of kids having babies, and they needed to grow up.

That September, I got permission to have Kyle meet us for Josh's first trip to the zoo. I do not know what had changed, but that day was a huge turning point for Kyle and his relationship with his son. For the first time, Kyle chose to be Josh's dad. I saw his face light up every time Josh smiled. I watched as he pointed out all of the animals and held Josh up so he could see. Kyle never left his side. From that day on, Kyle's focus seemed to change from wanting to get even with Beth to genuinely wanting to get to know his son.

Over the next six months, I watched as the relationship between Kyle and Josh began to grow. Kyle was given two unsupervised visits each week, and Josh began spending every Wednesday and Saturday afternoon with his daddy. As time went on, I began to notice Josh's excitement when he knew that Kyle was coming over. He would run to the front door and list every fun thing that he and his daddy had ever done together. The change in Kyle was apparent as well. He would immediately get down on the floor to play with Josh as soon as I opened the door. He asked questions about Josh's schedule, and wanted to know about his favorite foods, games, toys, etc. Kyle was fully invested in being Josh's father, and when he said that he wanted sole custody, I believed that he now wanted it for the right reasons.

As the March permanency hearing approached, we began working with CPS to create a transition plan. Losing Josh was something that I did not want to think about, but his caseworker assured me that we would have a good transition. The plan was to move to terminate Beth's parental rights, get a three-month extension, and start to transition Josh into Kyle's care.

That plan changed considerably when four weeks before the hearing, Beth resurfaced. She had decided that she wanted to see her son after two months of no contact. Suddenly, Beth wanted custody. I later learned that Beth's newfound interest in her son was due to prompting from her new foster mother. Beth had previously expressed her desire to relinquish her rights and allow Kyle to have sole custody. She acknowledged that she had no bond with Josh and no desire to be a mother, but her foster mother convinced her to try again. After two months of no contact, Beth was granted supervised visitation at her new home.

The month leading up to court was so difficult. Kyle could not understand why CPS was allowing Beth another chance when she had messed up so many times before. Josh was, once again, being used as the rope in a custody tug-of-war. His behavior began going downhill fast after visits with Beth began. It was bad enough when they lived with me and Beth ignored him. He, at least, had me to love on him the majority of the time. Visits were clearly different because Beth was forced to care for and entertain him for several hours at a time. Josh began hitting again as well as kicking at the cat and screaming, "MOVE!" He was one angry little boy, and he had every right to be. The system that was supposed to protect him was once again failing him.

The week before the permanency hearing, Josh's caseworker came out to the house. I expressed my concerns over Josh's regression in behavior since the visits with Beth had begun. I was very worried that the multiple visits throughout the week and lack of any kind of routine was more harmful than helpful when it came to providing Josh any kind of stability, but I assured her that I was doing my best to maintain some kind of routine and normalcy for Josh amidst the chaos. We went over the new plan for court that included a few changes based on Beth's desire for custody. According to his caseworker, they were still getting a three-month extension in order to transition Josh into Kyle's custody. Kyle had never spent more than eight hours with Josh, so we all wanted to give him the opportunity to build up to being a full-time parent. Visitation with Beth would continue, but the goal was still that Kyle would have primary custody. As much as the thought of saying goodbye to my baby boy broke my heart, I had begun to make peace with the fact that Josh would be well loved and cared for with Kyle. I was very relieved that I would have a few more months to fully accept it though.

The day of court began like any other. It was a Wednesday, so Kyle would be picking Josh up from daycare for his weekly afternoon visit as soon as the hearing was over. I dropped Josh off like any other morning, gave him a quick kiss, and said, "I love you, baby! Be good for Daddy! I will see you tonight!" Then I headed up to the courthouse. I sat with Kyle and his grandfather while we waited for the attorneys and caseworkers to arrive. We talked about starting overnight visits and things that Kyle would need to buy. We talked about some of Josh's new "tricks" and things that he had recently started doing. Beth was there as well, but was already in a hearing for her case as a child in care so we did not see her before Josh's case was called.

About five minutes before the hearing began Kyle's attorney arrived, and I stepped away so they could speak privately. Just then, Josh's caseworker pulled me aside and gave me the news that left me numb. CPS had decided to skip the transition and to give Kyle and Beth joint custody. I stared at her, completely dumbfounded. "What?" Surely I had not heard her correctly. She repeated the news. "When?" That is when this woman who had been so open, friendly, and caring over the previous ten months looked me straight in the eye with complete indifference and said,

"Well, Kyle has a visit this afternoon anyway, so I do not see any reason why he should have to bring him back." Then she walked away.

I stood there speechless, in total disbelief as I watched her walk away. The bailiff called Josh's case, and everyone walked into the courtroom. I sat in the back and attempted to listen to the judge through the storm that was raging inside my head. "Primary custody to the father...Every other weekend with the mother...Two weeks with mother during the summer...Congratulations!" That is when one of the attorneys spoke up and wanted to state "for the record" how very proud she was of these young kids. She raved about how hard they had worked for their son and how she was positive this arrangement was going to turn them into a wonderful young family. I remember thinking, "Oh! I am in the *wrong courtroom!*" Surely anyone who had actually followed Josh's case would know that this was a disaster in the making. I knew that Josh would be okay with Kyle, but with Beth in the picture on a long-term basis, the potential for fighting, Beth's lack of desire to care for Josh, and the stress the entire situation would put on my baby boy made me burst into tears.

My crying did not seem to matter though. As far as everyone else was concerned, I no longer mattered. I had been the hired babysitter for the past ten months, and I had just been let go two minutes prior to the ruling. There was no "Thank you for loving, protecting, and caring for this child as your own over the past year." There was no "Are you going to be okay?" There was not even a glance in my direction. I had never felt more disposable than I did at that moment.

I composed myself the best I could and went to find Kyle. I had to force myself to switch into "business mode" or I never would have made it through the rest of the day. None of us were prepared because we had all been expecting a three-month extension and time to transition. I had not packed a thing, and Josh had never even spent the night with Kyle. I told Kyle that I would go home and at least get Josh's important bedtime things together so he would have something familiar while he tried to go to sleep in a new place without me. Kyle was going to run to the store and come by my place to pick them up later that afternoon.

Before I left the courthouse, I stopped to talk to Beth. I am not sure what I was expecting, but it was not at all what she said. She was angry that her parents were going to have to pay child support for her until she aged out of care. She never mentioned Josh. She showed no excitement over getting joint custody when, only a month prior, CPS had planned to request termination of her rights. She expressed no anxiety over being required to parent the little boy she had chosen to ignore for the past 17 months. She was simply angry that the court was forcing her parents to pay child support. It took every ounce of what little strength I had left not to shout at her, "Your parents will be just fine! They have someone else raising their kid! I think they can give up one or two of the 'recreational purchases' that they make every month and come up with the $50 they are being required to pay for their daughter." Instead, I took a deep breath and mumbled, "I am sure they will figure it out." Then I walked out the door to find a way to start my life without my baby boy.

There is a huge difference between sorrow and grief. I do not think I ever realized that until I lost Josh. I expected to be sad when my foster children left my home. I expected pain and tears, but nothing could have ever prepared me for the all-consuming heartache and flood of emotions that encompassed me in the days and weeks after I lost Josh. I was numb. My heart had a gaping hole that physically ached. My arms were empty where Josh should have been. I did not leave my house or talk to anyone for days. I simply allowed myself to feel every emotion that washed over me; rage at CPS and the way they handled his case, denial that it was happening at all, fear for Josh and what might be in his future, and the suffering of a shattered heart.

If I had known the morning of court when I left Josh at daycare that he was not coming home, I never would have taken him. I would have spent the morning at home with my baby boy. I would have studied his face. I would have tickled and cuddled and held him until his father came to pick him up and take him to his new home. I would have told him just how much I loved him over and over, and I would have said goodbye.

But I had not known, so I had to do my best to accept that I would never see my baby boy again and try to move on without him. I went back to work. I went through the motions. I listened as people tried to offer condolences that they did not know how to offer. What exactly does one say to a person who lost a child who was not actually "theirs" to begin with? As time passed, the day-to-day tasks grew easier, but nights were still hard. Bedtime was always when Josh and I bonded the most, and there were more nights than not when I cried myself to sleep.

Just when I thought I was starting to heal, something would happen that would rip the wound open again. I would dream of Josh, and wake up in tears just wanting to go back to sleep so I could hold him again. I would see his favorite episode of Barney on the DVR because I could not bring myself to delete it, or someone would ask if I had heard how he was doing. I wanted to shout that, "No, I have not heard how he is doing! I am never going to know how he is doing again! I was the hired help, and I was fired!"

Fostering as a single person with no forever children of your own adds another dimension of loss. Families who foster have each other. They have spouses to lean on through the hurt. They have forever children to hold. They are able to busy themselves with the day-to-day tasks of being a family while they find ways to help each other cope with the loss. I did not have that. I went from being a busy mom of a precocious toddler to a single lady with a cat. I came home to an empty, silent house with no responsibilities other than to clean out the cat box. I had been a mom for nearly a year, but Mother's Day came and went, and once again my arms were empty. I knew I could not do it again. I just knew that I would never heal from another hurt this deep. So I gave up my foster care license, and tried to move on.

Beth contacted me in June to tell me that she had decided to relinquish her rights to Josh. She told me that she was not ready to be a mom. She had only seen him a few times since the hearing that spring, and told me that she thought it would be best if Kyle had sole custody. I did not have the heart or the energy to tell her that I knew the truth. I had found out through a mutual friend that Beth was pregnant again, and that she was told by CPS that if she did not voluntarily relinquish her rights to Josh before the final hearing the next month that they were going to move to terminate. CPS informed her that if the state terminated her rights, they would likely remove the baby she was carrying as well. Regardless of the real reason that she decided to relinquish, I knew that letting him go was probably the most parental, responsible, and loving decision that she ever could have made for Josh. By signing away her rights, she was giving Josh the stability of a loving home.

Knowing that Josh was safe and finally had permanency with Kyle was a huge relief, and I think it was the first major step towards helping me heal. Time went on, and my heart began to mend. Then, one afternoon in July, I logged onto Facebook and saw it. Kyle had reactivated his account, and I was able to see pictures of Josh for the first time in four months. My baby boy was getting so big! I studied every photo with an intensity that I had never felt before, and I cried again for the first time in weeks. Only this time, they were tears of relief and joy. Josh was clearly happy, healthy, and very, very loved.

I think being able to see firsthand that foster care can work helped me make a decision that I had been struggling with most of the summer. Should I listen to the pull in my heart or the voice of reason in my head? My heart had been pulling me harder and harder towards going back to foster care. It told me that I was a great mom, and that there were more children out there, like Josh, who needed what I had to offer them for however long it might be. My brain, on the other hand, was telling me that I was nuts and needed to get back on some medication. Seeing the pictures of Josh convinced me that my heart would be the winner in that particular battle. Seven months after I said goodbye to my little boy, I made the decision to welcome another little one into my home.

I am not certain how it happened, but during that time I somehow reconnected with Kyle. What started with me sending an out-of-the-blue email to Kyle telling him that I had put together a baby book for Josh's second birthday quickly turned into an online friendship with Kyle and his girlfriend, Anna. I learned that Anna had moved in with Kyle and Josh the day that Kyle was able to take Josh home. The day that Josh left my arms, he went into Anna's, and she had loved my little boy every bit as much as I did from that day on.

I had not seen Josh since the morning that I took him to daycare in March, and the first time that I got to see him again was a complete surprise. It turned out that Kyle and Anna were expecting a baby girl early the next year, and they had quite a bit of clothing that they had received from family that they thought I might be able to use for any new little ones who came into my home. When I heard the knock at the door, I expected Kyle to drop the clothes and run. Imagine my shock when I opened to the door to see all three of them!

Josh walked in like he owned the place. I could tell that he thought that he should know who I was, but that he could not quite place me. Josh sat there and talked to me like we were the best of friends for 20 minutes straight. I did really well holding back all of the emotions that had come flooding in the second I opened the door until they were getting ready to leave. I knew there was only one thing that I had to do in case I never saw them again. I thanked Anna. I tried my best to hold back the tears as I thanked a 17-year-old girl for stepping up and being Josh's mom. She had dropped everything to step in where I left off and to be the mom that Josh so desperately needed, and I needed her to know how much that meant to me.

The next weekend, Josh's baby book arrived, so I asked if the three of them would want to meet at the park to pick it up. I told them that I would, most likely, have my five-year-old niece and nephew with me, and they quickly suggested having a picnic. The twins were really worried that Josh would not remember them, but Anna did a great job the night before putting together presents for the twins with Josh and talking about them so he would know their names. When they got to the park, the twins asked, "Do you remember us, Josh?" He just smiled really big and replied, "Yeah!" The three of them picked up right where they left off, and right then I knew that Anna was something special. The fact that she had taken the time to make two little people feel important and remembered by a two-year-old was not something that a normal 17-year-old would even think to do, and I found myself wanting to know more about this girl.

Over the next few months, Anna, Josh, and Kyle started coming to our family get-togethers. They decorated Christmas cookies with us, and went to the twins' birthday party in January. Anna and I chatted online almost every day. What started as a bond that we shared from the two of us being "mommies" to Josh developed into the kind of mother/daughter relationship that I had always wanted. Anna's relationship with her own mother was very strained, and I was honored that Anna trusted me enough to come to me for advice and support when she needed it.

February came, and Kyle and Anna asked if I would be willing to babysit Josh while Anna was in the hospital giving birth to their little girl. I was beyond thrilled to be able to spend some one on one time with my little guy, but I found myself torn because I also wanted to be there for Anna. Ultimately, I knew that she would feel much better knowing that Josh was with me, so we took lots of pictures and messaged each other constantly until Josh's baby sister, Leah, arrived. I was there when Josh met Leah for the first time. I was there when they were able to head home as a family of four. Being a part of such an important time in their lives was a blessing that I never expected.

The next few months were a whirlwind of activity as we somehow started creating our own little family. Kyle worked on Saturdays, so Anna, Josh, Leah, and my niece and nephew usually ended up at my house where we would decorate cakes, do arts and crafts, walk to the park, and have spray bottle fights. Just when I thought that my life could not get any better, I got a call from my agency about a two-month-old baby boy named Tommy. He was the perfect fit for our little family. Tommy was three weeks younger than Leah and six weeks older than my newest little niece and nephew who had just been born a few weeks prior.

My dream of having a gaggle of kids had become a reality, and I did not even realize it until one day in October. Anna, Josh, Leah, Tommy, and I had piled into my minivan and headed over the Pumpkin Patch. As we were navigating our way through the corn maze, Josh exclaimed, "We have got to get out of here! Are we lost? We're lost, aren't we?" I felt my heart smile as I thought about that dream that I had dreamed so long ago. I was munching on kettle corn with my kids, and we were most definitely lost in that corn maze.

The following spring, as Tommy's permanency hearing approached, it had become clear that his dad would be granted custody if he was able to arrange childcare. Tommy's father worked nights, so I knew that would be an issue. I began taking Tommy to his weekly visits with his father, and what I saw was reminiscent of Josh and Kyle before Josh went home. Tommy's face lit up when he saw his father, and his dad beamed with pride and joy every time he saw his son. That is when I knew what I had to do. I offered to keep Tommy four nights and three mornings a week while his dad was at work.

I never would have had the courage to do that if I had not seen firsthand how foster care can work. If I had not been able to see Josh happy, healthy, loved, and completely cherished by his family after he had returned home, I do not think I could have trusted that a situation like the one I was considering with Tommy's father could work. Josh had taught me differently though, and I trusted that what I saw between Tommy and his father was something special. They just needed my help. The day that Tommy's dad was granted custody, he stood in my living room and cried. He thanked me for being Tommy's mother. He apologized for the pain that I was feeling, and he assured me that Tommy would be back in my arms on Sunday night. Then he said, "I know I only got Tommy back right now because of you." I knew differently though. It was because of Josh.

We received an early Christmas gift last year when two-month-old Jacob came through my door the day before our family Christmas celebration. Anna fell head over heels for her newest "baby brother" and sat spoiling him rotten. Kyle, Anna's sister, and the twins sat in a corner playing video games, and my mom sat on the couch snuggling with Leah and Tommy. I was standing back smiling at all of my kids in their coordinating Christmas pajamas, when four-year-old Josh pulled me aside because he wanted to give me my gift from him. I opened it up to see a heart necklace with a "J" inside. "It's so you'll know I'm always in your heart," he exclaimed. Oh, I know it, baby boy! Believe me, I know it.

They say that everything happens for a reason, and I believe that saying is true. Today, when I look back on that heartbreaking afternoon in the courtroom, I know exactly why I had to lose Josh the way that I did. Losing him in a way that brought me to my knees and slowly feeling myself heal taught me that I am much stronger than I ever thought I could be. Watching Josh and his family as they continue to grow and create a life together is absolute confirmation that what I do as a foster parent makes a difference. My relationship with them is what gave me the courage to offer to help Tommy's father when he regained custody of his son. Without Josh, I would not still be Tommy's mommy over a year after he returned home.

Losing Josh as my son brought me a family. If Josh had not left my arms that day, he would not have found his place in Anna's, and I never would have met the amazing young woman who quickly became the daughter of my heart. I would not have a young man who I am proud to call my son-in-law like I have in Kyle. I would not have a granddaughter who loves her "Mimi," as she calls me, like crazy, and who I get to spoil rotten and send back home like a real grandmother should. Because of Josh, I know that biology is not everything and that families created out of nothing but love are unbreakable.

I look at Josh now, four years after that two-toothed little guy crossed my threshold and swept me off my feet, and I see the "reason" my life is so full of love.

Conclusion

S*ome people might* wonder why we chose to share the stories that we did. Some have happy endings. Others are heart-wrenchingly sad. Some of our stories have no closure at all. The answer is simple. That is how foster care works. No two stories are the same, but all have emotional highs and lows that often leave us breathless with an ache in our hearts.

This book was written by a group of women who have seen the best and the worst that foster care has to offer. They knew that the foster care system was a broken mess when they signed up for it. Regardless, they held on to the hope that the system could work. They thought they were prepared, but in reality they had no clue what they were getting into. There is no way that one can ever be fully prepared for the flood of emotions or the overwhelming stress that come hand in hand with being a foster parent. No one can easily prepare for the heartache of being an anchor of security for a hurting child. Yet in hindsight, these women would do it all again if given the chance.

That is the interesting thing about foster parents - the good ones anyway. We read all of the stories. We try to prepare ourselves for the worst, while hoping for the best. We sit through the training classes. We immerse ourselves in a world that often leaves us questioning humanity. We listen to the horrifying details of what these children have been through. We hear our friends and families as they often try to steer us away from the inevitable hurt. Yet we know that, no matter what anyone says, we are going to do this anyway. Plain and simple, there is something within us that knows we need to help these kids, even if it means we get hurt in the process.

While writing this book, many of us have gone back to some of our darkest days that we would rather forget. Having to say goodbye to a child we were absolutely in love with is truly one of the hardest things anyone could ever do. We chose to share our heartaches along with our triumphs because we wanted to paint an honest picture of what the foster care experience can look like. We wanted to reach out to fellow foster parents to let them know they are not alone in their journeys. We hoped that by telling our stories, we might inspire others to join us on this roller coaster ride of a lifetime.

You might have to endure the fallout of a broken and flawed system. Yes, you might be inconvenienced. Yes, you might get your heart broken. The simple truth is you could also gain so much more than you ever risked losing. What if you were to find your daughter? What if you were to find your son? What if fostering opened your eyes to a world that you never knew needed you so badly? What if fostering changed you in all the ways you needed to be changed?

• •

We foster parents are a special breed. We have a fire inside of us that will not be ignored. We will not accept status quo for our lives. We would not be able to sleep at night knowing that a child needed us and we ignored them. We were made for more than the normal life we see others living around us. We have been called to bigger and better things. We see the roller coaster before us and face it head-on, knowing that we have been called to change the course of a child's life. No matter the risk, we will fight to give these children a chance.

Made in the USA
Lexington, KY
26 March 2017